The World Colonization Made

EARLY AMERICAN STUDIES

Series Editors
Daniel K. Richter, Kathleen M. Brown,
Max Cavitch, and David Waldstreicher

Exploring neglected aspects of our colonial,
revolutionary, and early national history and culture,
Early American Studies reinterprets familiar themes
and events in fresh ways. Interdisciplinary in character,
and with a special emphasis on the period from about
1600 to 1850, the series is published in partnership with
the McNeil Center for Early American Studies.

A complete list of books in the series
is available from the publisher.

The World Colonization Made

The Racial Geography of
Early American Empire

Brandon Mills

PENN

UNIVERSITY OF PENNSYLVANIA PRESS

PHILADELPHIA

Published by
University of Pennsylvania Press
Philadelphia, Pennsylvania 19104-4112
www.upenn.edu/pennpress

Printed in the United States of America
on acid-free paper
1 3 5 7 9 10 8 6 4 2

Library of Congress Cataloging-in-Publication Data
Names: Mills, Brandon, author.
Title: The world colonization made : the racial geography of early American empire /
    Brandon Mills.
Other titles: Racial geography of early American empire | Early American studies.
Description: Philadelphia : University of Pennsylvania Press, [2020] | Series: Early American
    studies | Includes bibliographical references and index.
Identifiers: LCCN 2020001876 | ISBN 9780812252507 (hardcover)
Subjects: LCSH: Colonization. | American Colonization Society—History—19th century. |
    Free blacks—America—History—19th century. | Slavery—United States—History—
    19th century. | African Americans—Colonization—Liberia—History. | African
    Americans—Colonization—Central America—History—19th century. | Indians of
    North America—Colonization—History—19th century. | Imperialism. | United States—
    Race relations—History—19th century. | United States—History—1783–1865. |
    Liberia—Colonization.
Classification: LCC E448 .M57 2020 | DDC 305.800973/0904—dc23
LC record available at https://lccn.loc.gov/2020001876

CONTENTS

The World Colonization Made

At an 1825 meeting of the American Colonization Society (ACS) held in the U.S. Capitol Building, Robert Stockton delivered a warning about the nation's future as an empire. Only three years earlier, he had led the U.S. Navy's effort to create the colony of Liberia in West Africa with the intention that this set-tlement would ultimately become a republic governed by African Americans. Despite the organization's recent success in establishing this colony, Stockton addressed the ACS with a cautionary tale of imperial hubris. He pointed out that the Spanish empire, a once-dominant global power, had suffered a steep decline in the preceding decades, recently culminating in the loss of nearly all its colonial possessions throughout the Western Hemisphere. Anticipating a time when the United States would preside over its own sprawling empire, Stockton worried that the nation might follow Spain's fateful path, ultimately undermining its effort to build a republic rooted in "moral rectitude and the equal rights of man." For Stockton, Spain's empire was defined by "ava-rice" and stained by the "blood of thousands of unoffending natives," and he warned that the United States could similarly perish from "a heart blackened by atrocity and countless cruelties to the Indian and the African."[1]

To avoid this fate, Stockton encouraged Americans to support the Afri-can colonization movement and to model it around the United States' repub-lican institutions, which were, in his estimation, "the very capital of human freedom" and "the sublimest structure for the promulgation of human rights the world ever saw." For Stockton, planting a black republic in Africa and the parallel "colonization of our aborigines" in North America would allow the nation to forge a benevolent empire: one that allowed for the expansion of liberty through racially separate regimes of self-governance for whites, Afri-can Americans, and Native Americans.[2]

Although his speech warned about the dangers of excessive colonial vio-lence, Stockton failed to mention his own violent role in colonizing Liberia.

As a naval officer tasked with patrolling the slave trade for the United States, he landed the U.S.S. *Alligator* on West African shores in late 1821 along with several ACS agents in hopes of securing territory for a colony. Stockton and the prospective colonists entered negotiations with a local Dei leader, known to English speakers as "King Peter," concerning the terms of a potential American colony in Cape Mesurado. When negotiations faltered, Stockton allegedly pointed a gun at the man's head and pressed him into signing a treaty to cede land to the American settlers. Thus, Liberia's founding event reenacted, in microcosm, the use of force to coerce treaties on the indigenous peoples of North America in order to establish the United States' own settler republic. Conveniently omitting this history allowed Stockton to claim that the United States could build an exceptional empire based not on exploitation but rather on the principle of self-government.[3]

As Stockton's speech and actions suggest, colonizationism offered many white Americans a compelling racial framework for defining, and obscuring, the character of U.S. imperialism.[4] From the American Revolution to the Civil War, colonizationists envisioned geopolitical arrangements in which African Americans would be severed from the United States' body politic while remaining part of its broader agenda for expansion. A relatively small number of black migrants left the United States for these colonies, either in search of self-determination or as a requirement of their manumission from slavery. For the most part, free black people in the United States steadfastly opposed these schemes as an affront to their livelihood, natural rights, and basic humanity. On its own terms, the colonization movement was largely a failure, yet it remained an influential fixture for the first century of American political life. As a foundational set of racial ideas within the United States, how did colonizationism evolve to create, and recreate, the United States' ever-shifting imperial priorities?

To answer this question, *The World Colonization Made* traces this idea across a wide range of political and cultural debates concerning citizenship rights, strategies of settlement, foreign policy, and economic expansion. By examining the broad circulation of this concept in the early United States, it is possible to see why colonizationism remained so attractive and resilient to many white Americans despite its consistent failures. The colonization movement gained so much traction, in part, because it spoke to American aspiration toward empire and connected this vision of expansion abroad with ideas about race at home. The white citizenry that imagined and set into motion colonization proposals was both self-consciously committed to expanding the reach of its republican ideals and intensely concerned about how the principle of self-rule could coexist with racial hierarchies created through enslavement, settler colonization, and overseas expansion. Indeed, colonizationist views of race evolved along with Americans' reconfigurations of the racial terms of their empire. While white Americans initially created the ideology of colonizationism in order to manage the domestic racial threats posed by slavery and settlement, it ultimately developed into a thoroughly racialized worldview that foreshadowed later iterations of the United States' global expansion.

The expansive scope of colonizationism is apparent in the fact that Americans proposed colonies in such a wide range of territories both inside and outside current U.S. borders. The ACS campaign to settle Liberia was the central and most successful effort to create such a colony, but it was by no means the only one. At different moments, colonizationists contemplated a sprawling array of settlements in the far reaches of the Atlantic world, including locations throughout much of North America, the Caribbean, Central and South America, and West Africa. That the United States would eventually claim a significant portion of these sites as part of either its own national territory or its informal imperial domain underscores the fact that the nation's continental settlement remained in constant dialogue with its global aspirations.

For a movement literally dedicated to founding and settling colonies, colonizationism has remained largely absent from histories of U.S. imperialism. Most accounts view it primarily as a manifestation of domestic politics, positioning it in relation to antislavery activism, growing sectional tensions, racial ideology, and the emergence of black political identity in the United States.[5] To some extent, this tendency replicates the way that many Americans discussed colonizationism at the time. In the antebellum period, the concept became a central battleground in the war over slavery as a generation of white abolitionists, following the lead of black protesters, defined their movement by rejecting colonizationists' constrained vision of emancipation. Thus, for contemporary advocates and opponents of colonization, questions of empire were not front and center. While acknowledging the importance of these domestic contexts, this book approaches the subject from a different angle by showing that colonizationism held enduring appeal for white Americans precisely because it was multifaceted: it promised to manage the nation's internal racial dynamics by structuring them around particular visions of empire.[6]

Offering a powerful and flexible framework for racial thinking, colonizationism helped define the United States' evolving imperial outlook throughout its early history. Accordingly, the colonization movement revealed Americans' persistent ambivalence about the nature of their empire: the

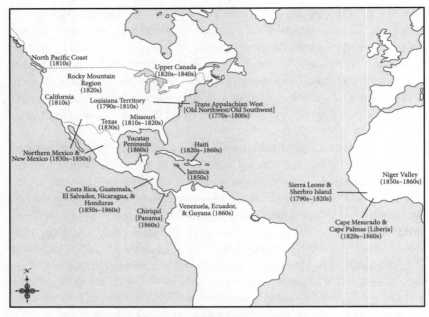

Figure 1. A map showing some of the proposed sites for creating colonies
for African Americans from the 1770s through the 1860s.

United States forged its republic through anti-imperial struggle and yet immediately set out to fashion itself as an expansive "empire of liberty" on colonized indigenous lands. As a settler empire, the United States sought to coalesce its expanding settlements into a single political entity by displacing Native communities through both military conquest and informal violence. At the same time, many Americans envisioned their nation as an aspiring world power and therefore aimed to exert authority over distant populations outside the nation's ever-expanding borders. Modeling itself both on and in contrast to European empires, the United States competed for resources and control in North America, the Western Hemisphere, the Atlantic and Pacific Oceans, and eventually throughout the entire world.[7] During the late nineteenth century, the nation became increasingly committed to extending its reach overseas but exercised its authority in ways that were often distinct from its practice of colonial rule in North America.[8] By viewing the story of U.S. expansion through the lens of colonizationism, we can see how deeply the legacy of the United States' settlement imprinted the nation's eventual ascent to global empire.

The World Colonization Made opens in the years immediately following the American Revolution as the young nation provisionally defined the racial contours of its emerging imperial agenda. The earliest colonization proposals sought to manage an unstable regime of racial slavery on contested indigenous land; therefore, this book's story begins by highlighting how colonizationism grew out of the United States' efforts to settle North America. By the time Robert Stockton helped found Liberia in the early 1820s, white Americans definitively favored locating such a colony in Africa. However, in the decades preceding the formation of the ACS, politicians and antislavery writers had debated a series of incipient colonization proposals that were primarily designed to eliminate the threat of slave insurrection in the United States by creating black colonies within various parts of North America. Proponents of these plans presumed that by establishing such colonies in the West, black settlers could remain separate from the United States yet perpetuate the nation's colonization of the continent.

These early colonization proposals reveal that Americans' ideas concerning the interaction between race and empire were open-ended, provisional, and subject to change. While colonizationism was increasingly popular in the decades following the revolution, by the late 1810s many of its proponents had come to believe that the existence of these colonies would only hinder the prospects of white settlement, and black slavery, in North America. As the context for the colony moved from the terrain of indigenous territories in North America to those in Africa, it retained its foundational logic of settler colonialism even as it suggested new prospects for U.S. expansion around the globe.

This shift resulted in a new concept for the colony in Liberia: one in which African Americans would not participate in the United States' settlement of North America but would rather reproduce it by becoming an independent settler republic. Despite attracting a dramatic range of support from prominent white Americans, the early colonization movement succeeded far more in popularizing this conceptual framework than in making it a reality. While whites were willing, often overzealous, settlers within North America, most free African Americans disavowed this position in Africa. Marginalized as citizens in the United States and unwilling to become settlers in Liberia, black anticolonizationists laid bare the contradictions of the movement from its inception.

As colonizationism became formalized under the ACS, its proponents developed a more consistent set of ideas rooted in the ideology of U.S. political institutions and foreign policy. Within this context, colonizationists advanced an ideal of racial republicanism in which nonwhite peoples could eventually become self-governing citizens, but within a framework in which they would remain perpetually subordinate.[9] In this conception, aspiring republics such as Liberia would remain racially distinct while ascending to nominal equality as independent nation-states.[10] By suggesting that African Americans might become unequal partners in overseas expansion, racial republicanism helped Americans envision new forms of U.S. global power while reinforcing white political supremacy and black disenfranchisement at home.

Even after colonizationists largely rejected North America as the location for a potential colony, their ideas remained preoccupied with defining the racial structure of the United States' settler empire. In his speech, Stockton advocated applying a colonizationist framework to Native Americans, a proposition then endorsed by several U.S. leaders, including President James Monroe. Such supporters believed that reorganizing Native peoples into colonies would help them dissolve their tribal affiliations and form parallel republican societies, thereby freeing up vast stretches of territory where white Americans could settle. While this colonizationist vision of Indian policy never fully came to pass, it would frame the conceptual landscape for the debate over Indian removal even as African colonization, and its distinct vision of U.S. expansion, ultimately faced a more ambiguous fate as national policy.

Despite African colonizationists' ability to secure only meager federal resources to support Liberia, their influential ideas continued to define both the limits and possibilities of U.S. empire. In forming state-level racial policies, white settlers could justify their claims to Native lands by arguing that Liberia, rather than their own states, provided the proper context for black settler citizenship. This was underscored by the prospect of Liberia's formal declaration of independence in 1847, which allowed the colony, in theory, to fulfill its republican promise and validate the United States' claim that its empire was wholly benevolent. While some free African Americans were intrigued by the prospect of an independent black republic, most remained skeptical about the implications of Liberian sovereignty, given that it remained embedded within the United States' ongoing racial and imperial priorities.

During the years leading up to the Civil War, several politicians reanimated colonizationism by advancing proposals to create colonies such as Liberia throughout Central and South America. Colonizationists of this era advanced more self-consciously global objectives, suggesting that the propagation of such colonies in the Americas could become stepping stones to the Pacific and help the United States establish broader networks of military and economic dominance in the Western Hemisphere. Even as they looked to integrate these colonies within the United States' budding overseas empire, the politicians advancing them frequently emphasized how they were consistent with the practices of U.S. settlement. By framing African Americans as international "homesteaders," advocates claimed they would serve as proxies for U.S. interests in the American tropics by becoming parallel settler citizens enacting their own versions of manifest destiny.[11] As a consistently renewable reservoir for imagining the nation's racial future, colonizationism allowed Americans to reconcile their vision of creating a white settler empire with the racially uncertain prospect of global expansion.

This book's chapters are arranged chronologically, tracing the life cycle of the colonization movement as a vital political force within the United States. Colonizationism had its roots in the crises of the Revolutionary era, ascended to national stature with the creation of the ACS, stumbled following attacks from both critics and defenders of slavery, and ultimately declined with emancipation during the Civil War. Although the rise and fall of the ACS partially frames the narrative arc of this book, the much larger story traces the path of colonizationist ideas as they moved through the early United States. As a result, each chapter is thematically organized, focusing on how the colonization movement both reflected and shaped a wide range of debates over race, settlement, citizenship, and empire in the early republic. By addressing these themes, this book interrogates how the specific case of colonizationism illuminates our understanding of broader issues of U.S. expansion, including the progression of federal Indian policy, the ideologies of the Monroe Doctrine and manifest destiny, and the growth of U.S. commercial and military power throughout the Western Hemisphere.

By recontextualizing colonizationism in this way, it is possible to see how ostensibly domestic debates among policy makers, activists, and ordinary citizens helped define the United States' outlook toward global engagement. This enduring conceptual framework allowed Americans to envision a world of self-governing nations that recentered their racialized political institutions. In the ensuing decades, the United States would pursue a wide range of approaches to expansion, elaborating on its prior practices even as it established new forms of rule abroad. The ongoing transformation of these ideas throughout the nineteenth century demonstrates how Americans situated their own nation amid other empires on the world stage. Ultimately, the enduring legacy of the colonization movement is that it provided one powerful way for Americans to integrate both their racism and republicanism with a boundless ambition for expansion.

CHAPTER 1

A Republic Once Removed

In 1801 James Monroe, then the governor of Virginia, wrote to President Thomas Jefferson to ask whether the federal government could help his state create a colony of former slaves somewhere within the western territory of North America. Monroe made this request in response to an event a year earlier when Virginia slaveholders thwarted an incipient slave insurrection that was partially inspired by the ongoing rebellions throughout the French Caribbean colonies. Along with other Virginian leaders, he believed that creating such a settlement for some of the state's free black population might prevent the prospect of a similar revolution in mainland North America. Monroe had reason to expect the president would be receptive to this idea. Since the Revolutionary era, several prominent writers and politicians, including Jefferson himself, had consistently discussed the possibility of creating colonies for former slaves.[1] Despite the growing constituency for such a proposal in Virginia, the recently elected president offered a lukewarm response. While not entirely dismissive of Monroe's plan, Jefferson questioned the fundamental wisdom of creating such a colony. Instead, he encouraged Monroe to envision a future in which white Americans would displace Native peoples as they settled the North American continent and cautioned that making black colonies part of this landscape would introduce a "blot or mixture in that surface."[2]

As this exchange suggests, the nation's most prominent leaders discussed colonizationism long before the ACS emerged to advance its plan for Liberia in the late 1810s. Throughout the 1790s the ongoing threat of slave rebellion helped inspire a series of colonization proposals that were aimed at combating the possibility of domestic insurrection in the United States. Eventually Africa would become the primary focus for most colonizationists, but at the turn of the nineteenth century, proponents of such colonies often looked westward to assuage anxieties that stemmed from the question of slavery and settlement in postrevolutionary America.[3]

During this era, colonizationists sketched out plans in which African Americans would create settler societies that were loosely aligned with the United States' expansion on the continent. However, Jefferson's response to Monroe demonstrates that the prospect of such colonies carried with it profound implications for the racial geography of the United States' expanding settler empire. Eventually other white Americans would come to have similar doubts about the long-term consequences of these early western proposals. This growing skepticism likely contributed to the failure of these plans to coalesce into a coherent movement, and ultimately the ideas only appeared in a scattering of books, pamphlets, private correspondence, and legislative debates during the decades immediately following the Revolutionary War. Indeed, when compared to the popularity, formalized ideology, and institutional strength of the later ACS, these plans for western colonies might appear to be trivial at first glance. Despite their relative marginality, these early proposals crucially reveal competing visions of the United States' settler state in the early years following the Revolutionary era. They demonstrate the ways that the eventual African colonization movement was both an extension and a reinvention of early American empire.[4]

This inchoate vision of a loosely coordinated and racially separate settlement of North America would not survive long. By the mid-1810s, colonizationists began to argue that the looming threat of slave rebellion, a fundamental argument for creating such colonies in the first place, actually made western settlements incompatible with the United States' plans for expansion. Increasingly, the proposed black colonies in North America were characterized as threats to national security, particularly when viewed through the lens of ongoing wars with Indian nations. Seen from this perspective, African Americans were more likely to be, as Jefferson argued, impediments to the United States' settlement rather than allies. The abandonment of these proposals highlights how discussions about the character of U.S. expansion helped frame the emergence of colonizationist ideas in ways that scholars have often overlooked. The failure of colonizationism in the West illustrates an early phase in the evolution of the United States' identity as a white settler republic within North America.

Colonizationist Counterrevolution

Colonizationism was born amid the anxious racial politics that followed the American Revolution, and no place exemplified this more clearly than Virginia. Here, the national debates about slavery and emancipation and the ever-present fear of slave insurrection were echoed and amplified nationally, leading the state to become a crucial incubator for the earliest colonization proposals that circulated within the United States. The Revolutionary War had caused major disruptions to Virginia's slave system and helped create the perception that the state suffered from a surplus of slaves. This factor, along with the declining profitability of tobacco, fueled white slaveholders' pervasive concern about a growing free black population. In this context, Virginia's politicians, many of whom were also prominent national leaders, increasingly questioned the long-term viability of slavery as an institution in the state.[5]

Thomas Jefferson, a key figure in the American Revolution and one of Virginia's most prominent planters, would also play a critical role in defining these unfolding debates over slavery, emancipation, and colonization. Approaching the subject as a revolutionary, an early national leader, and an anxious Virginia slaveholder, Jefferson likely did more than any other individual in the early republic to initially popularize the concept of creating colonies for former slaves. In the first years of the Revolution, Jefferson had helped draft a version of Virginia's constitution that included a proposal for the gradual emancipation of the state's enslaved population, with the provision that they "be colonized to such place as the circumstances of time should render most proper" where they would become a "free and independent people."[6] Although not included in the final version of the document, Jefferson's plan to relocate emancipated slaves received widespread attention when this earlier draft was published years later in *Notes on the State of Virginia*, and its prominence had a profound influence on the more detailed plans that would emerge in subsequent decades.[7]

Jefferson's early colonization proposals stemmed from his view that people of African descent amounted to an inherently antagonistic "nation" contained within the United States. Believing that these two nations would remain perpetually in conflict, he concluded that their separation into different political communities was the only viable solution to this dilemma. Underpinning this belief was Jefferson's concern that enslaved African Americans would be driven, like the American colonists had been, to demand their natural rights through revolution. As colonization plans circulated during the next few decades, both slaveholders and antislavery advocates alike echoed these sentiments and warned that if whites did not create favorable conditions for African Americans to achieve their political rights peaceably, they would inevitably seize them through a bloody conflict.[8]

As it turned out, these fears were prescient. Only a few years later, enslaved and free people of African descent led a series of revolutionary struggles that permanently transformed social relations within the colonies of the French Caribbean. In the early 1790s a political debate over extending citizenship rights to free people of color sparked a series of slave rebellions in France's richest sugar colony, Saint-Domingue. Toussaint L'Ouverture emerged as the primary leader of the struggle on the island and quickly became an international symbol of both the promise and threat of a wide-scale slave revolt. In 1804 Haiti became the world's first black republic by discarding the shackles of both slavery and colonialism.[9]

This rebellion rapidly spread to other French possessions in the region and radiated its influence out into other British and Spanish slave colonies, and, of course, to the United States. As a consequence, both the successful revolution and the resulting Republic of Haiti came to represent the first sustained challenge to the Atlantic world slave system as well as Eurocentric conceptions of republican citizenship. American newspapers, pamphlets, and books widely publicized lurid and sensationalized reports of slaves massacring white colonists, and, as a result, many Americans predicted that racial revolution was also imminent in the United States.[10] At the same time both enslaved and free peoples of African descent disseminated their own knowledge of these events throughout the Americas, serving as a testament to the prospect of successful resistance against slave regimes.[11]

As a result, these revolutionary events in the French Caribbean would serve to frame all discussions of colonizationism for the next several decades. Seen within this context, the early colonization efforts in the United States can be understood as an attempt at forging a counterrevolution in the wider Atlantic world: an effort to create the terms on which black republicanism might be cultivated, managed, and ultimately contained. During the 1790s and early 1800s, American politicians and antislavery writers discussed plans for black colonies as a response to the growing panic about slave rebellion. Thomas Jefferson's initial suggestion of creating black colonies during the Revolution was both provisional and open-ended; however, by the 1790s Americans began to advance more concrete proposals, inspired by British plans for creating a settlement for former slaves in the West African colony of Sierra Leone.

Although some Americans voiced support for these British efforts in Africa, at this early stage many still looked toward North America as a future home for former slaves. In many ways, this tendency illustrates how colonizationism was continuous with the long-standing dynamics of European settler expansion in North America. American colonists had long pushed to advance the boundaries of settlement, sometimes against the wishes of local officials who valued stable relationships with the powerful Indian nations who controlled borderland regions. After independence, the United States, unburdened by British imperial restriction on western settlement, claimed nominal, if not physical, control over a large swath of Native lands where they hoped to build an empire of their own. The sheer vastness of this territory seemed to offer the possibility that African Americans might be accommodated within these visions. While a colony in Sierra Leone might seem remote, costly, unpredictable, and wedded to a British imperial system that the United States had recently rejected, Americans possessed the knowledge, experience, and inclination they would need to support the further colonization of North America.

As a result, early colonization proposals hinged on the question of how they might be integrated within the United States' own settler empire, a preoccupation initially intended to avoid the uncertain pursuit of an African colony. For instance, William Thornton, a Quaker antislavery advocate who traveled throughout Rhode Island in 1786 and 1787, found considerable interest among the state's black population in the prospect of migrating to the proposed colony in Sierra Leone. However, when he raised the idea of securing transportation for these individuals with "members of the [Rhode Island] Legislature," they "expressed an unwillingness to send them out of the limits of the U.S., & wished a Settlement to be made in the most southern part of the back Country between the whites & Indians." Thornton disagreed with the view that a black colony could act as a kind of buffer between white settlement and Indian country and told the legislators that he "would never be instrument in placing those men, who were now comparatively happy & in a state of protection, between the Indians & Savages on their Borders, where they would become a prey to both." Moreover, he could see no way that black colonies could be properly integrated into the United States' empire, asking: "If they should prove capable of defending themselves against all their Enemies, & should preserve their political freedom, could they ever hope to be received as representatives in our Assemblies?" While many Americans would continue to look westward, this concern about a racially divided settler republic anticipated the arguments that would eventually lead most colonizationists, including Thornton himself, to support an African colony by the mid-1810s.[12]

The fact that Thornton consulted black residents on the subject of western colonies is notable because it was so rare. During this period, white colonizationists scarcely mention the perspective of the black men and women who they imagined would become willing colonists. Indeed, there is virtually no evidence that African Americans were interested in the prospect of venturing onto indigenous territory where they would be viewed as potentially hostile avatars of the U.S. settler state. Some free African Americans expressed interest in leaving the United States, but it was almost always for Africa, either to the British colony in Sierra Leone or another unspecified territory on the continent. Therefore, colonizationism, as it came to be expressed through these early proposals, was from its inception an expression of white imagination and designed to serve white interests. Colonizationists flagrantly disregarded the perspectives of African Americans by envisioning them as potential settlers whether they were willing to accept this position or not. While it is likely that most of these early proposals did not reach black audiences to any significant degree, they established a toxic dynamic that caused free black communities to stridently oppose colonizationism when it eventually arrived on the national scene in the mid-1810s.[13]

White colonizationists persisted in circulating a scattered array of proposals over the next few decades, largely without input from African Americans. Around the time when Jefferson's early colonization proposals became widely known, William Craighead, a magistrate in Lunenburg County, Virginia, locally discussed his own proposal to colonize African Americans in the western territories that the Northwest Ordinance laws had recently opened up for settlement in the late 1780s. Although Craighead clearly viewed these colonies as operating within the broader context of settling that region, he proposed a quasi-colonial relationship by which the proposed colonies' "relation to the government of the United States was to be something analogous to that in which the Indians now stand."[14] Craighead's proposal introduced the vexing question of precisely how such a colony might relate to the United States' other processes for colonizing territory, in addition to the existing Indian nations throughout the West. Shortly after Craighead made his proposal, an anonymously written antislavery article in the *American Museum* presented a similar idea by offering readers a stark choice: "Either we should set all our slaves at liberty, immediately, and colonize them in the western territory; or, we should immediately take measures for the gradual abolition of it." Appearing in one of the United States' most prominent early periodicals, and shortly following the publication of Jefferson's *Notes*, it suggests an elite national audience already familiar with, and receptive to, the prospect of creating black colonies.[15]

One of the most influential writings to suggest that the Americans should gradually emancipate slaves and resettle them on undetermined western territory was a pamphlet titled *Dissertation on Slavery*. Written in 1796 by a prominent and politically connected Virginia lawyer, St. George Tucker, it directly addressed the revolutionary implications of the ongoing slave rebellions in the Caribbean. Tucker was undoubtedly influenced by the prior colonization plans that had slowly begun to take root; however, his proposals were far more comprehensive than the thinly sketched outlines of his predecessors. Focusing primarily on a Virginia readership, he suggested that the state should emancipate all slaves born after a certain date and then compel them to leave the state by denying them any access to citizenship rights. In turn, the state would help create a colony of former slaves somewhere within U.S. territory. Explaining his proposal to a Massachusetts antislavery leader, Tucker noted that "the calamities which have lately spread like a contagion through the West India Islands affords a solemn warning to us of the dangerous predicament in which we stand." As a result, he believed that the United States faced a choice of accepting an inevitable revolution or following "the liberal sentiments of the national convention of France," which had recently abolished slavery in response to the ongoing revolutions in the Caribbean.[16]

While Tucker's proposed colony for African Americans was only one piece of the broader plan detailed in his *Dissertation on Slavery*, it connected colonization directly to the perception that the United States faced an impending threat of a black republican revolution. Addressing his plan specifically to Virginians, Tucker argued that the state could undertake gradual emancipation only by denying former slaves the very rights he believed they were poised to seize through rebellion. He asserted that "by denying them the most valuable privileges which civil government affords [Virginia could] render it their inclination and their interest to seek those privileges in some other climate." By providing the possibility of acquiring rights elsewhere in a separate colony, Tucker believed that such a plan would prevent the prospect that emancipated slaves would remain in the state and thus embolden both free and enslaved people to demand the recognition of these rights through violent upheaval.[17]

For a proper "climate" in which to realize these rights, Tucker suggested the "immense territory of Louisiana," then under Spanish rule, which would "afford a ready asylum for such as might choose to become Spanish subjects," even though he was skeptical as to "how far their political rights might be enlarged in these countries." While many subsequent colonization plans would repeat Tucker's recommendation of the Louisiana Territory, it is significant to note that he departed from many of the later proposals by not framing the colony as either an extension or a replication of the U.S. settler state. Rather, he envisioned it as a transfer of former slaves into the hands of a competing imperial power. While this might simply reflect Tucker's desire to absolve the United States of responsibility for administering this population by making them "Spanish subjects," it also highlights the degree to which the geographic and racial dimensions of American empire would dramatically transform in the next few years. Although Tucker looked to Spanish Louisiana, this land would soon shift briefly back to France before finally being claimed by the United States after 1803.[18]

Tucker was able to use his extensive political connections in Virginia to get his proposal for gradual emancipation and colonization considered by friends in the state's General Assembly; however, legislators quickly shelved the plan after facing considerable opposition from slaveholders who were loath to upset the status quo in the state. Despite this mixed reception, Thomas Jefferson wrote Tucker shortly after the *Dissertation* was published to offer encouragement. Acknowledging the difficulty of gaining support for slave emancipation and colonization, Jefferson nevertheless predicted that the gathering storms of revolution would eventually make such efforts a necessity: "Perhaps the first chapter of this history, which has begun in St. Domingo, and the next succeeding ones, which will recount how all the whites were driven from all the other islands, may prepare our minds for a peaceable accommodation between justice, policy and necessity."[19] Even so, Jefferson was more skeptical than Tucker about whether African Americans could become enlightened citizens. Nevertheless, he agreed that, at the very least, they were capable of seizing on the republican rhetoric of a revolutionary moment as they were then doing in the French colonies. In response to this situation he ominously warned that "if something is not done, and soon done . . . the revolutionary storm, now sweeping the globe, will be upon us." Jefferson's fevered predictions exemplified the thinking that fueled early colonizationism: if natural rights continued to be denied, they would need to be secured elsewhere or the United States would be overtaken by a "revolutionary storm."[20]

This sort of analysis was not limited to the anxiety-ridden imaginations of Virginia slaveholders. Writers from nonslaveholding states were equally motivated by the threat of revolution, and around the same time they also began to discuss similar plans for creating black colonies in North America. As in the South, prominent northern writers had advocated colonization schemes since the 1770s, when Anthony Benezet, an educator and early abolitionist, suggested that African Americans could be colonized "from the west side of the Allegheny mountains to the Mississippi." Like Jefferson, Benezet employed the revolutionary rhetoric of natural rights to argue that African Americans were "as free as we are by nature" and that they could realize that freedom in a western colony.[21] However, colonization proposals failed to gain much traction in the North until several states began abolishing slavery during the 1770s and 1780s. The resulting growth of free black communities made the issue of black citizenship a particular concern for northerners.[22]

Shortly before St. George Tucker wrote *Dissertation on Slavery*, Moses Fisk, a seminary graduate and instructor from Dartmouth College, published the first significant western colonization proposal written by a northern writer.[23] Initially published anonymously, Fisk's pamphlet, titled *Tyrannical Libertymen a Discourse upon Negro-Slavery in the United States*, was drawn from one of his Dartmouth sermons. While his proposal was more oriented toward ending slavery than advancing colonizationism, Fisk was similarly preoccupied with controlling the political forces that might be unleashed following emancipation. Like his southern brethren, Fisk's plan was borne out of the fear of rebellion, and he too believed that African Americans' inevitable desire to become citizens could be harnessed and contained through a process of colonization within western territory claimed by the United States. Acknowledging that emancipation could create a "dangerous parcel of vagabonds" who would become "the terror and vexation of the community," Fisk succinctly identified a solution: "If they are not fit for freedom, they must be fitted."[24]

To aid in this transformation, Fisk suggested that African Americans should be placed "under temporary guardians, governours, and instructors, to be educated, to be made acquainted with their rights and duties, and some honest method of acquiring a livelihood; to be prepared for citizenship." This instruction in citizenship was not designed to prepare "the great body of the negroes" for integration into the United States but rather for their separation into "a portion of our new territory [to] be assigned for the purpose." While Fisk imagined a relatively autonomous existence for the colony, he argued that independence would be managed tightly within the United States' geopolitical objectives: "They must be inured to industry and economy; defended, if any should invade them; and awed by soldiery, if they should rebel." While the pamphlet suggested that, in time, this independent settlement might "have a voice in Congress," the colonial hierarchy was a necessary step because "they will never be good citizens, till they know their duties." While he made no specific recommendation for the location of the colony, he explicitly envisioned it within the context of the United States' territorial settlement. Fisk's notion of transforming a formerly threatening community into a state that could serve as proxy for American expansion would become a hallmark of the early proposals for North American colonies and would persist into the ideology of the African colonization movement.[25]

The convergence between northern and southern proposals increasingly led colonizationists to advocate for creating black colonies as an instrument of federal policy.[26] But it was in Virginia, after a slave uprising known commonly as Gabriel's Rebellion took place in 1800, where politicians suggested the first concrete action toward creating such a colony. The primary leader of the revolt, Gabriel Prosser, planned to lead a march on Virginia's capital in Richmond with a group of slaves who would then seize the city and consequently spark a general rebellion throughout the state. The plot was never executed after two slaves aware of the plan alerted the authorities. As a result, Prosser and twenty-three of his coconspirators were captured and put to death. That his plans for the rebellion were influenced by both the French Revolution and the slave rebellions in the Caribbean confirmed the worst fears already voiced by early proponents of colonization. The failed uprising created a renewed impetus in Virginia for concerted state action to create a western colony for free African Americans.[27]

Only a few months after Gabriel and his collaborators were executed, the Virginia Assembly considered multiple resolutions aimed at circumventing future revolutionary actions. Some of this legislation was passed into law and implemented regimes of greater control over enslaved populations by expanding the power of state militias and strengthening the state's slave patrol system. On the heels of this legislative push, the Virginia House of Delegates also passed an open-ended proposal asking the federal government for support in "purchasing lands without the limits of this State" so that persons "dangerous to the peace of society may be removed."[28]

A few weeks after Virginia passed these resolutions, George Tucker, St. George Tucker's cousin, anonymously published a pamphlet titled *Letter to a Member of the General Assembly of Virginia, on the Subject of the Late Conspiracy of the Slaves with a Proposal for Their Colonization*. Tucker went further than the Virginia resolution, which had suggested something more akin to a penal colony for rebellious slaves, arguing that all African Americans in Virginia should be colonized on the "Western side of the Mississippi" in "some part of Indian country." While his cousin had previously proposed gradual abolition of slavery and colonization for a limited number of enslaved people, George Tucker believed that only the complete transplantation of Virginia's black population could prevent future waves of revolution within the state.[29]

Like other early proponents of such colonies, Tucker explicitly framed his plan as a response to the appropriation of the "rights of man" by free and enslaved people of African descent in the French Caribbean. He warned his readers that black populations in the United States were rapidly gaining knowledge of the same republican discourses of liberty: "In our infant country, where population and wealth increase with unexampled rapidity, the progress of liberal knowledge is proportionally great. In this vast march of the mind, the blacks, who are far behind us, may be supposed to advance at a pace equal to our own; but, sir, the fact is, they are likely to advance much faster." He also argued that slaves' awareness of civil institutions and republican ideas in the United States made this an even more dangerous situation: "The very nature of our government, which leads us to recur perpetually to the discussion of national rights, favors speculation and enquiry." Contending that this exposure had changed the consciousness of slaves in the few decades since British Loyalist forces offered emancipation during the Revolutionary War, he claimed: "The difference is, that then they fought freedom merely as a good; now they also claim it as a right." Tucker believed that this growing threat could only be alleviated by sending African Americans to a territory "under the protection and immediate government of this state, or the United States, until it contained a number of inhabitants sufficient to manage their own concerns." Due to such a colony's minimal resources and relative size, he imagined an asymmetrical colonial relationship with any resulting nation: "We may be to them a haughty and domineering neighbor; they never could be terrible to us."[30]

Tucker's aptly timed pamphlet made a significant impact in the wake of Gabriel's Rebellion. The tract proved so popular among the Virginian elite that a second edition was rushed out only a few months after its initial pressing.[31] Shortly after its publication, Governor James Monroe privately wrote to President Thomas Jefferson to inquire about the much-discussed concept of western colonies. As the newly elected president, Jefferson was in a powerful position to advance the colonization idea he had partially helped pioneer. While the correspondence was not made public at the time, their letters reflect the serious attention given to western colonization plans at the highest levels of government. As Virginia's governor, Monroe was writing on behalf of his state's resolution requesting federal support to remove "persons obnoxious to the laws or dangerous to the peace of society." He also hoped that this narrowly defined proposal would serve as an entrée into a broader federal policy for establishing black colonies in the West. In this vein, he urged Jefferson to contemplate the subject "beyond the contracted scale of providing a mode of punishment for offenders." Specifically, he asked Jefferson "whether a tract of land in the Western territory of the United States can be procured for this purpose, in what quarter, and on what terms?"[32]

In Jefferson's reply to Monroe, he signaled his continued support for colonizationism, but he also revealed his skepticism about integrating African
Americans into the United States' plans for settlement. While Jefferson, like
his fellow southern slaveholders, was profoundly disturbed by the prospect
of slave insurrection, he did not share their optimism about the possibility of
North American colonies for African Americans. Although he had broadly
entertained the idea in the early 1780s, by the time he became president in
1800 he was more explicitly focused on establishing the racial geography of the
United States' settler empire. In response to Monroe's query, he voiced some
practical concerns about the plan and questioned whether land could be easily
procured when it was controlled by several Indian nations and was subject
to the competing interests of the British, French, and Spanish empires. More
tellingly, Jefferson expressed his concern about the long-term consequences of
planting such colonies in North America and predicted: "It is impossible not
to look forward to distant times, when our rapid multiplication will expand
itself beyond those limits, and cover the whole Northern, if not the Southern continent, with a people speaking the same language, governed in similar
forms and by similar laws." Even before his monumental purchase of the Louisiana Territory from France in 1803, Jefferson was envisioning his "empire of
liberty," in which white American settlers would extend republican political
institutions throughout the continent. Jefferson saw no way for African Americans to be part of this expansionist project, concluding that the United States
must not "contemplate with satisfaction either blot or mixture in that surface."
Jefferson used this ambiguous, and racially loaded, turn of phrase to conflate
the imperatives of sustaining a settler empire in North America with the goal
of maintaining the white racial character of the nation, which he believed a
black colony would inevitably disrupt.[33]

This racial logic was also clear when, in the same letter, Jefferson somewhat facetiously entertained the idea of incorporating black colonies into the
established processes for settling territory organized by the Northwest Ordinance, which was set out under the Articles of Confederation in the 1780s.
Jefferson noted that while doing so would be an "expensive provision," there
was "nothing which would restrain the State of Virginia" from purchasing
"a very great extent of country north of the Ohio" that was currently being
sold and had already been plotted into townships. Yet he seemed to raise this
suggestion only to demonstrate the apparent absurdity of planting black colonies in North America altogether: "Questions would also arise whether the
establishment of such a colony within our limits, and to become a part of
our union, would be desirable to the State of Virginia itself, or to the other

States—especially those who would be in its vicinity?" While other white leaders at the turn of the century still imagined that black colonies might play some kind of role in the United States' growing continental empire, Jefferson had already come to believe that establishing independent black colonies was a dangerous impediment to the nation's plans of expansion. As a result, during his presidency Jefferson would largely eschew the prevailing notion of creating a North American colony; instead, he tentatively pursued the prospect of building on the existing British colony in Sierra Leone.[34]

Jefferson's resistance to this idea foreshadows the ways that the United States' settlement would become increasingly defined by race as the nation colonized more of North America in the coming decades. His widely influential racial views, most clearly expressed in *Notes on the State of Virginia*, were that peoples of African descent were inherently inferior to Europeans. In that same text, Jefferson judged Native Americans somewhat differently and argued that, while still largely inferior to Europeans, they might be racially fit to cooperate in the colonization of North America. Near the end of his second term in office, he famously told a group of Native Americans that "we shall all be Americans, you will mix with us by marriage, your blood will run in our veins, & will spread with us over this great Island." In other words, Native peoples might become part of the U.S. settler state if they abandoned their tribal identities and assimilated into whiteness, an assumption that largely underpinned federal Indian "civilization" policy at the time.[35]

While Jefferson's exchange with Monroe provides only a brief glimpse into his thoughts concerning the possibility of black settlements, it is telling that he implicitly framed the issue around how to maintain a settler empire. Whether Native Americans might be either peaceably or forcibly assimilated into a white settler population was a question that future generations would adjudicate. For Jefferson, African Americans were racially unassimilable; therefore, black colonies, whether loosely connected to the United States or constituted as independent nations, would represent a fundamental threat to the ongoing coherence of white settler statehood.

The Racial Geography of Settlement

In the short term, some early colonizationists, unlike Jefferson himself, could still envision a version of the Jeffersonian "empire of liberty" that also carved out space for black settlers. After the United States' 1803 purchase of the Louisiana Territory from France, Jefferson's divergence from fellow Virginians would become increasingly evident as it served to fuel hopes that part of that territory could be set aside for the purposes of a black colony.[36] Despite the president's discouragement of black colonies within western territories, the Virginia legislature persisted in passing more resolutions in January 1802, February 1804, and January 1805 asking the federal government to take action to establish such a colony. The text of both the second and third resolutions referred to the recent purchase of the Louisiana Territory, with the 1805 resolution urging the U.S. Congress to "exert their best efforts for the purpose of obtaining . . . a competent portion of territory, in the country of Louisiana, to be appropriated to the residence of such people of colour as have been or shall be emancipated in Virginia."[37]

That the Virginia resolutions specifically looked to Louisiana illustrates how the purchase of that territory had already begun to reconfigure many Americans' view of empire within North America.[38] Ultimately, the Louisiana Purchase would facilitate the two defining features of early American empire building: the rapid displacement of Indian communities in the Northwest and Southwest and an expansion of chattel slavery in the Deep South. Both of these actions would violently transplant nonwhite populations in vast numbers: dozens of Native American nations to a federally established "Indian Territory" and more than a million African Americans, through a "second middle passage," to newly colonized fertile cotton-growing lands. Although white Americans would eventually rationalize these actions by developing ever more elaborate justifications for expansion, at the time the United States acquired the Louisiana Territory, many Americans were skeptical about the benefits of such an unprecedented federal expenditure and questioned whether large-scale settlement in the region was possible or even desirable.[39]

In the short term, this initial uncertainty about the fate of this territory seems to have briefly sustained the idea of planting black colonies in the West. In a pamphlet published shortly after the Louisiana Purchase, St. George Tucker asserted that these newly claimed lands could finally help realize the colony he had envisioned since the mid-1790s. While Tucker's pamphlet was written primarily to extol the benefits of the newly acquired territory and convince Americans of its value, he also reflected the broader national anxieties surrounding the purchase. He cautioned against expanding white settlement into the region because he believed that an already sparse U.S. population would not be well served by further dispersal through such a vast territory. He suggested that Louisiana would be hospitable to black settlement, in part, by invoking popular climate-based racial theories that would later feature prominently in colonizationist arguments about the suitability of tropical lands in both Africa and Central America. Tucker contended: "The southern parts of Louisiana ... lie under a climate more favourable for the African constitution than any part of the United States," and he hoped that "we may colonize those unhappy people" there if "the great work of the abolition of slavery should be accomplished in Virginia." While Tucker loosely sketched these suggestions within his broader efforts to promote the colonization of Louisiana, they illustrate elite Virginians' continued interest in creating black colonies amid the expansionist horizons opened by the Louisiana Purchase.[40]

Northern antislavery writers were also enlivened by the territory's potential, and over the next few years they too persisted in recommending the creation of a western colony there. One of the most prominent voices was that of Thomas Branagan, an Irish immigrant to the United States who became an active participant in Philadelphia's antislavery community.[41] In 1805 Branagan published a pamphlet titled *Serious Remonstrances Addressed to the Citizens of the Northern States*, in which he renewed the case for a western colony among northern audiences. Like St. George Tucker, Branagan envisioned an independent settlement of African Americans in Louisiana that could stand separate from the United States even as it helped spread U.S. political institutions across the continent. Branagan recommended that African Americans should be given a "free and independent" state somewhere in "some distant part of the national domains." He argued that within such a territory, they could still remain connected to the U.S. settler state, being managed from afar and potentially reincorporated at some point in the future. Like most advocates of western colonies, Branagan was insistent upon the inevitable prospect of a "general rebellion" among African Americans, which he predicted could span "from Georgia to New Hampshire." This perspective led him to regard all African Americans, both enslaved and free, as domestic threats, contending, "The sons of Africa in America, are the inveterate enemies of Americans, and are at perpetual war with them." To underscore the gravity of this threat, Branagan included several pages about "the fate of St. Domingo" as a cautionary tale.[42]

John Parrish, a Quaker antislavery activist also based in Philadelphia, was similarly inspired to write a colonizationist pamphlet in the wake of the Louisiana Purchase. In *Remarks on the Slavery of Black People*, Parrish argued that sentiments of universal liberty within the Declaration of Independence and the Constitution needed to be extended to all people, and failure to do so would ultimately sow the seeds of revolt and undermine the republic. He contended: "If it were not meant as is declared, to form a more perfect union, it must have a contrary effect, and instead of securing domestic tranquility, it will consequently tend to promote insurrection, by depriving the coloured people of those rights." While Parrish believed the abolition of slavery was inevitable, like many of the early supporters of colonization, he was particularly concerned about how this process would unfold, warning that "the day is hastening when this people will become free; and it is desirable it should be with the consent of those who have authority over them." Anticipating critics, such as Jefferson, who worried that emancipation would result in racial mixture, he argued that his colonization plan, animated by republican principles, would actually aid the separation of racial groups. Parrish suggested that "when [former slaves were] colonized" they would enjoy "liberty and the rights of citizenship, the possession of property and attachment to domestic happiness," which would "promote" and "preserve the distinctions of nation and colour." Like Branagan, he suggested that the U.S. federal government could easily establish such a colony by assigning "a tract within some part of the western wilderness (where there are millions of acres likely to continue many ages unoccupied)." Employing the common settler rhetoric that imagined the West as largely "open" territory, Parrish implicitly envisioned the occupation of this land by black settlers as a process in which Native communities would be pushed aside and displaced.[43]

Two years later, William Thornton outlined an even more detailed plan for black colonies in North America. Back in the late 1780s, Thornton had rejected the idea that African Americans could be integrated into the United States' settlement strategy; however, the prospect of the Louisiana Purchase seems to have changed his mind by expanding the geographic scope for national expansion.[44] Like Parrish, Thornton was a Quaker antislavery advocate, but he argued that immediate emancipation would "endanger the repose of society" and instead proposed gradual emancipation. To begin with, former slaves would "be engaged on the public works" under temporary guardianship of the government for a period of two to five years. This would prepare them for emancipation while creating "the public roads, the bridges, the canals and ferries" necessary to build the nation. After this period, the former slaves, as wards of the government, would gradually colonize a region somewhere in the western reaches of North America.[45]

Thornton insisted that the United States was in the process of becoming a "great Empire," and he asserted that because the United States laid claim to "regions sufficiently extensive for all our people," emancipated slaves could be given "property in soil, suited to their constitutions" and would "soon be industrious and valuable citizens." Expressing the prevailing arguments about the inevitability of large-scale slave revolt, he asked, "Should they be condemned for laying waste the whole Empire to free themselves?" He continued, "While they are slaves they are dangerous to our welfare: they are our natural enemies; but if made free they become friends."[46]

Like many of the prior writers who proposed North American colonies, Thornton argued that former slaves could instead be loosely integrated into a conception of U.S. empire. Most proposals had very little to say about the indigenous populations already inhabiting the regions being suggested for colonization, generally implying that these territories were already possessed by the United States or that they were simply "unoccupied." However, Thornton imagined that black settlers could have a specific role as intermediaries to Indian nations, who he believed would ultimately have a similar relationship to the United States. While he conceded that "the Indians are said to have an antipathy to the blacks" because they have "been reduced to a state truly abject," he believed that coexistence between Native peoples and black settlers would be possible. Thornton contended that "if these same Indians were to find the blacks countenanced and supported by the whites . . . they would soon learn to respect them." Beyond this, he compared the position of a potential black colony to that of Indian nations who "themselves require protection" and the "fostering care of our government." In this sense, when Thornton argued that "nations of white, red and black men, all in peace, all in fraternity," could live together "under the wings of the American Eagle," he foreshadowed the critical decisions by John Marshall's Supreme Court two decades later that paternalistically characterized Native peoples as "domestic dependent nations." In such a view, Thornton expressed an optimistic vision of an American empire in which geographical spaces occupied by African American colonizers and colonized Native Americans could be both carefully managed and harmoniously reconciled.[47]

Thornton's plan was in line with the broader constellation of plans circulating during this era, albeit devoting more explicit attention to the complex racial politics that would be inherent to establishing any such western colony on Native lands. Like the majority of such proposals, Thornton's plan not only called for the exclusion of African Americans but also envisioned an affiliated settler society that would complement the United States' interests on the continent. Moses Fisk's early 1790s proposal argued that such a colony could channel African Americans' yearning for rights into a separate political structure where they could achieve autonomy, yet he suggested that it would be managed tightly within objectives dictated by the United States.[48] Similarly, Thomas Branagan envisioned an independent settlement of African

Americans in the Louisiana Territory where they could be integrated into a broader settlement strategy that held the possibility of reincorporation in the future.[49] Even George Tucker, whose Virginia audience was primarily focused on removing "dangerous" slaves after Gabriel's Rebellion, emphasized a quasi-independent colony that would be protected until it could manage on its own yet remain subordinate to the broader interests of the nation.[50]

The idea of using a black colony in North America to geographically engineer the nation's racial dynamics would remain an enduring theme of such plans until the mid-1810s, when the ACS began to dominate all discussions of colonizationism. One of the last published writings of this era to advocate a western colony was an 1810 pamphlet by Lewis Dupré, who framed the plan in precisely these terms. Dupré was an eccentric writer and inventor from Charleston, South Carolina. His antislavery views were increasingly out of step within his native South; however, he shared the belief of other early colonizationists that emancipation could be engineered through a reorganization of U.S. territory because "we are at no loss for a continent on to which we might transport emancipated Africans." Like other colonizationists of this era, he imagined that by settling the continent, former slaves could be turned from inveterate enemies to geopolitical allies. Unlike the more loosely sketched proposals of this era, Dupré viewed this black colony as having an explicit role in securing space for the United States' empire on the continent at the same time that it would neutralize the nation's internal threat from within. He argued that African Americans would be transformed from "an army of foes . . . dispersed throughout the very heart of our territory" into a "strong bulwark against the encroachment of neighboring or foreign invaders" because the United States could "purchase their friendship and services on cheaper terms than any other nation."[51] Dupré did not elaborate on the relations with Indian nations he envisioned for the colonies or why black colonists would willingly coordinate with U.S. settlement. Nevertheless, he believed that the colonies would inevitably become useful proxies for the United States within North America.[52]

Dupré's plan was the last in the crop of proposals published in the first decade of the nineteenth century that built on the momentum of Virginia's early colonization efforts and the promise of the Louisiana Purchase. Despite the regional diversity of authors, most of these plans were remarkably similar to each other and to the earlier proposals of the 1790s, sharing the premise that the United States could avoid a revolution by managing the process by which African Americans would come to realize both their freedom from slavery and their political liberty. Above all, these plans highlight the fact that colonizationism was always about far more than simply ending slavery or removing a population that was considered to be troublesome. Therefore, it is essential to frame the early colonization movement within an emerging and heterogeneous body of ideas about how the United States would settle North American territory. As such, they offer a glimpse into how politicians and activists were beginning, at this early stage of the republic, to map national space and even imagine alternative racial geographies.[53]

At the same time, all of these strategies for colonization in North America were either explicitly or implicitly dedicated to maintaining racial separation. As John Parrish suggested in his proposal, a black colony would be designed to promote racial distinctions rather than eliminate them. Prospective black colonists were seen to be neither equal nor fully independent and were to be ultimately subsumed within the logic of the U.S. settler state despite their explicit separation from it. While most colonization proposals were open-ended and highly provisional, they all imagined the possibility of a coordinated, yet segregated, continental settler empire.[54]

Preventing an "African Tecumseh"

In the mid-1810s the idea of creating black colonies in North America was rapidly overshadowed by the growing campaign to plant a similar colony in Africa. The declining prospects for North American colonies owe much to a factor that early colonizationists almost entirely ignored in their written proposals: the profound reality of Native Americans' ongoing resistance to U.S. settlement. In doing so, they largely sidestepped the critical question of whether black colonies might ultimately impede, rather than advance, U.S. expansion by aligning with Indian nations who were also struggling to assert their sovereignty amid the racial logic of the emerging settler state. In the years leading up to the formation of the ACS, such questions would help drive the conversation about colonizationism away from North America and toward Africa. Increasingly, white leaders cautioned that such colonies would complicate relations with enslaved African Americans and independent Native Americans, raising the frightening prospect they might even unleash the very revolutionary potential that colonizationists hoped to counteract.

This reveals the fact that colonizationism was inevitably bound up with the evolving dynamics of establishing a settler state and how the United States would respond to the renewal of Native resistance movements at the turn of the nineteenth century. White settlers expanded into more western lands in the 1790s after the Northwest Ordinance created a framework for colonizing and politically organizing the new territories that would eventually become "the Midwest." As a result, Indian nations east of the Mississippi River came under constant pressure as their relative strength in the region was diminished through U.S. military campaigns, federal Indian civilization policies, and a steady rush of white settlers onto their lands.[55]

In the first decades of the nineteenth century, the most prominent example of Native resistance to settler encroachment was the movement fostered by the Shawnee leader Tecumseh, in collaboration with his brother, the prophet Tenskwatawa. Together they helped organize growing discontent among several northwestern Indian nations and led the opposition to U.S. policies that often isolated individual tribal leaders in order to facilitate land concessions. Tenskwatawa represented a long prophetic tradition among Trans-Appalachian Native peoples who rejected Euro-American expansion and perceived European culture as fundamentally malevolent. Tecumseh built on his brother's religious movement and forged it into a political alliance of multiple Indian polities that were poised to rebel against land cessions, military violence, and civilizationist assimilation.[56]

Tecumseh's leadership facilitated the expansion of a new pan-Indian politics, which had been developing for several decades in response to rapidly diminishing Native lands and attempts by the United States to transform Native Americans into small-scale farmers who would be alienated from tribal claims to territory and political sovereignty.[57] In his efforts to facilitate a broad diplomatic coalition that could array multiple Indian nations against the United States, Tecumseh traveled to the Creek nation in Alabama and helped inspire a similar political and religious movement among a traditionalist faction known as the Red Sticks. When this group attacked Fort Mims in 1813, the conflict expanded into what became known as the "Creek War" in which the U.S. Army enlisted rival factions of the Creek nation to stop the rebellious Red Sticks. The United States forcefully suppressed pan-Indian resistance precisely because it aimed to impose permanent limitations on U.S settlement. Leaders of the alliance argued that when such a boundary was secured, Native Americans would be able to embrace a separate destiny that was free from the pernicious influence of whites. After a series of military clashes with the U.S. government, before and during the War of 1812, both Tecumseh's movement and aligned groups such as the

Red Sticks were defeated and the alliance between several northwestern and southern tribes fell apart. Like Toussaint L'Ouverture, Tecumseh became a powerful symbol of resistance to white supremacy, and his leadership suggested the possibility of organizing a different political reality in which Indian self-determination might undermine the unbounded expansion of U.S. settlement in North America.[58]

In response to these developments, colonizationists increasingly reflected on the connections between Native resistance movements and the threat of black rebellion as they began to shift their focus toward Africa in the mid-1810s. In one of the foundational texts of the African colonization movement, *Thoughts on the Colonization of Free Blacks* (1816), ACS cofounder Robert Finley directly addressed the feasibility of the prior North American proposals. Finley concluded that the risks were too great to have "in our vicinity an independent settlement of people who were once our slaves," and he wondered whether "there might be cause of dread lest they should occasionally combine with our Indian neighbors."[59] Samuel Mills, the other cofounder of the organization, voiced similar concerns to a British minister: "Should they [African Americans] ultimately obtain their freedom, which is more than probable, the position of the American government would be extremely embarrassing. To incorporate them into the Republic as an Independent part of it would be scarcely possible. To permit them to remain as a separate Nation, with political interests opposed to it, would be a dangerous expedient."[60]

After the formation of the ACS in 1816, the organization produced a widely circulated pamphlet that summarized its principles and used the same reasons outlined by Mills to dismiss the possibility of a western colony. The promotional literature for the newly formed ACS admitted that a black settlement in the West "would be cheaper, and more immediately under the eye and control of our government" but also expressed concern that "they might here after join the Indians, or the nations bordering on our frontiers in the cause of war, if they were placed so near us—that the colony would become the asylum of fugitive and runaway slaves." A growing number of colonizationists viewed African Americans' aspirations for sovereignty within North America as a dangerous prospect when paired with the potential collaboration of Indian allies.[61]

Such fears were not entirely unfounded. The actions of fugitive slaves, sometimes in concert with Native Americans, had demonstrated that independent communities of African Americans could both disrupt plans for white settlement and potentially threaten the continued expansion of slavery.

For instance, in the 1811 uprising on the German Coast of Louisiana, more than two hundred slaves marched on the city of New Orleans in an attempt to ignite a widespread rebellion. There is evidence that the plot resulted from both slaves' awareness of the successful Haitian revolution and support from independent maroon settlements of escaped slaves within nearby Louisiana swamps.[62] A few years later, the U.S. Army destroyed the so-called Negro Fort in the Florida Panhandle region because it was occupied by nearly eight hundred fugitive slaves as well as a handful of Choctaw and Seminole Indians. The existence of an ostensibly sovereign settlement of heavily armed African Americans near the U.S. border was intolerable to both the U.S. military and southern slaveholders, a prospect made all the more disconcerting by its connections to the surrounding Native communities.[63]

The collaboration evident at the Negro Fort was part of a long-standing tradition of intermittent and often fraught alliances between former slaves and Indians in the Southeast. In particular the Seminoles, although slaveholders themselves, provided occasional sanctuary for fugitive slaves by adopting them into their communities. African Americans played a decisive role in several Seminole conflicts with the United States during this era, including Payne's War from 1812 to 1814 in northern Florida. Furthermore, several African Americans acted as soldiers in the Tecumseh-aligned Red Stick War, and some black refugees from this defeat were involved in the construction of the independent military fort. Slaveholders feared that this instance of cooperation between former slaves and Native Americans might encourage other such communities to join together in combating the objectives of U.S. settlers, particularly those who wanted to expand slavery in the region.[64] John McIntosh, a white settler fighting Seminoles in eastern Florida, wrote to James Monroe, then secretary of war, arguing that if such alliances were left unchecked, "the whole province will be the refuge of fugitive slaves" and would be "detached to bring about a revolt of the black population in the United States." The collaboration of African Americans and Native Americans was even more threatening because some aligned with broader pan-Indian efforts and suggested the possibility of wide-ranging political coalitions against both U.S. expansion and white supremacy.[65]

During the mid-1810s, colonizationists foregrounded these questions when they began to largely abandon the concept of creating black colonies within North America. Shortly after the ACS formed in late 1816, Congress issued a report on the question of federal support for an African colony. The report disappointed many ACS members for its tepid endorsement of a federal role in colonization, but it did reflect the emerging consensus against planting a black colony within North America. While acknowledging that "every new territory established by our government, constitutes, indeed, a colony," the report argued that they had only been successful because they were "an extension of homogenous settlement," echoing Jefferson's previous sentiments in his correspondence with Monroe. The congressional report also noted that black colonies were problematic because "the rapidly extending settlements of our white inhabitants would soon reach them" and they would likely need to be "planted on lands now owned and occupied by the native tribes of the country," predicting that "it is not difficult to foresee the quarrels and destructive wars" that would result "should the colony so increase as to become a nation."[66] An editorial in the *National Register* concurred with the report's assessment of "the evil effects which would accrue to the nation by colonizing them anywhere upon this continent." Furthermore, it suggested that such a colony threatened not only the homogeneity of settlement but also the nation's security, because it could be "tampered with and brought over, as the Indians are, by an enemy, in the event of war with a foreign power."[67]

Within this context, Virginia's politicians, the vanguard of colonizationism since the 1790s, now began to shift their support firmly toward the new African colonization movement. Little more than a decade after the state's assembly had repeatedly asked the federal government for help in establishing black colonies in the West, it adopted new resolutions arguing that such a colony should be created in the "territory upon the coast of Africa, or upon the shore of the North Pacific, or at some other place, not within any of the States, or territorial governments of the United States." These resolutions were passed two days before the inaugural meeting of the ACS in Washington, D.C., providing further support for the growing campaign for a national African colonization organization.[68]

By the late 1810s the prospects for creating a black settlement in the West had faded to such an extent that most colonizationists now decisively embraced the emerging ACS vision for an African colony. In fact, once the North American colony was effectively rejected by African colonizationists, only a handful of antislavery activists, who were unconvinced of Africa's viability for a colony, continued to champion the idea. Only one year after the ACS was formed, the American Convention for Promoting the Abolition of Slavery (ACPAS), a prominent Philadelphia antislavery society, was unable to make any progress in promoting its plan to construct such a colony in the Missouri Territory. In 1818 the ACPAS issued an annual report that criticized African colonizationists and called their ideas "impracticable" with potentially "fatal consequences to those who shall embark on its purposes."[69]

Despite the distinct shift toward Africa among colonizationists, the ACPAS continued to argue that a western colony could become a subordinate partner in the nation's expansion onto Native lands: "By the cession of Louisiana, the United States have become entitled to the exclusive purchase of immense tracts of land westward of the Mississippi." Their 1819 report argued that a colony of free blacks could be settled there at minimal expense and would create a "territorial or provincial form of government, calculated for the protection of property and personal right." In advocating such a territory, the ACPAS pointedly targeted the prevalent arguments against creating an sovereign colony outside the borders of white settlement. While arguing that the erection of an "independent power" that could become "a dangerous enemy" was an "alarming prospect," it was not that different from "the political relations of the Indian tribes, who now use the same surface of territory." The ACPAS contended that black settlement in the West would have even greater prospects for the management of the territory because emancipated slaves would transport "a great portion of those civil arts, which they have acquired or observed among us." Furthermore, the report argued, like some earlier colonizationists, that the anticipated emulation of U.S. institutions by black settlers might make them a bulwark against Indian populations and a more pliable ally in westward expansion. The report rhetorically asked: "Will they not carry with them an attachment to, and a sense of dependence upon us? Will they not form a strong and useful contrast to the proud and jealous spirit of independence, which actuates the Indians?" Like the earlier generation of colonizationists, the ACPAS envisioned a colony that would retain strategic allegiance to the United States by expanding its political institutions throughout North America. However, by the early 1820s such notions were increasingly outmoded as most colonizationists were convinced that the United States' empire in North America should be reserved for white settlement alone and the movement should instead focus its energy on creating a colony that would become the "United States of Africa."[70]

In Missouri, as elsewhere on the western frontier, slaveholders dictated both the character and pace of white settlement and helped definitively foreclose alternative racial geographies of settlement that might have included independent black colonies. At the same time, the ACS worked to undermine fleeting efforts to shift the colonization debate back toward North America by aggressively gathering donations and planting auxiliary societies across the United States throughout the early 1820s. Shortly after the ACPAS report recommended North American colonies, Missouri was admitted to the union as a slave state. This dashed the organization's hope that the territory might be used for a black colony and highlighted how the westward advance of slavery was increasingly making any such plan inconceivable. By 1821 the ACPAS succumbed to these forces and revoked its prior recommendation for such a colony citing the widespread fear that "if slavery in the United States is permitted still to exist . . . the proposed colony [would] become an asylum for runaway slaves."[71]

The fact that such proposals persisted, even amid ACS consolidation, demonstrates that the organization was unable to completely sweep away alternative plans. Nevertheless, the capitulation of the ACPAS illustrates how quickly the concept of a North American colony was being eclipsed by the ACS vision of African colonization. It also shows how deeply intertwined the United States' empire had become with both expansion of slavery and the reproduction of a white settler citizenry. While earlier colonizationists had entertained the open-ended possibilities of settler expansion in Louisiana, only two decades later the Missouri Territory, carved out of its eastern reaches, no longer seemed so distant, and the nation's leading colonizationists now found it virtually unthinkable that this land could harbor an independent black colony.[72]

As the United States displaced Indian nations within the former eastern borderlands of places such as Missouri, the remaining proponents of black colonies in North America found that they had virtually no base of political support even as they looked further west to ever more distant settler frontiers. In 1825 George Tucker, by then a U.S. representative from Virginia, attempted to introduce a congressional resolution that would appropriate "a part of the country beyond the Rocky Mountains to the free people of color." While wishing the African colonization movement "all possible success," he argued that they did not "promise any effectual remedy for the evil" because North American colonization would be far cheaper and more attractive to black settlers than West Africa. Tucker proposed to set aside a portion of territory west of the Rockies that would have "the benefit and protection of a territorial government, until they were able to govern and protect themselves." He dismissed the now popular idea that the colony would become a haven for fugitive freed slaves or that it would become a "troublesome neighbor," because it would be "weak and insignificant" and "dread of our superior power would ensure their respect."[73]

Although such sentiments echoed colonizationists' earlier claims that North American colonies would ultimately be subordinate to the United States' broader imperial interests, Tucker's proposal was clearly out of step with the prevailing political climate. The fact that members of Congress greeted his new proposal with open hostility reveals how the conceptual and geographic scope of the United States' empire had shifted in the quarter century since Virginia's political elite had seriously considered George Tucker's earlier proposal.[74] In the intervening decades, the U.S. settler frontier had advanced well beyond the former boundary of the Mississippi River. In Tucker's estimation, the Rocky Mountains now formed a natural border where the United States could be separated "from them by a mountain and a wide desert" to "prevent the escape of our slaves." Tucker's proposal did not acknowledge any threat posed by the settlement's potential collaboration with Indian nations because it failed to mention Native populations at all. His implicit assumption was that the northwestern portion of North America would be governed by colonizers, rather than Native people, and that "it certainly seems better for us that it should be settled by two or more nations than by one—partly by Africans, and by Russians, if you please, than wholly by an Anglo-American population." Acknowledging the United States' weak settler presence in that contested portion of the continent, Tucker suggested that a republic governed by "Africans" would serve as a useful proxy for the United States in the region.[75]

Tucker claimed that a strategy of multiracial settlements could have numerous advantages for the United States, yet his ideas contrasted the prevailing consensus that the nation's settler empire had no place for black colonies, regardless of their presumed benefits. Although an earlier generation of politicians had seriously entertained Tucker's proposals, by 1825 a majority within the House of Representatives refused to even consider the resolution. Shortly after this failure, he took to the press to defend his ideas and point out that he "hardly expected to hear a policy denounced as dangerous which has received the sanction of the highest names on the list of American patriots and sages." While George Tucker could certainly claim prominent supporters of similar plans in decades past, by the mid-1820s he was among a dwindling minority as most colonizationists had judged such a plan to be incompatible with the United States' expansion on the continent.[76]

By the early 1820s Americans increasingly rejected Tucker's ideas, in part because they had come to see the prospect of both African American and Native American sovereignty as distinct yet overlapping threats to the coherence of a white settler empire. Leonard Bacon, a Congregationalist minister and early African colonizationist, voiced these converging fears when he asked Americans to support the ACS colony in Africa by warning that "a Toussaint, or a Spartacus, or an African Tecumseh" would lead slaves to insurrection "and we shall witness scenes—which history describes, but from the thought of which the imagination revolts." With his allusion to Toussaint L'Ouverture, Bacon echoed the early colonizationist refrain that revolution always loomed around the corner, but he also suggestively linked it to this era's primary figure of Native resistance by evoking the dangerous prospect of racial hybridization with the phrase "African Tecumseh." Such a rhetorical formulation highlights why African colonizationists such as Bacon increasingly found the notion that black colonies could be planted on indigenous lands incomprehensible.[77]

* * *

During an era that witnessed the acceleration of white settlement throughout the West and the growing entrenchment of slavery within the Deep South, the demise of proposals for black colonies in North America might seem inevitable. Nevertheless, influential white leaders had entertained this idea for more than two decades, so it is remarkable how quickly the fledgling colonization movement definitively embraced an African colony over other alternatives. Before the ACS achieved hegemony for its vision of the colony, colonizationists suggested that African Americans could be mutual, if inherently unequal, partners in the United States' colonization of North America and that the resulting colonies might function as a buffer between white settlement and Native populations. Over time, such a view fell by the wayside as colonizationists came to see these colonies not as bulwarks but as obstacles of settlement. By the mid-1810s many Americans had grown concerned that independent black colonies would pose the same threats as sovereign Indian nations: they could serve as havens for fugitive slaves while creating impediments to a settler empire that was increasingly oriented around expanding the reach of slavery. While American leaders proposed such colonies, in part, to maintain the foundations of white supremacy in North America, they increasingly feared that these settlements could have the opposite effect by providing a foundation for greater alliances between independent communities of Native Americans and African Americans.

These overlapping concerns about autonomy among nonwhite populations reflect a broader shift in how white Americans envisioned the racial geography of settlement within their rapidly expanding continental empire. By the early 1820s the ACS had popularized the concept of an African colony, a plan that promised to sidestep the fraught racial politics of expansion within North America. As a parallel settler society charged with planting republicanism in a distant territory, the eventual ACS colony in Liberia maintained some continuity with the earlier North American proposals. However, this new colony's supporters envisioned it as a "United States of Africa" that would formally exist outside the bounds of continental settlement and thus embody the global dimensions of early American empire.

CHAPTER 2

Colonization Doctrines

Three years after the formation of the ACS, an anonymous writer under the pen name "Warburton" advocated a plan for creating a colony of African Americans in California. On its face, this proposal resembled some of the recently abandoned plans for western colonies. However, its specific details reveal how thoroughly the ACS had already come to define colonizationism in the few short years since the organization was founded. Unlike the writers of many earlier western plans, the editorialist did not envision a California colony as part of the United States' settler empire. Instead, like the ACS, he maintained that such a colony "should be constituted [as] an independent government" and ultimately to become "a distinguished nation." He also joined many ACS members in the view that the ultimate goal of colonization was to shape the United States into an exclusively white republic and he predicted that "in a century, there would not be among us a black slave, or perhaps even a black man." Addressing a key concern that had driven colonizationists to look toward Africa, he argued that California's great distance from the United States' current settlements meant that white Americans could embrace, rather than fear, collaboration between black settlers and indigenous populations. In this respect, he joined African colonizationists in envisioning California as a kind of racial republic in which African Americans would "disseminat[e] the blessings of civilization" to the "multitude of demi-savages" who could "knit together by a government of perfect equality" people descended from "all nations and colors" because they would "not have an antipathy to mingle their blood with the natives."[1]

That these themes appeared in a proposal that was pitched as an *alternative* to African colonization is a testament to the ways that colonizationist doctrines had been both widely circulated and increasingly consolidated following the creation of the ACS. The proposal was published as an editorial in the *National Intelligencer*, a prominent political journal that had played a crucial role in supporting and publicizing the early African colonization movement. Within this context, the plan might be viewed as a fleeting effort to shift colonizationists' attention back toward North America. In some respects this is true, but strikingly it articulated a shape for the colony largely modeled on the foundations of emerging ACS ideology. While nominally a continental proposal, it signaled the organization's increasing emphasis on internationalist vision for colonizationism. As a separate and independent racial republic, the proposed California colony, like the eventual ACS colony in Liberia, would be structurally distinct from the United States' colonization of North America yet part of the nation's broader global ambitions. While many earlier proposals had set their sights on relatively proximate or contiguous territories, California, then still tenuously claimed by the Spanish empire amid the ongoing war of Mexican independence, remained a distant horizon for most Americans. While it was contained within North America, the difficulty of overland continental travel meant that it would be effectively, like the ACS settlement in West Africa, an overseas colony.

The fact that this California colony was pitched at a far remove from the boundaries of the United States' current settlement bears the direct imprint of the emerging African colonization movement. Since the Revolutionary era the idea of creating black colonies had been bound up with lingering questions concerning the racial geography of the United States' settlement. However, ACS rhetoric increasingly emphasized the question of how the United States would assert itself on an international stage. During this period, the ACS defined the conceptual contours for its colony alongside the Monroe Doctrine, a foundational framework for U.S. foreign policy that shared with the African colonization movement an anticolonial imperial worldview.[2]

Like the eventual ACS colony in West Africa, the proposed California colony converged with this emerging vision of internationalism. Warburton speculated that a U.S.-modeled republic on the western coast of North America could serve a crucial role in advancing the United States' global interests at a time when the Spanish empire was struggling to maintain a hold on its colonial possessions in the Western Hemisphere. Spain faced growing national independence struggles throughout its colonies, while U.S. expansion externally threatened its empire in places such as Florida. With the treaty for annexing Florida from Spain pending, the editorialist believed it might be possible for the United States to also "acquire the possession of California, in addition to the Floridas" and set it aside for an independent black republic there that would serve to further undermine the Spanish empire in North America. In his view, planting a black republic in California would help end

European colonization in the hemisphere by "extending the blessings of a free
and equal government on the domain intended by heaven for the residence
of liberty."[3] Four years later, James Monroe would use very similar language
to frame his influential foreign policy doctrine, noting that "any European
power" interfering with "the Governments who have declared their independence and maintained it" was "the manifestation of an unfriendly disposition
toward the United States."[4]

This chapter examines an era in which colonizationism, previously inchoate and ill formed, began to coalesce around an increasingly consistent set of
doctrines. Given that most colonizationists had largely rejected earlier plans
for creating black colonies in North America, perhaps it is unsurprising that
this speculative California proposal quickly vanished without a trace, a prospect its author admitted was almost inevitable given the momentum of the
ACS at the time.[5] Nevertheless, this failed proposal demonstrates how easily
colonizationism meshed with the anticolonial imperialism of U.S. foreign
policy during this period. During the late 1810s and early 1820s, supporters
of the African colonization movement engaged with questions of empire,
republicanism, and national independence as they considered the implications of British rule in Sierra Leone, continental versus global expansion,
and the United States' relationship to republican independence movements
in Latin America, Greece, and the Republic of Haiti. If the initial wave of
colonization proposals raised persistent questions about the racial character
of the United States' North American empire, then the prospect of African
colonization foregrounded questions about how racial republicanism might
connect to the nation's broader global agenda and imperial self-definition.

Anticolonial Colonizationism

Although Americans circulated an array of proposals for North American
colonies in the decades immediately following the American Revolution,
it was actually the British empire that laid the groundwork for creating an
African colony composed of former slaves. As colonizationists began to shift
their attention toward Africa in the late 1810s, much of their early debate
was framed by this existing colony, a settlement that had persisted in various guises for nearly three decades: Sierra Leone. The ensuing discussion
reflected the divergent approaches that each nation had to colonizationism,
but also the ways in which each related to the concept of empire. During
the first decades of its existence the United States was defined by its weak

position, both within North America and on the world stage. Therefore, when Americans first formulated plans for creating black colonies, they initially imagined them as part of a presumed, but largely unrealized, continental settler empire. By contrast, Britain situated its own plans for a black colony in Sierra Leone within the context of an already well-established overseas empire that featured a diverse and wide-ranging colonial apparatus and governance. Within this framework, Britain explicitly designed Sierra Leone in order to manage compounding crises from within a mature empire that was beginning to come under attack from an increasingly confident antislavery movement. The British government helped create the colony to reorganize some of its far-flung black subjects as well as address the concerns of its critics. Under this conception, the eventual colony in Sierra Leone was aimed at civilizing the British empire by making it a "Province of Freedom" for former slaves. For colonizationists in the United States, Sierra Leone served as an inspiration but also as a crucial counterpoint. Not only did Sierra Leone represent a contemporary model for the sort of colonies that Americans were envisioning, it also served to raise important questions about how the United States related to colonialism more broadly. The ensuing debate over the merits of Sierra Leone and the Americans' decision to form an independent settlement reflected the vision of expansionism the United States would endorse in its eventual African colony.[6]

To appreciate these distinctions, it is worth considering how the early colonization movement in the United States interacted with ongoing British efforts to establish Sierra Leone. The settlement was initially created within the context of British imperial reorganization after the United States' Revolutionary War. During the war, several thousand enslaved British subjects accepted offers of freedom in exchange for taking up arms against the rebellious American colonists. After the war, many of these soldiers joined the migration of Loyalists from former British colonies, and several thousand were eventually relocated to various parts of the British empire: some in England, some in other parts of the Caribbean, but the largest group was sent to the British colony in Nova Scotia. However, the disruption caused by these migrations created new problems, particularly in Nova Scotia, where British settlers largely rejected the free black population within their midst, and the black migrants, for their part, protested their isolation and lack of access to the land and provisions the British government had promised them. In London the nearly five thousand former slaves who landed there became a highly visible and much-fretted-about segment of the city's poor. Finally, at the urging of several leading figures within the early antislavery movement, including Henry Smeathman and Granville Sharp, the British government helped create a colony at the mouth of the Sierra Leone River in West Africa.[7]

Like earlier U.S. proposals for North American colonies, the settlement in Sierra Leone was inspired by the republican principles of the Revolutionary age. Granville Sharp, one of the most prominent spokespersons for abolition in Britain during the 1770s and 1780s, shaped the colony's early utopian ambitions. Originally calling it the "Province of Freedom," Sharp envisioned the settlement as a place where benevolent white leaders would help prepare former slaves to create a self-governing colony. Sharp was sympathetic to the ideal of representative government embodied in the American Revolution and sought to extend these republican sentiments to the new colony. White antislavery activists initially administered the settlement, partially supported by a British government anxious to replace the slave trade with "legitimate commerce" in West Africa. Despite this early idealism, the colony struggled to achieve stability during its first decades of existence. Black colonists were quickly disillusioned with the conditions of the settlement and challenged the authority of white colonial officials. After multiple reorganizations of its leadership, the colony's governing authority, eventually called the Sierra Leone Company, was facing bankruptcy by 1807. At this point, the British government stepped in to assume full administration of the settlement, making Sierra Leone its first crown colony in Africa. Thus, a colony that was set to become a free and republican society became a harbinger of direct colonial rule in Africa by the British empire.[8]

The creation of Sierra Leone was one of Britain's first efforts to grapple with the imperial legacy of slavery. The existence of free people of African descent in both British colonial and metropolitan societies threatened the hierarchies of race inherent in the system of slavery. Thus, Sierra Leone was conceived, in part, as an attempt to contain and manage this racial uncertainty. These early efforts suggest that the British pursuit of such a colony, just as in the United States, was also intimately tied to the management of an empire. Undoubtedly, some supporters were attracted to the idea of an African colony because of the possibility for expanding Britain's economic empire, and many argued that such a colony could help transition the economic base of the region away from the slave trade and into more acceptable forms of commerce. Thus, British officials saw the colony as a means of solving several significant problems at once, even if the primary focus for its promoters was ostensibly humanitarian.[9]

The fact that Britain was able to swiftly execute this proposal within a few years offers a powerful contrast to the Americans, who would not act on their long-discussed plans for a black colony for several more decades. Whereas Britain increasingly asserted a self-conscious presence as a liberal empire on the world stage, the United States had a conflicted relationship with its own imperial identity. British officials were both willing and able to draw on the apparatus of their empire, while leaders in the United States were restricted by persistent anticolonial sentiment and constitutional qualms about the limits of imperial expansion. These distinctions serve to highlight how the settlement of Sierra Leone functioned as a contrast to the United States' eventual efforts to foster a colony in Liberia.[10]

In the early 1790s James Madison acknowledged the growing interest in creating black colonies in North America, but he expressed his preference for an African colony like the one recently planted in Sierra Leone. In his "Memorandum on an African Colony for Freed Slaves" he indicated that either the "interior wilderness of America" or the "Coast of Africa" could be made a "proper external receptacle" for "slaves who obtain their liberty." However, unlike later colonizationists in the 1810s who feared nonwhite collaboration, Madison instead worried that any such North American settlement "would be destroyed by the Savages who have a peculiar antipathy to the blacks." He also had little hope that black settlers could effectively coordinate with white colonizers and believed that "peace would not long be expected to remain between Societies, distinguished by such characteristic marks, and retaining the feelings inspired by their former relations of oppressors & oppressed."[11] Ultimately, these concerns led Madison to favor planting a colony in Africa similar to Sierra Leone, rather than establishing one in North America. Viewing such settlements as inherently disruptive to the processes of U.S. settlement, he anticipated this eventual shift among colonizationists toward Africa.[12]

Given that the British empire was already a powerful global empire while, by contrast, the United States remained relatively weak, it is unsurprising that many Americans would be drawn to the concept of amending the existing British colony in Africa more than the prospect of creating their own colony. As a result, during the first decade of the nineteenth century there were scattered efforts to merge British and U.S. plans for an African colony. During the early years of his presidency, Thomas Jefferson pursued the prospect of sending African Americans to Sierra Leone with some enthusiasm, despite the prevailing interest among his fellow Virginians for creating a North American colony. From 1801 to 1804 President Jefferson corresponded with members of the Virginia state government, most prominently Governor James Monroe, about the fate of emancipated slaves. In addition to discussing the possibility of colonies in Louisiana and the Old Northwest, these letters considered several possible sites for black colonies, including various locations within South America, the Caribbean, and Africa. To Monroe, Jefferson wrote that "Africa would offer a last and undoubted resort if all others more desirable should fail us." Although Jefferson viewed Africa as a last resort, he pursued the idea, in part, because it did not suffer from the complications raised by his ambitions for expanded white settlement amid the decline of Spanish and British interests in North America.[13]

To this end, President Jefferson did explore the prospect of coordinating with British efforts to establish a colony in Africa. In a letter to Rufus King, the antislavery politician from New York who was serving as the minister to Great Britain, he dismissed the idea of creating a stand-alone American colony in Africa, saying that "it would seem better, by incorporating our emigrants with theirs [British emigrants] to make one strong, rather than two weak, colonies."[14] In 1802 and 1803 Jefferson initiated contacts with British diplomatic officials, who were receptive to the idea; however, when his administration communicated with the directors of the Sierra Leone colony, they were wary of accepting former slaves from the United States because, in King's opinion, the "idle and disorderly character of the negroes who . . . joined the British army in America . . . has produced an unfavorable opinion of our slaves."[15] Nevertheless, King pressed forward with the inquiry until the prospects for American colonists in Sierra Leone were soundly defeated because the newly created Sierra Leone Company was in a "treaty with the [British] government to receive the colony under its exclusive control."[16] Ultimately, the fact that Sierra Leone came under the direct colonial control of the British helped end Jefferson's pursuit of Africa as an option for colonizing black populations from the United States.[17]

Following President Jefferson's efforts, the main impetus for the United States to work with the colony came from the work of Paul Cuffe, a successful black ship captain who had become the most prominent spokesperson for resettling African Americans in Sierra Leone. In the early 1810s he not only attempted to establish trade relations with the colony but also tried to help African Americans migrate there. Notably, Cuffe hoped to achieve these ends not by attaching himself directly to the goals of either the United States or Britain but by privately navigating the diplomatic politics between the two empires. During his visit to Sierra Leone in 1812, he secured informal trading partnerships with leaders of the colony but ran into difficulties when the rising tensions between the two nations caused Britain to impose a trade embargo on the United States. After the War of 1812 ended, British leaders again gave Cuffe permission to trade and facilitate settlement in Sierra Leone. His initial project was to fund the transportation of thirty-eight free African

Americans to the colony and establish trade relations there; however, his success was short-lived. His trading partnerships dissolved, the land for settlers did not materialize, and he was financially ruined by the endeavor. By the time of his death in 1817, Cuffe had lost hope of securing Sierra Leone as a destination for African American emigration.[18]

Although Cuffe's venture had ended in failure, it helped reignite interest in an African colony at a time when the momentum for North American colonies had begun to stall. By the mid-1810s it seemed increasingly unlikely that white leaders would support the idea of creating black colonies that might become part of the United States' settler empire. When Americans initially explored the concept of an African colony, they largely deferred to the established British colonial system, implicitly acknowledging the limits of American power on the world stage. During his early presidency, Thomas Jefferson had recognized this inherent weakness and hoped to yoke American ambitions to superior British resources in Sierra Leone. While this approach avoided thorny questions about the racial character of U.S. settlement in North America, both Jefferson and Cuffe had been thwarted to some extent by exigencies of British imperialism. Consequently, as colonizationists now shifted their attention toward Africa, they would be forced to consider what it might mean for the United States to cooperate with the existing efforts or to establish its own colony overseas.

Initially, the public debate focused on whether to support the British colony in Sierra Leone or to create a new settlement to be administered exclusively by the United States. By the time the ACS was formed in late 1816, its ranks included powerful white politicians, whose stature prompted several influential periodicals to devote extensive coverage to the ideas of this incipient movement. As a result, questions about where black colonies would fit into the overall schema of U.S. expansion were increasingly voiced. Although these discussions were ostensibly aimed at selecting the most effective colonization policy, they also illuminate the particular colonial vision that would undergird the eventual settlement in Liberia. ACS supporters usually pointed to Sierra Leone in order to demonstrate that African colonization was feasible; however, they often minimized or ignored the fact that the colony had experienced a series of fundamental crises over governance since its founding.[19] Alluding positively to the precedent set by Sierra Leone, one such article argued, "African colonization is no novelty. . . . It is not a dream," and noted, "It has the support of past observation and the demonstration of real fact."[20]

During this period, several newspapers reprinted an 1811 letter by Thomas Jefferson arguing that African Americans could meaningfully contribute to

the settlement of Sierra Leone. Interestingly, these publications provided little context for the letter, which was in fact written in response to the inquiries of a friend of Paul Cuffe about the feasibility of African colonization.
Cuffe's work for a black-organized emigration to Africa was almost entirely
erased from press accounts; the emerging colonization movement was linked
instead to the ideas put forth by prominent white elites.[21] The wide reproduction of this letter served to highlight the fact that Jefferson had long supported various colonization proposals, as well as suggest that Sierra Leone
might remain a viable alternative to a U.S.-sponsored colony. While the early
meetings of the ACS immediately ruled out colonies in North America,
members of the society initially considered a more open agenda for potential
African settlements, including the possibility of merging their efforts with
the existing British colony.[22]

Despite persistent interest in Sierra Leone, it was not long before critics
began to openly question the wisdom of connecting the American efforts,
either literally or symbolically, to those of the British. Colonizationists began
to push back against enthusiasm for Sierra Leone by professing distaste for
colonialism, more generally, and for the British variety, in particular. This
debate played out within prominent periodicals that covered national politics
and began to comment on congressional deliberations over colonization proposals during the months following the creation of the ACS.

Little more than a week after the first meeting of the ACS, an anonymous editorial in the *National Advocate* strongly criticized U.S. Speaker of
the House Henry Clay's praise for Sierra Leone.[23] Citing recently published
letters by a judge within the colony, the author condemned the settlement
as fundamentally corrupt and argued that it was an inadequate foundation
for Americans' colonization efforts, because "it has been established, and still
exists like various other of the *humane* establishments of England, calculated
to make rich a few hungry parasites who must be provided for." The editorial
went on to argue that "the colonization of the free blacks should exist, we
conceive, independently—form its own laws, and have no connexion with
the U. States, further than the protection which it might afford them in their
infant settlement—and be as different, in every respect, from Sierra Leone
as the government of the states is from Great Britain. Let the precedent of
humanity thus be fairly claimed as American, and as fairly denied that we
are in any manner indebted for it to England." This anticolonial rhetoric,
reignited by the recently concluded War of 1812, echoed the heated anti-
British sentiments of the Revolutionary era. Moreover, the article argued
that the United States should not simply engraft its proposed colony onto an

inherently flawed British colonial structure. The colony should be based on the United States' particular "precedent of humanity," unlike Sierra Leone, which had devolved from its ideal of self-governance to become a "corrupt" and "dependent" British crown colony.[24]

Despite some initial hostility to Sierra Leone, advocates of a stand-alone American colony were discouraged a few months later when the congressional committee on the slave trade formally suggested that U.S. colonizationists should pursue some degree of cooperation with the existing British colony. While the committee seems to have encouraged this course of action to avoid the complications of direct U.S. support for an African colony, their report qualified this recommendation by expressing deep reservations about the prospect of entangling the United States with British imperial objectives. The committee was concerned with the degree of control the United States would have in shaping Sierra Leone: "Would that government agree that at the period when the colony shall be capable of self-government and self-protection, it shall be declared independent? In the meantime, will it desire to monopolize the commerce of the colony? This would be injurious to the colonists, as well as to the United States." In short, the committee was concerned that British imperial interests might undermine the very aspects of the colony that supporters in the United States hoped to secure: free access to the development of commerce and an independent republican government for the colony.[25]

Shortly after the congressional committee issued its report, the *National Intelligencer* published an article noting that both of the committee's options were problematic because, on one hand, supporting Sierra Leone would "be promoting the colonial interest of England at our own expense" and, on the other hand, an independent U.S. settlement "would bind us to protect the infant colony, and consequently involve us in war with some sovereign whose avarice would excite him to conquer it." In particular, the report noted that creating a new colony would have negative consequences for the United States with the result being that "much money and numbers of troops would be left at the disposal of the executive" and "the attention of the nation would be diverted from local to colonial affairs," which would entangle the United States in an expansive imperial agenda. To avoid this fate, the editorial suggested that colonization should offer true republican independence without a formal colonial role for the United States: "For the moment a citizen of the U. States becomes a member of another independent state, our right to his services, and his claim to our protection, are cancelled."[26] Similarly, an article in the *National Advocate* suggested that the United States' unilateral expansion into Africa could result in problematic colonial commitments and questioned "whether it would be politic for the government of the United States to give official sanction to this attempt at colonization, as involving us in foreign disputes, and leading, by their consequences, to the agitation of questions of a more serious and important nature."[27]

Hezekiah Niles, a prominent newspaper publisher, similarly cautioned against the prospect of creating foreign entanglements for the United States in West Africa. Niles published an editorial in his influential weekly newspaper that sympathized with the aims of establishing an independent colony but warned that "people have placed too great a value upon" the pursuit of "*foreign* affairs," fearing that "by having our attention directed *abroad*, we may neglect our means at *home*."[28] A month later, the same paper published a rebuttal to Niles's critique by an anonymous writer who defended colonialism as a fundamental fact of human history, arguing that "since the earliest periods, at which we have any knowledge of mankind as living under any regular forms of government, the *establishment*, or *acquisition*, of colonies, has been part of their policy." The writer went on to argue that the question was not whether the United States should have a colonial policy but what kind of policy it should be: "There remains no necessity for pursuing such a policy, *as it has generally been pursued by other nations.*" The African settlement could embody an exceptionalist vision of U.S. colonialism because it would be "planted and protected, from *motives*, differing in their origin and tendency, from those which have generally actuated other nations in such cases." In the case of the proposed African colony, he wrote that the colonial relationship would be fundamentally distinct because "our after conduct, in relation to the jurisdiction, which we should attempt to exercise over this settlement would be materially different" from that of previous empires. In this view, the United States would encourage an independent government that would not permit restraints placed on "their lives, their liberty, or their property." As a result, the colony would "in fact not deserve to be considered as an appendage to the government of the United States." This sentiment reflected the convictions of many early colonizationists who believed that the proposed African colony could represent a benevolent expansion of U.S. republican institutions without eliciting the negative consequences of creating a more formal overseas empire.[29]

Other early colonization supporters focused on the fact that the United States would be required to again subordinate its own interests to those of the British empire if it were to assist or amend the settlement in Sierra Leone. On this subject, an early ACS auxiliary in Virginia released a public statement that rhetorically asked: "If there is such an asylum already prepared for them at Sierra Leone, what need of providing any other?" and, in response, argued that Sierra Leone "belongs to another government" and asserted that Americans should be "ashamed to ask" the British government to make an "enlargement of [its] territory on our behalf," nor should the United States "submit to it" if such an enlargement were offered. The organization wondered if there were to be "either duty—honor—or profit attached to such a settlement, ought we not be willing to make them our own?" implying that the United States could assert itself as an equal power on the world stage by demonstrating its ability to build a new colony rather than supporting the British colonial system.[30]

Some newspaper coverage argued that a colony designed by the United States would be well equipped to improve on the British precedent in Sierra Leone. One publication noted that "free people of colour in the United States" could be instructed in "all civil, literary and religious rights, with strong assurance of order competence and propriety."[31] In a similar vein, the *National Register* published a series of editorials that objected to "aid of British means, British information, or even British humanity itself" because it would unduly give them "the glory and greatness of an enterprise which had its origin in the bosoms of independent Americans." These articles recounted the brief history of the Sierra Leone colony from its origins as a humanitarian enterprise through its eventual fate as a British crown colony and used this to demonstrate that its government was "wanting in every feature of liberality and independence" as a direct result of "British [colonial] principles." The articles also condemned the economic imperatives of British colonialism as detrimental to establishing a free and independent colony, asking: "Did Great Britain ever give the world the example of her sacrificing a lucrative commerce at the shrine of humanity? And how can we suppose that the commerce she enjoys by furnishing all Africa with the manufactures of India, as well as those of her internal fabrication, should be relinquished in a government where *policy* always prevails over *principle*?" The writer concluded that the only way Sierra Leone would ever succeed was by imitating "the government of that colony" planted by "this society of freemen" in the United States.[32]

Newspapers advocating for an independent U.S. settlement in Africa argued that the United States could avoid the flaws of the British empire by forging its own model of overseas empire based on republican principles. The *Georgetown Register* applauded the ACS, in the middle of 1817, for having "no intentions whatsoever of making any attempt to connect their colony with that at Sierra Leone" in their efforts to create a "settlement totally distinct from and independent of any other" and "establish and regulate it upon principles wholly American." A Baltimore-based periodical employed similar arguments to reassure African Americans, who were already beginning to voice their dissent against the emerging colonization movement, that the United States' particular brand of anticolonial imperialism would promote independent republicanism: "Let the free people of colour be well assured, that they are to revisit their native country, civilized, free, and independent; that they are to be protected by the American Eagle, and to assume their proper rank among the nations of earth." The article argued that giving such assurances would not only hasten emigration but also ensure colonists' continuing allegiance to the United States: "Forever will they hail with joy, the star-spangled banner, under the protection of which they were made *freemen*."[33]

While this drama unfolded primarily among a small group of elite political leaders within the relatively narrow confines of national press outlets, these early discussions had a decisive and long-lasting role in shaping the course of colonizationism. While colonizationist ideas had circulated for more than three decades by this point, they had focused primarily on vague proposals for North American colonies, only to be rivaled by occasional interest in the existing colony in Sierra Leone. As colonizationists began to definitively reject the notion of making black colonies part of the United States' settler empire or appending them to British colonialism in Sierra Leone, they defined a new framework for their ideas to the American public by claiming a different set of prerogatives for asserting the United States' power around the world. As colonizationism formalized into a national movement, this context motivated some of its proponents to advocate for a colony that they claimed would be different from other imperial projects.

The Bounds of Empire

Even as most colonizationists abandoned the prospect of North American colonies, the question of empire refused to die. Public debate over Sierra Leone ostensibly centered on selecting the most effective method for building a black colony, yet it inevitably rekindled earlier questions about the boundaries and character of U.S. expansion. While both colonization advocates and skeptics debated the merits of supporting an established British colony in the national press, ACS leaders continued to push the issue to the fore through its politically powerful members. In 1818 the ACS sponsored an expedition to West Africa in order to scout out an acceptable location for the settlement and strengthen its case for federal support. Initially pursuing an independent colony on Sherbro Island near Sierra Leone, the colonization lobby succeeded in securing a generous interpretation of the 1819 Slave Trade Act by President James Monroe, who, over time, had become fully committed to an African colony.[34] When disease devastated the short-lived Sherbro Island colony, the ACS drew on a limited pool of federal resources and a growing base of private donations to fund another 1821 expedition, led by ACS agent Eli Ayers and U.S. naval officer Robert Stockton, which secured land in Cape Mesurado, the seed for the eventual Liberian colony. While the U.S. government offered crucial financial and military support to bring the colony into existence, federal involvement fell far short of the full funding desired by colonizationists and this situation led to an often murky public-private partnership that would define the colony's status for decades. The ACS settled for a sympathetic President Monroe using his executive powers to broadly interpret the slave trade law without explicit congressional approval for a directly funded colonization program. In the near term, this support was still encouraging to colonizationists, who reasoned that partial federal support was better than none at all.[35]

While the ACS was able to leverage its impressive roster of political connections in order to get the colony initially established, the debate over colonization policy continued within the Monroe administration. The pursuit of a colony in Africa raised the same question about the scope and constitutionality of U.S. expansion that Thomas Jefferson had wrestled with during his first term as president. Although Jefferson considered himself to be a "strict constructionist" when it came to the federal constitution, he flagrantly ignored this position when claiming vast federal powers to expand the boundaries of U.S. territory with the Louisiana Purchase in 1803. While the constitutionality of this action was debatable, it did establish a precedent for acquiring new territory. Furthermore, it laid the groundwork for potential black colonies through purchasing more North American territory or by setting aside part of Louisiana, as Jefferson's fellow Virginians advocated. Jefferson was wary of reserving any of this territory for a black colony because this would interfere with his vision of a republic of white agrarian settlers. Like Madison, he believed that the creation of an African colony was potentially unconstitutional and that such an act would require an amendment to the Constitution. After already expanding his constitutional powers in order to purchase Louisiana, Jefferson was likely sensitive about the possibility of further criticism if he used his executive authority to acquire a colonial possession overseas. Of course, this distinction was largely arbitrary. Having claimed the authority to purchase an enormous territory contiguous to the nation, it is unclear why Jefferson could not also invoke the same author- ity to purchase a small territory on the coast of Africa that would be more accessible than many remote portions of the Louisiana Territory. Neverthe- less, Jefferson chose to tentatively pursue the Sierra Leone option with Brit- ain, hoping to avoid making black colonies part of his "empire for liberty" or confronting the thorny question of whether a U.S. territorial acquisition in Africa would be constitutional.[36]

When the prospect of federal support for an African colony revived these issues in the late 1810s, politicians once again framed the issue as a constitu- tional question that reflected deeper concerns about the scope of the United States' empire. The 1819 Slave Trade Act, which opened the door to federal funding, was introduced by a key ACS supporter, Congressman Charles Fen- ton Mercer, but it made no specific reference to African colonization. How- ever, it did include language that gave the president open-ended authorization to "make such regulations and arrangements, as he may deem expedient, for the safeguarding, support, and removal" of those persons who were rescued by the United States in the course of patrolling the slave trade, and this pro- vision would provide the eventual justification for financial and military support within the colony.[37] Immediately after the law was passed, the ACS employed several constitutional lawyers, including Francis Scott Key and Bushrod Washington, to lobby President Monroe. Their intent was to elicit a broad interpretation of the law that would allow the United States enough latitude to secure and purchase territory for an African colony. Apparently, these efforts had a favorable impact on Monroe. Shortly after talking to the group, the president apprised members of his administration that he strongly supported the African colonization movement and asked his cabinet how he could use his authority to help establish a colony.[38]

However, subsequent debates within Monroe's cabinet raised some of the same concerns about creating colonies that had surfaced in the public discus- sion about British colonialism in Sierra Leone. Monroe had hoped to use the $100,000 appropriated by Congress, and perhaps even more, to help secure territory in Africa, as urged by the ACS, but Secretary of State John Quincy Adams argued forcefully against the idea. Adams contended that it was "impossible that Congress should have had any purchase of territory in con- templation of that Act." However, the secretary of state's objections to Afri- can colonization went beyond his belief that this would be an inappropriate use of the Slave Trade Act and reflected his fear that federal support for an African colony would lead to unconstitutional and, in his view, undesirable precedence for expanding the scope of U.S. colonial policy. Adams acknowledged that the constitutionality of the Louisiana Purchase was now a settled question in U.S. law, but he judged it to be entirely distinct from the purchase of territory in Africa. Like Jefferson, Adams rested this claim on a distinction between contiguous and noncontiguous territory, arguing that "the acquisition of Louisiana, and the establishment at the mouth of [the] Columbia River, being in territory contiguous to and continuous with our own, could by no means warrant the purchase of countries beyond the seas, or the establishment of a colonial system of government subordinate and dependent upon that of the United States." This critique questioned the constitutionality of an African colony and, in choosing to use politically charged words such as "colonial," "dependent," and "subordinate," signaled Adams's concern that emulating British imperial practices would inevitably corrupt the republic.[39]

Adams was not so much articulating a robust anticolonial stance as he was attempting to define the ethos of U.S. continental expansion by placing it outside of his narrow definition of colonialism. Of course, he did not acknowledge that the United States already had a de facto colonial system, structured around subordinate relationships with "domestic dependent nations" of Native peoples. In his memoirs, Adams reflected on this issue: "The world shall be familiarized with the idea of considering our proper dominion to be the continent of North America. From the time that we became an independent people it was as much a law of nature that this should become our pretension as that the Mississippi should flow to the sea." Here, Adams was embracing an early iteration of the ideology of manifest destiny in a way that helped him both justify his rejection of an African colony and deny that U.S. expansion constituted a "colonial system."[40]

Adams maintained his position in the face of concerted efforts by a committee from the ACS Board of Managers to persuade him that the Louisiana Purchase provided sufficient precedent for acquiring an overseas colony. Eventually, Adams also succeeded in persuading Attorney General William Wirt and Secretary of the Navy John C. Calhoun that the Slave Trade Act did not authorize federal support for African colonization. Rather, he argued that it would permit "the engrafting of a colonial establishment upon the Constitution of the United States" that would cede "power to the National Government transcending all its powers." As a result of such prominent backing for this interpretation, Monroe initially informed the ACS that he could not provide them with the robust support they desired.[41] However, after several months of persistent lobbying by ACS officials and President Monroe, Wirt changed his official construal of the law. He conceded that Congress had authorized the executive branch the power to return recaptured African slaves and that this provided the implied power they needed to create a colony.[42]

While Wirt's decision allowed Monroe to support the ACS's effort to establish a colony in Africa, it still avoided Adams's broader concern that federal support for African colonization would dangerously redefine the boundaries of the United States' empire. The Monroe administration's legal maneuvering did not give the United States direct power to purchase the colony, but its legalistic interpretation allowed the government to claim that it was not erecting a new system of colonial powers. Naturally, this compromise did not end the debate about whether an African colony constituted a new manifestation of U.S. expansion. The fact that these issues would continually resurface throughout the antebellum era illustrates persistent concerns about how the United States was going to inherit or transcend the British mantle of empire. Throughout the 1820s and early 1830s, this question would recur as colonization supporters attempted to establish a precedent on which to expand federal involvement in colonization, while anticolonizationists echoed Adams's argument that direct U.S. involvement in an African colony would create a wholly new and undesirable colonial system.

Colonization and Republican Revolution

Both the public debate about Sierra Leone and high-level political discussions about the constitutional boundaries of overseas colonialism highlight the fundamental questions at stake concerning the extent and character of the United States' empire. Most American leaders seemed to agree that an overseas colony should exist firmly outside the bounds of the United States' "empire for liberty" in North America. Critics used this distinction to condemn the concept because it would introduce a purportedly new system of colonial governance. Supporters, on the other hand, believed such fears to be unfounded because the proposed settlement was framed by the ACS to be an anticolonial republic that was separate from the United States and distinct from European colonialism. Such a seemingly contradictory colonial project was nevertheless comprehensible to Americans, situated firmly within their broader worldview that would come to be expressed by James Monroe's central foreign policy doctrine in the early 1820s.[43]

Both the African colonization movement and the Monroe Doctrine were shaped by an era in which Americans fervently debated the implications of ongoing republican revolutions in Latin America and Europe. As with the

French Revolution two decades earlier, U.S. observers were inclined to interpret the international events of the late 1810s and early 1820s simultaneously
through the lenses of the United States' revolutionary anticolonial struggle
and its emerging identity as an expanding continental empire within the
Western Hemisphere. While many American leaders were eager to lend both
material and political support to anticolonial republican movements around
the world, their enthusiasm was tempered by the need to remain disentan-
gled from the affairs of more powerful European empires.

   Amid the backdrop of republican revolutions in Greece and throughout
the Spanish empire in the Americas, President James Monroe chose to make
a definitive, yet open-ended, statement of U.S. policy in his 1823 annual message to Congress. Within a few decades, this statement would become the
cornerstone of U.S. foreign policy, eventually widely known as the Monroe
Doctrine. The foundational ideas in Monroe's speech were that the Western
and Eastern Hemispheres should remain distinct zones of influence and
that Americans and Europeans should not directly intervene in each other's
political affairs. Most crucially, Monroe soundly condemned the notion that
European powers had the right to recolonize parts of the Americas that had
declared themselves independent republics.[44] Far from being a wholly novel
set of policies, Monroe's doctrine distilled many commonly held ideas about
the United States' role in the world, positioning it as both an anticolonial
force and a nation that presumed imperial domain over the hemisphere. In
his influential history of the Monroe Doctrine, Dexter Perkins noted that it
did not create a new ideology so much as it captured "ideas that . . . were in
the air." Indeed, well before the policy was officially announced, many of the
same ideas were already contained within the initial framework for the African colony being proposed by the ACS.[45]

   The ACS based its earliest appeals for an African colony on the notion that
the settlement would be an embodiment of the United States' republican and
anticolonial ideals. When the ACS presented its first memorial to Congress
in 1817, it claimed the eventual colony would become "the glorious edifice of
well ordered and polished society" built on the "deep and sure foundations of
equal laws" and the "power of liberty." In this statement the ACS envisioned
the African colony as a self-governing nation that could demonstrate the
"capacity of a race of men" that "had yet made no progress in the refinements
of civilization," enabling the colony to become "the orient star revealing the
best and highest aims and attributes of man."[46] The *National Intelligencer*, an
early and consistent ACS booster, encouraged African colonizationists to
view the colony as crucial to the dissemination of republican ideas around

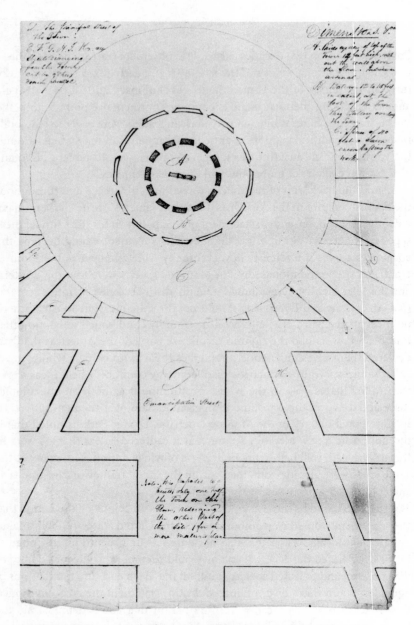

Figure 2. Town plan for Mesurado, Liberia, 1821. As the architect of the
U.S. Capitol and several other government buildings in Washington, D.C.,
William Thornton sketched a proposed street layout for Cape Mesurado,
eventually the site of Liberia's capitol in Monrovia. This plan reflected
the ACS's vision of a "well-ordered" republic modeled after U.S. political
institutions. American Colonization Society Papers, Library of Congress.

the world by asking, "While we are viewing with such deep interest the struggles of the people of South America for freedom, how can we look with cold indifference on the situation of the people of Africa?" Such rhetoric would become a recurrent theme, situating colonizationists' later efforts to export republicanism to Liberia as part of the global struggle for liberation.[47]

Beyond the context of the Americas, the passionate support of politicians and reformers for the Greek independence struggle in the early 1820s often overlapped with this sort of colonizationist rhetoric. Several prominent public figures, including Henry Clay, Daniel Webster, Edward Everett, and Matthew Carey, straddled both movements, making the case for Greek independence and Liberian colonization on the grounds that both would help found parallel republics composed of Christian citizens.[48] An 1823 *National Gazette* editorial typified this sort of appeal by arguing that Americans should support the Greek revolutionaries because they "will establish a Republican Form of Government. . . . The similarity of political institutions would make that nation our friend and ally."[49] Carey, an eminent publisher and prominent spokesman for African colonization, was at the forefront of an active Philadelphia community of reformers making the case that the United States should lend greater support to the Greek struggle, in part because it offered an opportunity to promote the establishment of republican institutions elsewhere in the globe. Carey would later make similar assertions in favor of colonization, contending that the purpose of such a colony was to create a republic "where they [African Americans] may enjoy the benefits of free government" and "spread civilization, sound morals, and true religion through the vast continent of Africa."[50]

While most colonizationists characterized the effort to establish a republic in Liberia in similar terms to the struggles of Greek or Latin American revolutionaries, some actually situated the proposed colony in Liberia as the vanguard of the United States' global republican mission. An 1824 newspaper editorial argued that the establishment of a black nation, rooted in U.S. political institutions, would benefit the world more than any "holy alliances of emperors and kings." It would do so because African Americans were "more fortunate than two-thirds of all mankind" as they had lived "in a nation where all are free (except themselves)," and their observation of "the pleasures and comforts of liberty" would teach them how "wretched man is without freedom, secured by general principles, organized by a constitution, and administered by elective agents." As a result, a black republic would demonstrate the power of the "freedom of conscience," "liberty of the press," "jury privilege," and "equal taxation" and enable Liberia to surpass the recently independent

nations of South America that had not renounced "Catholic supremacy."⁵¹ A
similar article, written a year later, argued that Liberia's efforts to bring the
"blessing of civilization and religion" to the "midnight darkness of Africa"
were in concert with the other "struggles for civil liberty which so powerfully
engage our sympathies" in both the Americas and Greece. However, the article argued that the colonization movement was ultimately of "more importance to mankind" because Liberia would not be destined to suffer a lapse
into colonial dependency. The author argued that even if the "new republics
. . . lately arisen on the American Continent" were to be "reduced beneath the
dark despotism of Spain" or the "[Ottoman] crescent [were to] again triumph
over the cross in unhappy Greece," Liberia would persist and remain a reason
"to rejoice in the progress of the holy cause of justice, truth and liberty."⁵²

African colonizationists would also point to the Greek revolutionaries'
success in achieving independence from the Ottoman empire in 1829 alongside the establishment of Liberia as indicators that the global tide of civilization was advancing. Rev. Reuben Smith, in an 1830 sermon given to the
Vermont Colonization Society, framed his call for donations to the colonization movement in these terms: "I ask the statesman, who hates oppression, and rejoices in the extension of civil and religious liberty, how much
he is willing to give towards rending another nation free and independent?"
Specifically, he pointed to the success of the Greek independence movement as well as the recent French colonization of Algiers as evidence that
the "Mahomedan power" had "experienced an extensive diminution of its
resources" opening "all northern Africa to the influence of civilization." In his
view, the remarkable success of Liberia portended the "renovation of Africa"
toward the path of civilization, Christianity, and republicanism. Reverend
Smith placed the American colony in Liberia alongside the resilient Dutch
"Christian settlements" in southern Africa and the Greek and French victories against Islamic regimes in the Mediterranean. For him, these events
collectively represented a "belt of light" that would penetrate the "dark and
unknown interior of this vast continent."⁵³

This sort of rhetoric reflected the way that African colonizationists col-
lapsed anticolonial and settler-colonial frameworks within a common ethos
of Eurocentric civilizationism. Significantly, Smith connected Liberia to
republican movements for independence in Greece but also to French and
Dutch settler colonies in northern and southern Africa. Like many African
colonizationists, Smith elevated the stature of Liberia in relation to these
other examples because it was built on U.S. institutions. In a short time the
colony had "attained to all the advantages of a free and civilized community"

because its "laws and customs are changed, and the energies of its children are turned to more rational pursuits." For African colonizationists, Liberia both echoed and transcended these other global reference points because of its purported ethos of anticolonial republicanism.[54]

Such inflated rhetoric illustrates that although colonizationists sometimes situated Liberia alongside both other global independence movements and instances of European settler-colonial expansion, they also held it up as unique and exceptional, just as they often set the United States apart from the history of other nations. Many Americans cheered the Greek revolution because they viewed it as restoration of a classical republican tradition the United States had hoped to embody. They similarly encouraged Latin American revolutionaries because their success could potentially validate the United States as the leader of a new network of postcolonial republics in the Western Hemisphere. Within this broader context of U.S. republican sympathies, Liberia represented a parallel yet distinct phenomenon. Unlike the revolutionary struggles against the Spanish and Ottoman empires, colonizationists were not calling for the enactment of a republican government by throwing off the yoke of colonial rule. Instead, they were attempting to create a republic out of whole cloth by acting as the colonizing force in another part of the world. Indeed, Americans could more easily connect with the idea of supporting a nation that mimicked their own settler-colonial origins and transplanted the political institutions they held sacred. Even if colonization supporters did not directly seek to advance the geopolitical goals set forth by a policy such as the Monroe Doctrine, they assimilated its worldview by taking an anticolonial stance to assert expansive prerogatives for U.S. power abroad.

Racial Republicanism

Although colonizationists forged the template for Liberia amid a backdrop of other anticolonial struggles for national independence, these analogies also raised a vexing question about the relationship between race and republicanism. The United States' persistent refusal to diplomatically recognize the Republic of Haiti since its independence from France in 1804 indicated that many U.S. leaders were unwilling to accept the possibility of a self-governing black republic, even as it had begun to recognize several Latin American republics with nonwhite citizenries by the early 1820s. Within this context, it was no trivial matter for ACS supporters to explicitly design Liberia as a republic governed by persons of African descent. The inherent tension in this position is evident in the political firestorm that erupted when President John Quincy Adams decided to send delegates to the 1826 Congress of Panama, a conference of the independent nations within North and South America. Several U.S. politicians opposed sending a delegation because the gathering included recently independent Latin American republics that had abolished slavery and included nonwhite citizens. Furthermore, they feared that these nations might push the United States to recognize the Republic of Haiti, even though the nation was not formally participating in the conference.[55]

Opponents of the Congress of Panama often couched their objections in overlapping racial and religious terms by questioning the ability of these republics to govern themselves, given their mixed populations of European, indigenous, and African descent and adherence to a "despotic" Catholic religion. For instance, in a congressional debate concerning the conference, John Randolph, a senator from Virginia, argued that the Republic of Guatemala, whose revolution had notably featured slave rebellions, should be considered just as diplomatically problematic for the United States as the Republic of Haiti. In particular, he objected to the idea that American delegates would be compelled to take their seats next to representatives of a nation characterized by a "so motley a mixture" of "the native African, their American descendants, the mixed breeds, the Indians, and the half breeds."[56] Randolph was one of many colonizationists who ostensibly endorsed a movement aimed at building a black republic while categorically rejecting diplomatic relations with republics that had included significant populations of former slaves and indigenous people. The colonization movement's efforts to situate Liberia within a narrative driven by American exceptionalism would be consistently undermined by racial politics that sought to deny the legitimacy of nonwhite republicanism.[57]

Like the prior generation of colonizationists, early ACS supporters consistently framed the speculative black republic of Liberia as a counterpoint to the existing black republic in Haiti. In the 1820s Haiti briefly also became the most significant rival to Liberia as the potential site for black emigration. The short-lived Haitian emigration efforts illustrate how the African colonization movement laid claim to a particular vision of black migration by framing its settler republic as the only state capable of credibly enshrining rights for African Americans. Shortly after the ACS had established its colony in the early 1820s, the prospect of emigration to Haiti challenged its primacy as a destination for black migrants. During this period the new Haitian president, Jean-Pierre

Boyer, presided over a recently reunited nation that he hoped to rebuild after nearly a decade and a half of civil war.[58] At the behest of an African American educator named Prince Saunders, Boyer hoped to attract free black immigration to the island, in part to bolster the nation's shortages in agricultural labor. The prominent newspaper editor Hezekiah Niles, a well-known skeptic of African colonization, promoted this plan to his wide readership.[59]

This publicity helped generate considerable interest within some northern black communities, such as Philadelphia, where residents had stridently rejected African colonizationism in recent years but remained interested in black-led emigration efforts. Significantly, Niles was also one of the few prominent American writers to argue that the United States should recognize the Haitian republic, and he connected this stance to his support for immigration to the island. President Boyer was well aware of the African colonization movement's popularity among whites as well as the fact that African Americans viewed his nation with ongoing interest, despite its decades of political turmoil and disunity. As a result, Boyer portrayed Haiti as a superior alternative to Liberia because of its robust commitments to abolitionism and black self-determination, goals notably different from those of many white ACS supporters.[60]

Although Boyer situated Haitian immigration in opposition to African colonization, some white colonizationists initially hoped to demonstrate that the two proposals need not be mutually exclusive. As black audiences were increasingly attracted to the Haitian plan in the early 1820s, Loring Dewey, an ACS agent from New York, began to promote it as an option alongside African colonization. Initially, Dewey had found it difficult to convince African Americans to migrate to Liberia, but he found audiences far more receptive when he mentioned the Haitian proposal. In 1824 Dewey published a pamphlet outlining a multisite approach to colonization. It addressed white colonizationists' concerns about black resistance to the ACS and Liberia's difficulties becoming established during the early 1820s.[61] After reviewing Dewey's tract, the *United States Literary Gazette* endorsed the Haitian plan by contending that "the republic of Hayti holds out stronger inducements and brighter prospects" and connected the subject of Haitian immigration to the broader question of diplomatic recognition for a black republic. While admitting that "we could not expect the same promptitude in the case of the Haytiens as was shown toward the inhabitants of South America" because of "prejudices existing against the descendants of Africa," the article urged immediate recognition of Haiti because "we consider their existence as a nation, established beyond the possibility of a doubt." Echoing Hezekiah

Niles, the writer implied that recognition of Haiti was essential to any strategy of promoting emigration or colonization because it demonstrated a good faith acceptance of black republicanism.[62]

Although Dewey and his supporters felt that encouraging black migration to multiple locales, including to the symbolically significant Republic of Haiti, offered greater opportunities for success, the ACS quickly reprimanded the agent for his divergence from official policy. The ACS Board of Managers accused Dewey of contravening "the fundamental object of the Society" and demanded that all agents "discourage any attempt at this time to send emigrants to Haiti."[63] Not only was Dewey privately dissuaded from advocating other emigration proposals in the name of the ACS, but the *National Intelligencer*, arguably the colonization movement's most prominent advocate in the national media, publicly campaigned to undermine the Haitian emigration proposal. The paper attacked Boyer's plan as "at variance with the very fundamental principles, and with some of the most important reasons for colonizing in Africa." Echoing earlier arguments against cooperating with the British in Sierra Leone, the article contended that a plan should be created that does "not depend upon any foreign power. Now, there can be no colonization in Hayti, because the moment the emigrants are landed, they become the subjects of that government." The newspaper also alluded to the widespread fear that Haiti remained a threatening bastion of radicalism, noting that "it is pretty well ascertained that most, if not all, of these persons would not send their slaves to Hayti, for various reasons, which it is unnecessary to state." After questioning the credibility of the Haitian republic, the article compared the nation unfavorably to Liberia, which was best suited "to give [freed slaves] full civil and religious rights, under a government best calculated to promote the happiness of them and their descendants" because "if properly supported, [it] will soon be in a situation to realize all these expectations."[64]

At the most basic level, the ACS wanted to maintain political and financial backing for its tenuously established African colony and feared that rival efforts would only serve to erode this support. However, colonizationists denounced the Haitian plan in terms that suggested that what was really at stake was the hegemony of their own vision for racial republicanism. Even though some ACS members adopted an explicit antislavery stance and endorsed the concept of Liberia as an independent black republic, they criticized the Haitian plan by drawing on widespread public perceptions of a nation that remained a threatening symbol of radical opposition to slavery and a maligned example of black self-government.

Dewey's efforts demonstrated central tensions in the colonization movement by highlighting the fact that free African Americans might be more likely to participate in such a plan when it involved an established black republic with an abolitionist history rather than a speculative colony supported by white men who expressed dubious antislavery views at best and virulent racism at worst. Furthermore, the concept of colonization proposals, dating back to their earliest iterations, was predicated on the notion that they offered white audiences an orderly and nonthreatening alternative to the Haitian revolution. In contrast to Haitian emigration plans, the colonization of Liberia achieved success precisely because it offered the possibility that white Americans, rather than former slaves, might shape the future of racial republicanism.

Later, in 1824, the *National Intelligencer* continued its campaign against "yielding to the intimation of Boyer's Agent [Dewey]" by arguing that Liberia offered an "independent Colony of colored people . . . enjoying the same privileges [Americans] enjoyed." In contrast, immigrants to Haiti would not have "an unbounded theatre for generous effort to raise [themselves] into notice" and would miss out on the "glorious prospects of success" to create a republic that surpassed those of "even South America." The paper contended that "the Haytien scheme carries on its face no advantages like those presented by the colonization plan" because it denied the possibility for black colonists to "erect themselves into an empire . . . based upon the republican principle" just "as we have" in North America.[65] Unlike some slaveholders who simply objected to black self-government on the grounds that it was an affront to the United States' system of racial slavery, some colonizationists made it clear that Haiti was the *wrong kind* of black republic. The African colonization movement developed its ideology through constant dialogue with Haiti as an already existing, yet inherently unacceptable, model of black self-government. At the same time, the notion of creating a black settler republic in Africa drew its power from the notion that the United States was simultaneously constructing a white settler republic within North America. In this context, colonizationists defined Liberia's racial republicanism as both a repudiation of Haiti and a reproduction of the United States.

Over the course of the antebellum era Americans' evolving conceptions of race would shape and be shaped by this ACS-defined vision of racial republicanism in Liberia. After gradual slave emancipation throughout the North, white leaders increasingly characterized free African Americans as a "degraded" and "disorderly" threat to the social order that needed to be contained. Although racial thinking would increasingly become grounded

View of the Colonial Settlement at Cape Montserado.

Figure 3. "View of the Settlement at Cape Monserado in Africa," 1830. This etching of the settlements at Cape Monserado (Cape Mesurado) was printed in one of the early issues of the ACS publication, *African Repository and Colonial Journal*. It is notable for the presence of three American flags, showing the early ACS efforts to represent the colony as a reflection of U.S. values and political institutions. Some versions of the engraving labeled the buildings, noting "Stockton Castle," the military fort named after the U.S. naval officer and depicted next to the leftmost flag. American Colonization Society Papers, Library of Congress.

in conceptions of innate inferiority, early colonizationists largely followed prevailing Enlightenment notions that attributed the condition of African Americans to the detrimental effects of slavery in the United States.[66] They theorized that removing African Americans from this environment would allow them to advance as they created a republican government modeled after that of the United States. For instance, Leonidas Hamline, a prominent Methodist bishop, argued that African colonization "is equal to the American revolution" through "its promise of security to the rights of man." As the colonization movement elaborated on these arguments over the course of the 1820s, its proponents increasingly promoted the concept of a black racial republic that could globally export the "rights of man" beyond the United States' own North American settler empire.[67]

Colonizationists often claimed that African Americans were perfectly suited to bring republican governance to Africa because they could thoroughly integrate indigenous Africans into their nation by harnessing the apparent binding power of race. In a typical example of this thinking, the *North American Review* argued that Africa was an ideal location for sending African Americans because it would "see the sons of Africa returned to the home of their fathers, establishing good governments among themselves, and communicating the influence of their example to their degraded brethren."[68] Although encounters between African Americans and indigenous Africans would involve each group mobilizing very different conceptions of race and ethnicity, many white supporters simply assumed that having an essentially similar racial identity would provide a foundation for the nation in the same way that whiteness functioned to bind together Europeans in the United States. Colonizationists often used a religious variant of this argument to claim that slavery was, in fact, divinely ordained so that Africans would be brought to North America in order to ultimately redeem their native continent by bringing it Christianity and U.S. political institutions.[69]

Although racial thinking always undergirded narratives about African redemption, some colonizationists explicitly emphasized the congruence between racial republicanism in Liberia and racial republicanism in the United States. At the ACS annual meeting in January 1828, Charles Carroll Harper, a leader of Baltimore's ACS auxiliary, argued that Liberia was positioned to become an outpost for black liberty and enjoined fellow colonizationists to take seriously their support for the colony because he claimed, "We are the guardians of a nation in the bud,—a miniature of this Republic,—a colored America on the shores of Africa." While holding up Liberia as a "colored America" that could protect black rights, Harper suggested that the United States' own white racial republicanism had created a "mockery of freedom" that would only be remedied by creating a racial republic in Liberia that would serve as "the only resting place and refuge of the coloured man." Such sentiments reflected the fact that by the late 1820s the ACS had marginalized competing colonization proposals by proclaiming that Liberia would mirror the United States in the racial foundations of its political institutions.[70]

*   *   *

In 1817 Samuel Mills, one of the architects of the ACS, argued that the movement's goal was "to lay the foundation of a free and independent empire, on the coast of poor degraded Africa." Mills's vision of the colony as both independent and imperial demonstrates the intention for Liberia to reproduce the United States' settler empire rather than become part of it. In the immediate wake of the Haitian revolution, the first generation of colonizationists focused their efforts on preventing revolutionary insurrection within the confines of North American settlement. By the mid-1820s, with the founding of Liberia, whites could envision the realization of African American self-governance within a safely distant and nonrevolutionary context. The colony was shaped by both the anticolonial ethos of the era and a specific vision for racial republicanism as its supporters imagined that it would reflect the United States' ability to mold the world in its image. As the doctrines of this movement came into clearer focus, many Americans began to consider whether these same models of colonization and racial republicanism might also be applied to the crises created by the displacement of indigenous communities within North America.[71]

CHAPTER 3

Colonization Policies in an Age of Removal

In his final address to Congress before departing from office, President James Monroe recommended that the federal government undertake an ambitious effort to resettle the remaining Native peoples of the East to a region west of the Mississippi River by making this a permanent territory where they could establish their own government. Monroe presented a broad outline for the future course of federal Indian policy that bore a striking resemblance to the plan for African colonization he had supported earlier in his presidency. By casting Indians as would-be settlers alongside whites in the West, Monroe argued that the "conflicting interests" between Native peoples and "frontier settlements will cease." He claimed that with the adoption of "civilized" government, Indians' "movement will be in harmony with us, and its good effect be felt throughout the whole extent of our territory to the Pacific . . . the condition of all the tribes inhabiting that vast region may be essentially improved; that permanent peace may be preserved with them, and our commerce be much extended."[1] Up to this point, federal Indian policy was primarily designed to diminish the political and territorial claims of eastern Indian nations by theoretically "civilizing" and absorbing them into the U.S. body politic. Monroe's plan shifted from the goals of these earlier efforts by aiming to turning Native Americans into settlers who would eventually colonize the western territory with an Indian republic, just as African American colonists were doing in Liberia.[2]

The idea of relocating Native communities within North America was not entirely new. In the preceding decades, the United States had negotiated several treaties that offered eastern Indian nations territorial exchanges for western lands. However, Monroe's ambitious plan envisioned the federal government as being instrumental to both removing Native populations and playing an active role in helping them build a new kind of nation. This approach to federal Indian policy self-consciously echoed the ACS agenda

in Africa and reflected the growing influence of colonizationism among politicians, missionaries, and federal officials throughout the 1820s and early
1830s.[3] White colonizationists often explained their vision of racial republicanism for both African Americans and Native Americans as manifestation
of the benign and exceptional character of U.S. imperialism by purportedly
avoiding the coercive tendencies of other empires. Richard Barton, a Maryland colonizationist leader, employed this logic in his 1829 speech when he
argued for the exceptional character of U.S. empire: "Ours is not to follow
the conquest of arms, the blood-stained path of the victor—its progress indicated by the violation of rights" because "it neither contemplates invading
the rights of others abroad, nor of violating rights at home." Barton placed
the transmission of liberal enlightenment to Africa within the history of
"improvement" brought about by great empires that stretched back to ancient
Greece and Rome; "Europe in modern centuries enlightened America, and
to America is reserved the greatest of benefactions; for around this western
hemisphere a bright halo is spreading which will reflect a retributive light
upon benighted Africa!"[4] Both Indian and African colonizationists sanitized
the violence behind empire building by claiming nominal commitment to
the ideals of political independence and self-governance.

While these colonizationist ideas overlapped in significant ways, they suffered notably different fates as federal policy. By the early 1830s President
Andrew Jackson and his supporters had transformed the concept of creating Indian colonies into a federal removal policy that all but abandoned the
benevolent pretenses of earlier colonization proposals. Meanwhile, the ACS
campaign to expand the federal government's role in supporting African colonization ended in complete failure. Although the United States never fully
implemented the initial conception of either colonization plan, the intersection between these two efforts reveals both the contingencies and the limitations of U.S. expansionism in the antebellum era.

Colonizationism Proliferates

Advocates of resettling Native peoples in the West drew from colonizationism
at a critical turning point for federal Indian policy. For decades the United
States had pursued a "civilization policy" that aimed to compel Native Americans to adopt more individualist agricultural practices, abandon collective
tribal political identities, and eventually assimilate with white settler populations. While architects of these policies sometimes rooted them in notions of

Enlightenment universalism, they were ultimately driven by the need to displace the Indian nations that occupied territory that white Americans viewed
as critical for settlement and resource extraction.[5] In this vein, Thomas Jefferson often advanced the idea that Native Americans could assimilate with
white settlers as the nation expanded, famously telling a delegation of several
Indian nations in 1808, "You will unite yourselves with us, and we shall be
Americans. You will mix with us by marriage. Your blood will run in our
veins and will spread with us over this great island."[6] However, years earlier, Jefferson had already begun to voice his growing skepticism about the
success of the civilization policy. For him the overriding imperative of U.S.
settler expansion created an inescapable choice for Native peoples: "They will
in time either incorporate with us as citizens of the United States or remove
beyond the Mississippi."[7] In subsequent decades, U.S. officials would often
echo this rhetoric, demonstrating how easily a civilizationist ethos could
reinforce a brutal logic of displacement.

While early U.S. Indian policy was nominally rooted in the assumption
that Native Americans could eventually become citizens of the United States,
increasingly politicians began to heed Jefferson's skepticism and gradually
abandoned the notion that Native peoples could be easily integrated into the
United States' body politic.[8] Meanwhile, white settlers in borderlands regions
violently challenged the sovereignty of Indian nations and repeatedly pushed
both the states and the federal government for policies that would remove
Native communities and free up more territory in the East.[9] With mounting
pressure on the frontiers and dwindling political enthusiasm for absorbing
Native populations, proponents of Indian colonizationism refashioned the
basic premises of federal policy by claiming that the ultimate goal of civilization was best served by moving the continent's indigenous people away from
the pernicious threat of white settlement.

Although this change in thinking was already in the air by the early 1820s,
a Baptist minister, Isaac McCoy, would come to play a critical role in shifting the terrain of Indian policy toward colonizationism over the course of
the decade. McCoy began working as a missionary to various Indian nations
on the western frontier of Indiana during the 1810s, and initially his efforts
aligned with the stated objectives of federal policy as he worked to transform
his Indian congregants into Christians, farmers, and eventually U.S. citizens.
However, he soon grew weary of establishing missions he felt were being
constantly undermined by the destructive influence of settler populations. As
a result, he began to dream of colonizing eastern Indian peoples somewhere
west of the Mississippi River.[10]

McCoy's shift away from the framework of federal civilization policy reveals how the African colonization movement influenced the evolution of his thinking. By the early 1820s the ACS had gained a considerable following within reform-minded evangelical communities, and as a consequence, McCoy became one of the founding members of the Indiana auxiliary of the ACS.[11] Around the same time, he adopted an orphaned African American boy who had attended his missionary school and intended to prepare him for a leadership role in Liberia.[12] As a result of his participation in the ACS, McCoy increasingly argued that African Americans and Native Americans faced parallel problems: "I have supposed that Indian calamities, as they now exist, originated in their degradation, and have until this time been cherished by the same general cause. This is not a solitary case; the condition of the wretched Africans is fully in point, and strikingly illustrative of the position we have taken. . . . The fact is, Africa, that portion at least of which we speak, is too destitute of national character to command respect, and therefore, in the usage of other nations, its natives cease to be treated as human beings entitled to common rights."[13] For McCoy, the creation of an independent republican nation was the only mechanism by which both African Americans and Native Americans would secure political rights.

McCoy was particularly concerned with the question of how a pan-Indian racial state might be able to combine and reconcile several disparate and often antagonistic tribes into a single nation once they colonized a new territorial domain. In this respect, he echoed African colonizationists, who claimed that the binding power of racial nationhood in Liberia would sort out the vast differences between African American settlers, multiethnic recaptured African slaves, and indigenous Africans. Indian colonizationists endorsed this approach based on the commonly held belief that North America's native populations were rapidly "vanishing" and needed to be preserved through a dramatic federal intervention.[14] Presuming that African Americans were racially inferior to whites, African colonizationists similarly speculated that emancipation might lead to the "extirpation" of African Americans, thus making their colonization an imperative for "protecting" black populations.[15] McCoy claimed that encroaching white settlement onto Indian lands had dramatically weakened existing communities. From his perspective, the only way to protect Native Americans from the advance of white populations was through the creation of a new and separate political state that would be protected permanently.

Both Indian and African colonizationists argued that the process of settlement itself would dramatically transform the would-be colonists. One missionary publication endorsed Indian colonization by claiming that "removal to some distant point, and concentration, as far as possible, into one body, appears to be the only means which can guard the Indian name and interest against total extinction."[16] Such explicit calls for the consolidation of Native peoples reflected the fact that some white reformers hoped to cultivate this proposed Indian nation into a self-consciously racialized settler state. The article suggested several possible outcomes of such an arrangement: "They would be under a regular polity, would possess inducements to acquire property, would feel a sort of national importance and would be more accessible to missionaries and other agents of reform and civilization." Therefore, Indian colonization proposals sought to create an Indian state that, like Liberia, would mirror the United States' racial republicanism. In his *Remarks on the Practicability of Indian Reform*, McCoy claimed that his plan "proposes to place the Aborigines on the same footing as ourselves; to place before them the same opportunities of improvement that we enjoy. . . . The colony would commence and improve, much after the manner of all new settlements of whites."[17] In creating a body politic of this new racial settler republic, Indian colonizationists argued that eastern Indian nations would civilize, acculturate, and eventually incorporate the western Native communities in the proposed nation. This expectation that such a colony would facilitate a civilizing process paralleled African colonizationists' assumption that black colonists would be well suited to civilize indigenous Africans because they could form a state organized around their shared racial identity.

Despite the overlap between African and Indian colonizationism, they were characterized by very distinct relationships to the question of U.S. expansion. By the early 1820s African colonizationists emphasized the importance of building politically and territorially separate nation-states not on lands that were destined to be incorporated into the United States. In contrast, Indian colonizationists envisioned the creation of a quasi-independent Indian civil society that would unite Native peoples while remaining embedded within U.S. settler expansion in North America. In his *Address to Philanthropists in the United States*, McCoy argued that Indians in a new western territory, unlike those who had lived as separated tribal cultures, "are to be united in one common bond of civil community, and constituted an integral part of the United States."[18] In this vision of independence, an Indian republic would theoretically inhabit a territorially and politically autonomous space, yet its sovereignty would always remain subordinate to the United States' settler imperial objectives.

Although McCoy was a very influential figure among American politicians, he occupied a particular niche within the increasingly contentious missionary politics of his era. Beginning in the mid-1810s, missionaries dramatically expanded their presence within Indian nations, particularly among the large southeastern tribes that were increasingly becoming targets of federal removal. For the next two decades, Congregationalist, Presbyterian, Methodist, Baptist, Quaker, and Dutch Reformed missionaries played a crucial role in the growing national debate over the sovereignty of Indian peoples, a struggle that came to be intensely focused on the fate of the Cherokee nation. In particular, the American Board of Commissioners for Foreign Missions (ABCFM), a multidenominational missionary organization founded by New England Congregationalists, helped organize opposition to federal Indian policy starting in the late 1810s and culminating with civil disobedience to protest removal that resulted in the Supreme Court decision of *Worchester v. Georgia*.[19]

This created dramatic schisms both among and within several denominations practicing missionary work among Indian nations. When federal removal efforts accelerated following the election of Andrew Jackson, the ABCFM-affiliated Congregationalists, supported by many Presbyterians and Quakers, had become the public face of opposition to the policy. Meanwhile, Isaac McCoy had succeeded in convincing many Baptists to support removal policies through his colonizationist framework. However, aside from some support from a few smaller denominations, most missionaries working among Indian nations at the time either implicitly or directly opposed removal policy, even in its colonizationist guise. Thus, McCoy was a particularly unique figure who had the ear of policy makers despite lacking a significant constituency among either the Native peoples he claimed to support or the missionaries with the closest contact to those communities. However, because the most prominent public opponents of removal were also missionaries, he served as a crucial political ally for politicians who sought to employ the rhetoric of benevolent colonizationism in order to push back against an increasingly organized opposition.[20]

Although McCoy remained a contentious figure, his vision of colonizationism helped legitimize the United States' Indian removal policy in the 1820s by lobbying influential policy makers, such as the territorial governor of Michigan, Lewis Cass, and Kentucky senator Richard Johnson. By 1824 his persistent advocacy helped him gain an audience with President Monroe and his secretary of war, John C. Calhoun, and while both men were impressed with McCoy's colonization proposals, the meetings resulted in no immediate changes for federal Indian policy. However, when Monroe announced his recommendation to move toward Indian colonization at the end of his term, it was clear that McCoy's lobbying was beginning to have an effect. From the time of Jefferson's presidency, the federal government had promoted civilization policies and supported the voluntary removal of Cherokee, Shawnee, Delaware, Kickapoo, and Wea bands who signed away eastern lands in exchange for western lands in parts of Arkansas and Missouri. These discrete instances of removal policy had operated alongside the government's civilization programs, and none were patterned after the large-scale colonization proposals envisioned by reformers such as McCoy. However, with Monroe's parting recommendation it appeared that these scattered efforts might be transformed into an Indian colonization program that would exceed the meager federal support Monroe had helped secure for African colonization a few years earlier.[21]

Although a shift toward colonizationism was taking place within the highest levels of government, it was also gaining traction among key federal Indian agents such as Thomas McKenney. McKenney had served in the Bureau of Indian Trade since the mid-1810s, and President Monroe appointed him to become a superintendent for the Bureau of Indian Affairs. Within this position he remained a vocal advocate of the prevailing federal civilization policy. He claimed that Indians were "our equal" in "intellectual and moral structure" and that he never doubted "the capacity of the Indian for the highest attainments of civilization."[22] Increasingly, McKenney began to express full-fledged support for a colonizationist framework, particularly after President Monroe proposed resettlement as a precondition for civilization efforts in late 1824. While such a policy amounted to moving away from a long-held government position, this shift in McKenney's thinking appears much less abrupt considering that he had already demonstrated consistent support for African colonization. Indeed, he viewed both Indian and African colonization as efforts to fortify a white settler republic against both internal and external racial threats, arguing that "the two problems yet to be solved" were "the black population, which we carry in our bosom," and the "red population which we carry on our back."[23] Over the second half of the 1820s, McKenney served to bridge the policies of Presidents James Monroe, John Quincy Adams, and Andrew Jackson by becoming one of the most important federal advocates for the colonization, and later the removal, of Native Americans.[24]

Monroe's proposal likely emboldened Indian colonizationists, yet as an outgoing president he could not directly implement this policy. Nevertheless, Monroe's message helped spur Congress into action. Less than a week after his speech, Missouri senator Thomas Hart Benton introduced a bill that proposed to "provide a permanent residence" for a wide range of Indian nations throughout the Southeast and Midwest, including the Cherokee, Creek, Choctaw, Chickasaw, Delaware, Kickapoo, Shawnee, Wea, Osage, Wyandot, Seneca, Kaskaskia, and Miami nations. Benton's bill drew on a racial republican framework wielded by both Indian and African colonizationists, claiming that it would make provisions to bind these disparate Native peoples together by "forming a system of government suited to their situation, and which shall tend ultimately to ensure to them protection and rights similar to those enjoyed by the citizens of the United States."[25]

In the ensuing debate, one of the bill's supporters, Georgia senator John Elliott, justified it as a means of "preservation" of Native peoples because he believed that "two independent communities of people, differing in color, language, habits, and interest cannot long subsist together—but that the more intelligent and powerful will always destroy the other." This justification for reconstituting existing Indian nations within a new national formation inverted colonizationist rhetoric about the necessity of separating African Americans because they threatened revolt. In this self-serving logic couched in humanitarianism, it was Indians who needed to be protected from whites. Echoing earlier proposals for black colonies in the West, Elliott contended that an Indian colony would become a proxy for the United States in the region rather than an impediment to it because Indians living in this colony would not "make war upon those whose power they *know* they cannot resist and the preservation of which, they *feel* to be necessary to their own safety." Ultimately, Elliott's arguments won the day in the Senate, but the bill languished in the House of Representatives and was never passed into law.[26]

Despite the defeat of this measure, President John Quincy Adams's incoming administration initially pursued a policy similar to the one outlined in both President Monroe's final speech and Benton's bill. In 1826 Adams's secretary of war, James Barbour, proposed an expansive federal colonization program that elaborated on Monroe's loosely sketched plan. In a letter to the congressional Committee on Indian Affairs, Barbour pushed for the creation of an Indian territory on the other side of the Mississippi, which would remain permanently guaranteed as a federally governed possession and therefore face no conflicts with various state governments. Along the lines suggested by McCoy, he also proposed that within this territory tribal identities would be dissolved, and this would help promote a sense of national unity within the colony that would eventually eliminate any need for the United States to manage competing tribal claims. Barbour's conception of a permanent yet ambiguously sovereign Indian republic within the heart of North America was decidedly less idealistic than McCoy's. Nevertheless, it reflected the growing influence of colonizationist ideas among federal officials focused on Indian policy. However, like Benton's bill in the late Monroe administration, Congress did not adopt Barbour's plan, and in 1829 Andrew Jackson would ascend to the presidency with a hard-nosed removal policy that showed little trace of Indian colonizationists' prior idealism. Although McCoy's colonizationist ideas gained traction shortly after President Monroe's outgoing policy recommendation, ultimately Andrew Jackson's vision of removal would prevail in the longer term.[27]

During the 1828 presidential campaign, Jackson garnered crucial support in the southern states by promising an Indian removal policy that purported to protect states' rights to their territory. While Jackson's election that year would initiate a distinct shift in Indian policy objectives, benevolent colonizationism remained a popular rhetoric for masking the more coercive aspects of removal policy. In the early years of his presidency, Jackson met with McCoy several times for advice, and legislators frequently consulted him as an expert during congressional debates.[28] Jackson even informally endorsed some of the missionary's suggestions from *Remarks on the Practicability of Indian Reform*. Meanwhile, McCoy attempted to promote his own version of an Indian colonization society that would mirror the ACS, called "The Indian Board, for the Emigration, Preservation, and Improvement of the Aborigines of America." While this organization failed to attract enough interest among reformers and evangelical ministers to counter the growing antiremoval campaigns, it did garner the support of similarly minded government officials such as Thomas McKenney, who had continued to serve in Andrew Jackson's administration.[29]

The influence of Indian colonizationism remained evident in President Jackson's first annual address when he advocated removal of Native people to the west of the Mississippi where "they may be secured in the enjoyment of governments of their own choice, subject to no other control from the United States than such as may be necessary to preserve peace on the frontier and between the several tribes. There the benevolent may endeavor to teach them the arts of civilization, and, by promoting union and harmony among them, to raise up an interesting commonwealth, destined to perpetuate the race and to attest the humanity and justice of this Government."[30] Perfunctory declarations of support for Indian self-determination such as these punctuated Jackson's rhetoric, even as his speeches suggested that removal was inevitable and might even require military force to execute. While scholars have commonly characterized this transition to a removal policy during the Jackson administration as primarily reflecting a hardening of racial attitudes in the United States, this narrative downplays the fact that both Indian and African colonizationists insisted on improvability *and* exclusion, a contradiction that was highlighted in the famous case of the Cherokee republic.[31]

The Contradictions of Racial Republicanism

As colonizationists advanced their proposals for creating racial republics during the mid- to late 1820s, some Indian nations had already taken steps toward building similar governments on their own terms. In the preceding decades, several tribes, such as the Creek, Choctaw, and Cherokee, reformed their governance structures by adopting many of the bureaucratic functions of a Euro-American nation-state. The Cherokee, like many other Native peoples in the 1820s, found themselves in a difficult position following the rapid encroachment of American settlers. Perhaps more than any other Indian nation at the time, they attempted to legitimate their political sovereignty by emulating the logic of the United States' racial republic. In contrast to later proponents of Jacksonian removal, Indian colonizationists argued that they should remain entitled to their territory, and they lauded Cherokee efforts to present themselves as a civilized republic. While Isaac McCoy hoped to amalgamate several Indian nations by dissolving tribal identities, he made exceptions for the "civilized" Cherokee, Creek, and Choctaw nations because he believed that, in fact, the Cherokee provided a template for the kind of Indian republic he envisioned in his proposed colony.[32]

While McCoy viewed the Cherokee republic as a sort of model, unlike the colony he and other Indian colonizationists proposed, that government had not been created from whole cloth through the efforts of white reformers. Cherokees forged new political structures through several decades of internal tribal debate that responded to the growing crises created by U.S. settlement. Beginning in the 1790s, some Cherokee leaders attempted to maintain their sovereignty by presenting themselves to U.S. authorities as a "civilized" people through methods that included the adoption of southern plantation farming and the use of African American slaves, the creation of a system of writing the Cherokee language, the development of written laws, and the formation of a more formalized governance structure through a political body called the National Committee.[33] Throughout the 1810s and 1820s, a concerted faction of Cherokee leadership advanced these changes in response to the mounting pressure to cede land posed by the U.S. federal government, the Georgia state government, and renegade U.S. settlers who routinely violated the nation's political and territorial sovereignty. These forces ultimately led the Cherokee to adopt a written constitution in 1827 that was modeled on that of the United States and transformed their National Committee into a form of republican government.[34]

Through this process, the Cherokee created a political state that, in some respects, resembled the republics envisioned by both African and Indian colonizationists. The Cherokee conception of racial nationhood was deeply inflected by the United States' self-conscious effort to forge a white republic during this era. Some Cherokee may have even been attracted to the African colonization movement, in part, because it helped legitimate their own vision of racial nationalism.[35] On this point, the federal Indian agent Thomas McKenney remarked that the consolidation of Cherokee national identity would naturally facilitate African colonization. He noted, "There is hardly an intermixture of Cherokee and African blood. The presumption is, that the Cherokees will, at no distant day, co-operate with the humane efforts of those who are liberating and sending this proscribed race to the land of their fathers. National pride, patriotism, and a spirit of independence mark the Cherokee character."[36] McKenney was likely encouraged by the fact that some Cherokee elite were taking a growing interest in African colonization, a development facilitated by some white colonizationist missionaries living within Cherokee territory. In 1829 one white missionary noted that "I have assisted the black people in Wills Valley in forming themselves into a society, called the Wills Valley African Benevolent Society. Their object is to aid the cause of civilization and Christianity in Africa."[37] Several articles from the first Cherokee newspaper, the *Cherokee Phoenix*, attest to the growing interest in the movement and indicate that the African colonization movement was one of the several benevolent projects supported by Cherokee leaders who were influenced by the missionaries residing among them.[38]

Cherokee Phoenix articles on this subject often departed from the most racially inflammatory sentiments expressed by white colonizationists. On a few occasions, the *Phoenix* seemed to support limited rights for African Americans, even publishing an article that decried attempts by the Michigan legislature to expel black residents from the territory: "We do not believe that a human being who is a free man, although possessing a black or yellow complexion or being one or more shades darker than is common to white freemen, should be deprived of those rights and privileges, which are the common heritage of this happy and republican country."[39] This mixture of advocacy for African colonization and tentative claims for the rights of black people occurred at the same time that the Cherokee nation strove to present a clear racial hierarchy in support of their own claims to nationhood.[40]

In many ways, the Cherokee created a republic that mirrored the race, class, and gender stratifications of the United States by locating greater power among the land-holding Cherokee elite, excluding women, poorer farmers, black slaves, and many African-descended Cherokee. Most crucially, the new Cherokee constitution focused considerable attention on the nation's racial composition, and it systematically prohibited most African Americans from participating in the government. Thus, in pursuing a path toward greater self-determination, Cherokee leaders increasingly advanced appeals to Indian racial statehood, which undermined potential interracial alliances with African Americans against white supremacy.[41] Within this light, Cherokee support for African colonization aligned with their efforts to demonstrate that the nation's citizens were, unlike African Americans, already fit for self-government. The inherent contradiction of this position highlights the fundamental instability of racial republican ideas. Despite colonizationists' claims, a white nation, a black nation, and an Indian nation could never be practically or functionally equivalent. This would become starkly evident as Jacksonian proponents of Indian removal easily jettisoned the benevolent version of colonizationism when they claimed that the imperatives of an expanding U.S. settler state ultimately overruled any Cherokee claim to autonomy.

This racial framework for the Cherokee republic helps explain why some of the nation's leaders might have supported African colonization. This was despite the fact that whites also used colonizationist arguments to cast African Americans and Native Americans in the same position and thus diminish the prospect of Cherokee self-determination. Indeed, in the state of Georgia, where most of the Cherokee nation was based, the efforts to colonize African Americans had often dovetailed with the campaign to remove Native populations from the state. Some Georgian officials, including Governors Wilson Lumpkin and George Troup, were strong advocates for both projects and often used the language of removal and colonization to turn popular sentiment against the state's black and Indian populations.[42] In such a context, the fact that some Cherokee leaders aligned themselves with white colonizationists could have signaled that they, unlike African Americans, did not need to be removed from their present territory because they had already formed a civilized republic around their own version of racial nationhood.

An 1830 article in the *North American Review* suggested that some Cherokee leaders could have supported African colonization because they hoped to created distance between themselves and African Americans: "If ardent spirits and other adopted agents are not removing [eastern Indian populations] fast enough much may be gained in point of time, by colonizing them to the coast of Africa; or sending the recruits to Key West. It matters little, to a wild, red man, in what forests he pursues his game, or from what river he draws his fish." The writer justified removal by observing, "Government is unknown among them; certainly that government which proscribes general rules and enforces or vindicates them. They have no criminal code, no courts, no officers, no punishments." In suggesting that any "forests," including those of Africa, were suitable for removal, the writer implicitly linked Native Americans to African Americans while rejecting the claims to civilization made by nations such as the Cherokee. An editorial in the *Cherokee Phoenix* directly responded to the *North American Review*'s suggestion that Indians be removed to Africa by characterizing it as an insult to the Cherokee nation's efforts to adopt aspects of Euro-American civilization. The *Phoenix* critiqued the article's attempt to "ascribe to the whole race of red men one uniform and fixed character" but sharply highlighted the contradiction of its racial logic: "The writer raises a note of alarm, because this obstinate son of 'nature' who has no government and cannot be persuaded to submit to any—whose character is as fixed from age to age, as the character of a rock or a tree, has already organized 'a government de facto, within the limits of the State of Georgia, claiming *legislative, executive,* and *judicial* powers, and all the essential *attributes of sovereignty.*'" The writer concluded by exclaiming, "What a change a few pages have made in the unchangeable character and condition of the Indian!"[43]

This exchange also illustrates that while some Cherokee deployed a particular version of racial republican ideas by supporting African colonization, this rhetoric could easily be turned back against them to reveal the fundamental incoherence of colonizationist racial logic. The *Cherokee Phoenix*'s response indicates the difficulty of navigating these overlapping racial characterizations without ultimately upholding white supremacy. Sensitivity about being characterized as incapable of self-government was understandable considering that the adoption of a U.S.-style government was a crucial strategy by which the Cherokee nation attempted to distinguish its claims to territory and sovereignty. The mere suggestion that Native Americans should be compared to African Americans threatened the efforts of Cherokee leaders to claim racial and national legitimacy by supporting African colonization themselves.

As debates over both Indian removal and African colonization intensified, abolitionists would begin to further expose the instability at the core of

colonizationist ideas. Increasingly, they pointed out that federal removal policy was undermining Native sovereignty in ways that mirrored African colonizationists' disingenuous claims to support the self-determination of black
colonists. In 1835 a British traveler named Edward Abdy remarked on the
similarity of the ways that Native Americans and African Americans were
regarded in the United States: "It is curious to observe, in the treatment they
both have received, the same principles in operation, and the same profes-
sions put forward. Under the plea of kindness they are plundered of their
lands and their labor, and driven from their native country to find a grave in
the waves of the Pacific, or the pestilent marshes of Africa. The legislature of
Georgia uses the same sort of language, when speaking of the Indians, that
the Colonization Society employs to describe the descendants of Africa."[44]
Abdy's analysis captured the views of American abolitionists at the height of
the twin debates about Indian removal and African colonization in the early
1830s. As a result of their participation in the campaign against the Indian
removal policy, many antislavery activists turned away from supporting African colonization and moved toward an abolitionist stance during this period.
Drawing on the criticisms of colonization made by northern black communities, several former colonizationists refashioned their activism about removal
policies into a more pointed critique of white supremacy. Black and white
abolitionists condemned both Indian removal and African colonization, in
part because they offered a false vision of self-determination that was both
severely limited and inherently coercive.

White abolitionists increasingly voiced this perspective after some black
activists expressed their long-standing concerns about colonizationism
alongside their criticism of the devastating effect of U.S. settler colonialism on Native American communities. One such example was the critique
by Rev. Peter Williams of white settler expansion: "The colonies planted by
white men on the shores of America, so far from benefiting the aborigines,
corrupted their morals, and caused their ruin; and yet those who say we are
the most vile people in the world, would send us to Africa, to improve the
character and condition of the natives."[45] In drawing on this parallel, Williams
focused on settler expansion, which he argued had treated the Native populations of North America with injustice. Having encountered a similar logic in
both projects, Williams identified the inherent contradictions of colonization
and removal policy by framing his objections through the language of anticolonialism. The black abolitionist Maria Stewart was even more explicit about
the destruction wrought by white settlers in North America. Stewart drew
a parallel between the removal of Native Americans and the denial of black

citizenship within the colonization movement: "The unfriendly whites first drove the native American from his much loved home. Then they stole our fathers from their peaceful and quiet dwellings, and brought them hither, and made bond-men and bond-women of them and their little ones. They have obliged our brethren to labor; kept them in utter ignorance; nourished them in vice, and raised them in degradation; and now that we have enriched their soil, and filled their coffers, they say that we are not capable of becoming like white men, and that we can never rise to respectability in this country. They would drive us to a strange land. But before I go, the bayonet shall pierce me through."[46] Stewart pointed out that whites had exploited and cast aside indigenous populations in North America just as they were now attempting to do with African Americans.

As white activists joined the growing movement against Indian removal, black leaders seized on this to mobilize opposition to colonization within antislavery circles. A set of resolutions in November 1831 by the black community in Providence, Rhode Island, condemned the hypocrisy of whites who opposed Indian removal yet wholeheartedly endorsed African colonization. One resolution stated: "We view, with unfeigned astonishment, the anti-christian and inconsistent conduct of those who so strenuously advocate our removal from this our native country to the burning shores of Liberia, and who with the same breath contend against the cruelty and injustice of Georgia in her attempt to remove the Cherokee Indians west of the Mississippi."[47] By placing the burden of moral consistency on white activists, African Americans were more successful in drawing attention to the injustice of colonization than they had been in the previous two decades of protest. Black leaders aimed their critiques of colonization and removal precisely at the quality of the idea most emphasized by their supporters: self-determination. In a protest by free African Americans against colonization, a speaker said, "We hope that those who have so eloquently pleaded the cause of the Indian, will at least endeavor to preserve consistency in their conduct. They put no faith in Georgia, although she declares that the Indians shall not be removed but 'with their own consent.' Can they blame us if we attach the same credit to the declaration, that they mean to colonize us 'only with our consent?' They cannot use force; that is out of the question. But they harp so much on 'inferiority,' 'prejudice,' distinction' and what not, that there will no alternative be left us but to fall in with their plans."[48] While colonizationists legitimated the republicanism of the project by consistently emphasizing that it was based on voluntary consent, black leaders recognized that colonizationism dramatically undermined their potential for self-determination, just as it had with those native peoples who faced the removal policy.

Highlighting this contradiction, white abolitionists began to argue that the logic behind African colonization and Indian removal merely served to foster an illusion of consent and republican self-governance. At the annual meeting of the New-England Anti-Slavery Society, Amasa Walker responded to colonizationists by invoking the contemporary crisis over removal in Georgia: "But, sir, I know I shall be met here by the declaration, that the friends of Colonization '*don't compel* the blacks to emigrate.' This is a wonderful discovery, truly. So said the government of Georgia, in regard to the removal of the Indians—we don't compel them to go. No, Sir, they *did not* compel the Indians *to go*; but then, they rendered them so uncomfortable, by their oppression and injustice, that the poor Indians *can't stay*." Walker argued that the rhetoric of colonization and removal was so successful that they had become the only solutions in the minds of many whites, and by shifting the conceptual terrain, these plans were becoming a "choice" of last resort. He went on to note that "it is but a short time, a few months, since the sympathies of this community were excited to the highest pitch, by the proposed removal of the Cherokees from the land of their fathers, to the western banks of the Mississippi. . . . All this was said and felt, because a few thousand Indians were to be removed from one part of the United States to another. And yet, Sir, *these very men*, who raised this lamentation, over Indian sufferings, look with entire complacency upon the expatriation of twenty-five hundred thousand of their fellow beings to the dark, sickly coast of Africa!"[49]

Abolitionists increasingly made this connection in order to persuade other white reformers to abandon colonizationism. In the pages of the *Liberator*, the flagship abolitionist newspaper, several articles highlighted this relationship in ways that echoed the sentiments of black activists. A typical article pleaded with its readers to confront the contradictions of both colonization and removal: "The American *Colonization* Society, then, stands in the same attitude to our colored population, as Georgia does to the Cherokees. It willfully disregards their earnest, unequivocal and reiterated desires; pretending at the same time to be actuated by the most disinterested and benevolent motives; promising to remove them to Africa only with their own consent; yet determining by every artifice to render their situation so intolerable here, as to compel them to emigrate."[50] Another article stated that "no scheme for the removal of a people from their territorial possessions, or native country, should be forced into operation contrary to their inclinations" and argued that "the remonstrances of our colored brethren deserve as candid an interpretation as those of our red brethren."[51] Abolitionists argued that while both colonization and removal may claim to embrace a spirit of republicanism, through their disingenuous claims of consent they were instead profoundly antirepublican in both spirit and practice.

Such appeals highlight how the fate of the Cherokee nation had increasingly become a cause célèbre among northern activists, many of whom had once been strong supporters of African colonization. Through their adoption of Euro-American customs and a republican form of government, Cherokees embodied the type of civilization that white reformers had wished to see in the colonists traveling to Liberia. While several antislavery activists became abolitionists simply because they viewed the ACS as a proslavery organization, the grounds on which they adopted the Cherokee cause displayed the influence of their former belief in colonizationism. Opposition to Indian removal seems to have helped many antislavery activists, particularly women, transition from gradualism to immediatism and ultimately hastened the abandonment of colonizationism among an increasingly radical core of abolitionists.[52]

William Lloyd Garrison's *Thoughts on African Colonization* was perhaps the most influential piece of writing for turning antislavery activists against colonization, and its rhetoric bears the strong imprint of the antiremoval campaigns that had been brewing within abolitionist circles. Garrison argued that activists should recognize that opposition to African colonization was naturally linked to a stance against Indian removal policy, a position that many in the antislavery movement had already adopted.[53] In a scathing critique of Cherokee removal, an editorial in Garrison's *Liberator* summarized the perspective of the abolitionist community that had developed in the past few years: "What more could be done in Georgia by a Cherokee Colonization Society, headed by their Excellencies Troup, Lumpkin and his Honor Judge Clayton? In regard to the principle I can see no distinction between the case of the Cherokee and that of the Africo-Americans, but this; the Cherokees had to contend with a single state,—to the black men we are all Georgians!"[54]

By equating the persecution of the Cherokee with the implicit support for colonization among many whites, the editorial demonstrated that complicity with white supremacy was evident in efforts that seemingly had the most benevolent of intentions. While African Americans had long expressed their skepticism about the rhetoric of consent and self-determination used to justify African colonization, the hollowness of the racial republic was finally revealed to many white activists by the fate of the Cherokee nation, who seemed to embody the ideals of civilized self-governance. Any illusions harbored by those in the antislavery community about whether colonization reflected the best interests of the colonists were put to rest by the ease with which the benevolent colonizationism for which Isaac McCoy had success-fully advocated in the early 1820s had developed into a set of policies that by the 1830s sought to remove Indian populations at any cost.

The Collapse of Colonization Policies

By the early 1830s both Indian and African colonization policies were in peril. African Americans, Native Americans, and white abolitionists had begun to expose the contradictions of both from a wide range of perspectives. More-over, Indian and African colonizationists envisioned ambitious programs that could not proceed without extensive federal involvement, yet govern-ment support for both of these efforts was tenuous, at best. The initial success of the ACS in the late 1810s and early 1820s had encouraged the notion that colonizationism might also be applied to Native Americans, but by the rise of Andrew Jackson at the end of the 1820s, colonizationist idealism faced a serious backlash.

Jacksonians increasingly questioned whether building, cultivating, and administering new nonwhite republics should be contemplated within the scope of the federal government. In a congressional debate on an appropria-tions bill for the Bureau of Indian Affairs, Samuel Vinton, a U.S. representa-tive from Ohio, reflected a growing wave of colonization skepticism among Jackson's supporters in the lead-up to the 1828 presidential election. Vinton sharply criticized the logic behind Indian colonization, as it had been out-lined by the recent Monroe and Adams administrations. He expressed open disdain, claiming that "[the Indian colony is] the boldest experiment upon human life, and human happiness, that is to be found in the history of the world. It proposes to take a whole people, nay, more, the remnant of forty nations from their abodes and place them down in the recesses of a distant and forbidding wilderness, and there, after creating a Government over them, to reform, amalgamate and civilize them."[55]

Vinton was not simply questioning the plausibility of Indian coloniza-tion; he was concerned that such a policy might actually result in a truly sovereign, and dangerously independent, Indian republic: "If you succeed in the plan of civilization, the increase of population and moral power that must necessarily result from the success of the measure, added to their pres-ervation as a distinct race of men, and the great extent of country occupied by them, must unavoidably, bring about the establishment of a Government independent of our own." He harshly rebuked Indian colonizationists for "execut[ing], by a single movement, the great plan of Tecumseh, that carried terror and dismay to every cabin beyond the Alleghenies. . . . He labored to bring about a concentration of Indian power, not for the purpose of civilization, but to resist and arrest the march of your population, and then to draw a perpetual line of separation between them and us. . . . If the name and the prowess of Tecumseh are so far forgotten here, as to induce us, voluntarily, to concentrate the whole Indian power on the frontier, it is far otherwise in the West—they are not forgotten there."[56] For Vinton, the prospect of creating a permanent Indian territory evoked still-recent memories of the pan-Indian insurrections in the midwestern region from which he hailed.

In the unfolding debate over removal policy, Vinton's concerns would eventually win out over the colonizationist notion that Native people be granted greater autonomy while organizing themselves as a nominally independent republic. African and Indian colonizationists imagined an expansive vision of the United States as an empire with both settler and global ambitions. In this conception, the government could presumably shape and manage the political existence of nonwhite populations both within and outside its borders. However, such a notion cut against emerging Jacksonian politics that idealized the autonomous, militarized white frontiersman. While not inherently incompatible with colonizationist ideas, this rhetorical stance emphasized a more decentralized, and explicitly violent, conception of U.S. settler statehood.

At the same time that Indian removal was being publicly debated, discussions about the extent and nature of federal support for African colonization during the 1820s and 1830s once again raised similar questions about what kind of empire the United States should be. The debate exposed a central tension in both African and Indian colonizationist rhetoric: if these nations were going to be truly independent, how could they be expected to reflect the interests of an expanding white settler empire? The colony in Liberia had been created through the limited support and funding of the U.S. government, which was only possible because President Monroe's administration took a broad interpretation of federal authority and set aside John Quincy Adams's constitutional qualms.[57] Internal debates within Monroe's cabinet, however, revealed that anxieties about the boundaries of federal power in colonizing new territory and the danger of creating a new "colonial system" persisted. The question about whether establishing a federal African colonization policy would redefine the contours of U.S. empire predated the passage of the Slave Trade Act of 1819 and would resurface continually in critiques of colonizationism throughout the 1820s and 1830s.[58]

The Monroe administration's initial funding and support for the ACS colony encouraged African colonizationists to try to expand the scope of federal involvement. In the mid-1820s the legislatures of Ohio, New Jersey, Delaware, and Connecticut all sent memorials to urge Congress to take an even more direct role in aiding the fledgling colony. However, several politicians from slaveholding states resisted these attempts to include colonization in national policy, suspicious that this would constitute a backdoor route to the abolition of slavery.[59] In his effort to demonstrate that an expanded federal colonization policy would not interfere with the institution of slavery, ACS secretary Ralph Gurley wrote articles in ACS publications fervently insisting that the organization had no abolitionist aims. He argued that the ACS was merely interested in removing "a people which are injurious and dangerous to our social interest, as they are ignorant, vicious, and unhappy," concluding that "the object is *national*, it demands *national* means."[60]

Supporters of slavery expressed their growing concerns about the extent of federal intervention into the Liberian colony and, in doing so, revived the same questions about the limits of U.S. empire that arose when the African colonization movement emerged in the late 1810s. A series of letters published in 1824–25 in Richmond, Virginia's *Enquirer* captured ongoing concerns surrounding the scope of the federal authority to build an overseas empire. The letters were so popular that they were later published as a pamphlet titled *Controversy Between Caius Gracchus and Opimius.*[61]

The public dialogue began in 1824 when an editorial, penned anonymously by "Caius Gracchus," warned that the ACS was being used by politicians to dangerously expand the power of the federal government.[62] In response, William Henry Fitzhugh, writing under the pen name "Opimius," made the case for the constitutionality of colonization. As a Virginian planter and the vice president of the ACS, Fitzhugh defended colonization against growing concerns that the federal government should only have the power to acquire territory that would become a permanent part of the nation. He argued that the acquisition of territory and relocation of populations both within and outside U.S. borders were constitutionally suitable and followed the precedent of previous federal actions, such as the purchase of Louisiana and the removal of Native populations within North America. He asked: "How else will he account for the appropriations made for the purchase of Louisiana and Florida?" or for "the repeated acquisitions of Indian Territory—for ameliorating the condition of the savages." [63] His anonymous opponent, Caius Gracchus, countered that a federally supported African colony could threaten the racial composition of the nation and challenge the boundaries of U.S. territory. He asked: "Does there live a man so blinded by fanaticism and folly as to wish to see the Federal Union extended beyond the Atlantic to the Western shores of Africa, to embrace a population already deemed so vile by the votaries of this scheme as to be unfit to live among us? I presume not." Fitzhugh countered that colonization would not saddle "the country with 'a permanent Colonial System,' or 'of extending the rights and privileges of the Federal Union to the shores of Africa, and to a negro population.' Neither will be necessary. The territory to be acquired will be acquired for a special purpose, believed to be conducive to the general interests of the nation."[64]

Although this dialogue ostensibly concerned the constitutionality of African colonization, it again revealed the deep divide over the question of the United States' authority over territories and populations both within and beyond its settler empire. Fitzhugh acknowledged that the prospect of a permanent "colonial system" or "Federal Union" that stretched across the Atlantic Ocean into Africa could present a troubling redefinition of the United States' power and lead to a more formalized overseas empire with limitless boundaries. Even more importantly, such an empire threatened to undermine the United States' own racial republicanism by potentially extending equal rights and privileges to nonwhite peoples. To reassure skeptics, Fitzhugh referred to the efforts already being undertaken to remove Native American populations onto federally managed lands, a set of actions that was beginning to be developed into Indian colonization policy by the Monroe and Adams administrations thanks to reformers such as Isaac McCoy. In drawing this parallel, Fitzhugh implied that African colonization was not distinct from other policies of U.S. expansion and would be analogous to the management of Indian territory. Therefore, a federally directed African colonization policy would promote the "general interests of the nation" without establishing a colonial system or endangering white republicanism.

The South Carolinian senator Robert Hayne voiced similar concerns about the perils of a U.S. overseas empire after another senator introduced an ACS memorial to Congress that called for an increase in federal support for African colonization in 1827. Hayne argued that although colonizationists claimed that Liberia would become an independent republic, the entire enterprise raised "the great political question" of "establishing Colonies abroad." Hayne wondered to which "part of the history of the world we are to look for argument in favor of the Colonial system." After cataloguing the "wars," "injustice," and "oppression" evident in the practices of the British empire, he asked, "What argument could possibly be urged in favor of its adoption, at this time, by us, whose habits, institutions, and fundamental principles, oppose an almost insuperable bar to all foreign connexions and alliances?" Hayne then read into the Senate record several ACS documents that detailed the colonists' conflicts with both indigenous populations and European empires in West Africa. His intention was to demonstrate that the United States' support for colonization would "engage this country in a war with the native tribes on that continent, and to involve us in serious dif-ficulties with other nations."[65] While southern critics such as Hayne likely opposed colonization for fear that it would cause an unwelcome disturbance to the institution of slavery, they framed their arguments in a way that again revived anticolonial rhetoric, which had remained a backdrop to debates over the African colonization movement since its inception.

Such debates highlight the fact that African colonization had become an increasingly contentious issue within national politics by the mid-1820s. During the 1828 presidential campaign, Jacksonian Democrats occasionally built on these arguments by using African colonization in order to highlight the perils of expansive federal power. Although Jackson had previously lent his name to a list of ACS vice presidents when the organization was formed in 1816, he did not become an active member and remained publicly silent on the topic. While Jackson may have broadly supported the aims of the organi-zation, it is just as likely that his ACS membership simply signaled the desire to bolster his rising political ambitions by associating himself with the influ-ential elite who backed the organization. Regardless of the convictions behind his initial support for African colonization, by Jackson's second presidential campaign in 1828, the idea of using federal funds to create far-flung overseas colonies and intervene in slavery was antithetical to the states' rights ideol-ogy that animated his campaign. An influential pamphlet published in 1828 by Robert J. Turnbull titled *The Crisis: Or, Essays on the Usurpations of the Federal Government* articulated the Jacksonian view of African colonization. In this pamphlet, Turnbull argued that the constitutional concept of "general welfare" to create a "*consolidated* national government" in the United States was evidence of federal overreach.[66] Andrew Jackson won the presidency in 1828, in part by opposing what he considered to be overly ambitious and meddlesome government efforts, including federally supported colonization programs.[67] At the same time, his campaign was also successful at mobiliz-ing support for federal Indian removal policy. The disjuncture between how Jacksonians came to view these two projects reveals competing visions of U.S. expansionism. For many, colonization was a dangerous step toward a boundless and federally managed overseas empire, while the removal policy was an outgrowth of the United States' presumed territorial claims within North America and was therefore essentially different and separate from the question of overseas colonies.

In the midst of the 1828 election, Littleton Tazewell, a Jackson supporter and Virginia senator, commissioned a report for the Senate Committee on Foreign Relations that argued against the concept of federal authority for African colonization. Tazewell's report raised familiar concerns about the creation of an overseas empire and particularly dwelled on whether the United States had the constitutional right to acquire territory in Africa. While the report admitted that the federal government had the authority to secure territory through "discovery, conquest, or negotiation," it contended that acquiring a colonial possession in Africa would not be appropriately placed in any of these categories. With regard to the United States' ability to make treaties for the cessation of territory, the report argued that this could only be executed with people who respected the rights and obligations of "intercourse between the different members of the family of nations." The report concluded that for this reason, "no civilized nation in modern times" entered into a treaty "with any of the savage tribes who wander over the deserts, or dwell upon the coast of Africa."[68]

Such critics of African colonization viewed the mode of empire it advanced as fundamentally distinct from the United States' settler expansion within North America. Conscious of the apparent contradiction this claim might present for the nation's numerous treaties with Indian tribes, Tazewell argued that "the peculiar character" of compacts with Native peoples did not acknowledge their "independent sovereignty." Furthermore, he argued that Indian titles to land were extinguished "under the permission of the United States, who long since acquired the acknowledged sovereignty and dominion over the territory so possessed." Moreover, the report argued that contiguous territories were very different from "distant territory . . . separated from the United States by a wide ocean" because such entities must "continue in a state of colonial bondage, deprived of all hope of being ever admitted into the Union." Most importantly, the report asserted that "the genius and spirit of all our institutions" are opposed to "holding distant colonies" or "creating new empires" that would be independent of the United States.[69]

While African colonizationists saw little distinction between the United States' colonial policies in North America and those proposed in West Africa, critics like Tazewell contended that colonization was a fundamentally distinct and dangerous new path for U.S. expansion.[70] The Jacksonian skepticism about African colonization was echoed by their approach to Indian removal. Unlike earlier supporters of Indian colonization, Jacksonian proponents of removal policy placed far less emphasis on the claim that resettlement would create a civilized Indian republic west of the Mississippi. While Jackson sought the counsel of Indian colonizationists such as Isaac McCoy and Thomas McKenney and occasionally employed their rhetoric of benevolence, he shared none of their utopian designs, preferring to focus on the objective of opening up territory occupied by Native peoples.[71]

Some members of Congress were discouraged by the manner in which earlier proposals for Indian colonization had shifted toward a hard-edged Jacksonian removal policy. During the debate for the Indian Removal Act of 1830, John Test, a U.S. representative from Indiana, criticized the law because he believed it undermined the autonomy and potential civilization of Native Americans. Test believed that it departed from the initial conception of Indian colonization by granting too much authority to individual Native leaders who had the power to cede collective tribal lands in a piecemeal fashion rather than maintaining their sovereignty through a coherent colonization process. In defending the long-standing sovereignty of Indian nations, Test stated, "I have always been in favor of colonizing the Indians as well as the negroes; but I wish, when it is done, it may be done in a manner that shall be agreeable to them—that it shall be done upon correct principles. Give them a territory over the Mississippi; let us take it under our protection; let us not undertake to govern them with our laws, but aid them in governing themselves with their own laws." Test believed that by fostering a unified Indian republic, the United States could eventually neutralize Native Americans' potential to threaten the nation: "Let them be Indians, not tribes of Indians; cultivate a good understanding with them; give them to know that we intend to treat them as our equals."[72]

Test echoed these sentiments two years later in an 1832 speech on behalf of African colonization to Congress when he argued that the failure of federal Indian policy had stemmed from the growing proximity of white settlers to Native people in parts of the West. Like Isaac McCoy, Test spoke from direct experience: both men occupied Indiana's recently contested frontier and had witnessed the effects created by violent and destructive relations between whites and Indians. For this reason, they argued that distance and separation from the United States was a prerequisite for the success of an Indian republic. Test said, "We have all seen and felt the difficulties of the Whites and the Indians settling in the same neighbourhood," which has resulted in "perpetual bickering" and "war and bloodshed" that "threaten the total annihilation of the unhappy race of Aborigines." He argued that the "weight in this argument . . . derives a double force when applied to the blacks." Therefore, he contended that "time, distance, and more dignified position to be assumed by the blacks" was necessary and could only be achieved in a separate African colony in the same way that he advocated for an Indian republic.[73] However, with the passage of the 1830 Removal Act, and the defeat of federal funding for African colonization two years later, the colonizationist policies endorsed by Test were beginning to fall by the wayside.

By the end of the 1820s, Jacksonian Democrats led the campaign to oppose federal funding for African colonization and helped shift the terms of Indian policy toward removal. These efforts unfolded against the backdrop of African colonizationists' consistent appeals for more direct federal involvement in Liberia. In 1825, for example, the New York senator Rufus King, having two decades earlier pursued colonization in Sierra Leone as a diplomat in the Jefferson administration, introduced a bill that would attempt to generate funds from public lands sales and use it to colonize African Americans "to any territory or country without the limits of the United States of America."[74] Meanwhile, the ACS increased their push for federal funding by drawing on a growing organizational base. During the 1820s the ACS continued to urge local auxiliaries to use their influence in state legislatures to pass memorials calling for action by Congress. Some colonizationists were even encouraged by federal support for Indian removal programs and attempted to use its overlap with colonizationism to make their appeals. In one such congressional memorial from 1830, the Kentucky Colonization Society called on the federal government to take a more active role in funding African colonization. The Kentucky auxiliary, encouraged by federal support for Indian removal, attempted to realign it with the aims of colonization, observing that "millions of dollars have been annually expended for the maintenance and comfort of the North American Natives." They argued that the Africans' claim "is at least of equal dignity with that of the savage."[75]

In an 1831 petition to Congress, the citizens of Buckingham County, Virginia, argued for the use of federal power in building the Liberian colony:

> We find that the General Government has uniformly passed laws which sanction the principle of colonizing the free negroes, and that those laws have received the approbation of the part which has been most rigid in their constructions of the powers of Congress granted by the constitution, by the purchases of Louisiana and Florida, by the erection of fortifications on Key West, and by the removal of the

Indians. We are unable to draw the distinction between the constitutional power of making purchases in America and making purchases
in Africa; between settling Key West and settling Liberia, (neither
of which can ever form an integral part of our Union) and between
removing the Indians and removing the free negroes.[76]

Like previous advocates of federal support for colonization, the peti-
tioners interpreted the idea within a much broader range of U.S. imperial
authority, which included the power to relocate nonwhite populations with
impunity as well as the ability to control land that would not formally become
part of the United States.

During Henry Clay's 1832 presidential campaign against Andrew Jackson,
he attempted to channel this persistent support for African colonization by
advancing a bill through Congress that would, among other things, initiate
massive governmental spending on its behalf. Clay had been one of the ACS's
most consistent supporters since it was formed and would go on to become
president of the organization in the late 1830s. When he introduced his "Distribution Bill" into the Senate in April 1832, he revived the idea that Rufus
King had advanced in the Senate seven years earlier. It was designed to dis-
tribute monies generated from public land sales by the federal government to
individual states to fund public education, internal improvements, and African colonization.[77]

The aim of this bill was to encourage white settlement of the vast reaches
of North America by acquiring territory through "extinguishing title" to
Indian lands. In effect, Clay argued for a public land policy that would use
the proceeds from settler expansion to develop these regions economically
and promote "general welfare" through a federally distributed infrastructure
investment in roads, bridges, and canals. This central plank in the Whig Party's "American System" emphasized building infrastructure that could link
eastern manufacturing to western agriculture and was expected to not only
foster the nation's geographic and economic cohesion but also strengthen its
social cohesion through African colonization and the expulsion of a "dangerous" black population that threatened white republicanism. In a lengthy
speech on the Senate floor in support of his bill, Henry Clay argued that distribution of public land was important to maintaining republicanism within
the United States' settler empire: "There is public land enough to found an
empire; stretching across the immense continent, from the Atlantic to the
Pacific Ocean, from the Gulf of Mexico to the Northwestern Lakes." Expanding on this theme, Clay asked, "What other nation can boast of such an outlet

for its increasing population, such bountiful means of promoting their prosperity, and securing their independence?"[78]

Clay connected his vision of an expansive and racially cohesive settler empire to African colonization: "The evil of a free black population is not restricted to particular States, but extends to, and is felt by, all. It is not, therefore, the slave question, but totally distinct from and unconnected with it." He concluded by weaving together nationalist, republican, commercial, and racial sentiments, arguing that the bill would result in "benefits of moral and intellectual improvement of the people, of great facility in social and commercial intercourse, and of the purification of the population of our country, themselves the best parental sources of national character, national union, and national greatness." In response to Senator Elias Kane's contention that colonization would not benefit his home state of Illinois, Clay countered that "every part of the Union was interested in the human object of colonizing the free blacks" and that "if any part were exempt from the evils of a mixed population, it would still not be indifferent to the prosperity of less favored portions." Clay rhetorically concluded this line of argument by emphasizing the long-term colonizationist vision of enabling a white racial republic: "Suppose that, fifty or a hundred years hence, the country could be entirely rid of this African race; would the gentleman from Illinois—would any gentleman—say that he should be indifferent to such an auspicious result?"[79]

While perhaps agreeing with Clay's assumption that Indian land must be privatized and parceled out before the United States could extend its far-reaching empire over North America, Jacksonian Democrats claimed that his bill excessively interfered in sectional interests and that infrastructure was not an appropriate field for federal action. During the debate, Senator Josiah Johnston opposed the colonization provisions of the bill on the basis that the idea should never be entertained "unless as the united desire of the slave-holding States themselves."[80] For similar reasons, the Committee on Public Lands opposed the colonization provision in their report, stating that "the existence of slavery is local and sectional. . . . If it is an evil, it is an evil to them [the southern states] and it is their business to remove it."[81]

Beyond criticisms of the bill's constitutionality, its opponents voiced the common concern that this legislation created a dangerous precedent for U.S. empire. In a last-ditch plea to sway fellow members of Congress against the bill's colonization provisions before a final vote, Senator John Forsyth argued that while he felt that removing free black populations could be done without the aid of the government, the other great colonizationist goal that "command[s] the approval of all" is the "civilization of Africa." Forsyth regarded this as a dangerous pursuit that went "beyond the European notion of acquiring justification" through "discovery and purchase." Instead, he noted that the ACS obtained territory "by purchase alone" and "on this sole ground of sovereignty" claimed to exert "authority over twenty thousand people, and expect soon to exert it over one hundred and fifty thousand." Noting that there had been several struggles between the Liberian colony and its neighboring indigenous populations, he argued that the bill would alter the previously tenuous colonial relationship between the United States and Liberia and force "a commitment of the Government to protect the colony against all the world." Implying that solid federal connection to the colony would inevitably propel the United States into the business of maintaining global empire, Forsyth noted that "Europe will not allow a colony in Africa thus to grow up and extend, unmolested, while under so feeble prohibition. They will wrest it from the society, unless Government interposes."[82] Although the bill faced significant dissent within Congress, it narrowly passed both the House and Senate. However, this legislative triumph was short-lived because Clay was decisively defeated in the 1832 election against Andrew Jackson. When the colonization bill came to President Jackson's desk in early 1833, he vetoed it, effectively ending the prospect of federal African colonization policy for several decades until the colonization movement's brief and final resurgence during the era of the Civil War.[83]

* * *

Historians have sometimes explained both the defeat of a federal African colonization program and the triumph of Indian removal policy by pointing to the hardening of racial ideology, a process that drove both the expansion of slavery and the accelerated displacement of Native people during this era. While this shift was certainly under way, African and Indian colonizationists were not simply racial moderates who were outpaced by a new, more virulent strain of racial thinking. Both of these colonization projects were, in fact, radically ambitious nation-building efforts aimed at both incorporating nonwhites within the republican project and actively reinscribing racial hierarchy. Because these colonizationist ideas emerged from the contradictions posed by Americans' ideological commitments to both self-governance and white supremacy, the racial republic was a fundamentally unstable construct. This is evident in the case of the Cherokee nation, whose sovereignty was eventually undermined despite its gestures toward both racial nationalism and republican governance. While white Americans were increasingly committed to fashioning the United States into a white republic, many were uncertain whether doing the same for other groups was feasible or even desirable.

This uncertainty stemmed, in part, from the questions that colonizationism raised about the character and scope of the United States' empire. Some feared that an Indian republic in the West would not work in concert with U.S. expansion but rather would threaten to rekindle the pan-Indian insurrections witnessed by the previous generation. At the same time, the colonization movement had looked to Africa precisely to avoid such a threat, yet many Americans remained worried that this might serve to redefine the United States as a global rather than a settler empire. In the short term, the ascendant Jacksonian Democrats characterized both Indian and African colonizationism as outside the bounds of federal authority: Indian removal policy would all but abandon the idealistic ambitions of the earlier Indian colonizationists, and the African colonization movement would languish for several decades without the support of full federal funding. Nevertheless, the colonizationist concept of an independent yet subordinate racial republic would prove enduring, and in the coming decades it would become the basis for an emergent conception of U.S. expansionism.

CHAPTER 4

Settler Republics in Black and White

In 1832 a group of black residents of New Bedford, Massachusetts, issued a series of public resolutions that denounced the colonization movement in no uncertain terms. While such protests had been common since the inception of the ACS in the mid-1810s, this particular statement focused on how colonizationist ideas undermined the ability of African Americans to settle and become citizens within U.S. territory. They charged that colonizationists were teaching "the public to believe that it is patriotic and benevolent to withhold from us knowledge and means of acquiring subsistence, and to look upon us as unnatural and illegal residents in this country."[1] New Bedford's free black community issued this protest during a period in which white Americans had increasingly employed colonizationist rhetoric, exclusionary laws, and violent street politics to discourage African Americans from settling within several northern states. Three years earlier, white colonization supporters in Cincinnati, Ohio, had led a campaign to drive out the city's black residents to a colony outside the United States. Vicious mob attacks helped convince several hundred residents of the city ultimately to relocate to British Upper Canada. In subsequent decades, the African colonization movement would become even more closely linked to removal and disfranchisement as white politicians within several northern states referenced it when passing laws that denied African Americans the ability to reside and acquire citizenship rights within their borders.[2]

As these events illustrate, the mobility of free African Americans presented a dilemma for an expanding republic that employed literal and symbolic violence to assert its sovereignty over indigenous lands and police the racial boundaries of its white settler communities. The federal government had used treaties, backed by the threats of both military force and removal, to establish settler control over a large section of North American territory east of the Mississippi River. However, by the early 1830s the African colonization movement had failed to secure federal support for a program on par with Indian removal policy. This raised concerns among white citizens about the prospect of free African Americans settling alongside them on recently colonized lands and attempting to participate in newly forming state governments.

Starting in the 1820s, colonizationist ideas became instrumental in defining how white Americans engaged with questions of black citizenship and the right to reside within an expansive settler empire. The United States' colonization of North America had been predicated on a firm distinction between the political and territorial sovereignty of indigenous nations and the settler communities that worked to displace them. Settlers consistently justified this process by arguing that they should be the rightful occupants of this territory. As the black residents of New Bedford recognized, colonizationism served to reinforce the perception that African Americans were not a "natural" or "legal" part of the United States' settler community. Since the Revolutionary era, whites had attempted to resolve the problem of where freed slaves might reside by suggesting different configurations of colonization: they imagined African Americans as parallel settlers, first in North America and eventually in Africa. In this regard, the colonization movement's effort to reposition African Americans as inevitable African colonists would serve to separate and exclude them from the white settler citizens who claimed a natural right to colonize North America and form new political communities on indigenous lands.[3]

These ideas spread rapidly through two very different forums: urban mobs and state constitutional bodies. The street-level politics of the "colonization riot" and the formal political processes of state conventions and legislatures effectively cultivated the assumption that African Americans had no place within the territorial or political boundaries of the United States. Colonizationists presented African Americans as illegitimate settlers within lands claimed by the United States and denied them the ability to occupy certain urban and rural spaces. The legitimacy of African Americans as settlers was further called into question by attempts to curtail their mobility within U.S. territory, particularly in the anxious communities that occupied the recently colonized lands of the Midwest.

The presumed illegitimacy of black settlers served to further enshrine black disenfranchisement. Indeed, the ability to settle territory was so intimately linked to the formation of political communities that several states crafted laws attempting to definitively curtail black citizenship rights at the same time they were erecting restrictions to end black migration within the United States. While white politicians were increasingly working against black settlement at home, they were simultaneously encouraging the settlement of Liberia. By claiming that political rights for blacks could only be protected by the creation of a racial settler republic in Liberia, colonizationist ideas reinforced the notion that African Americans were a "foreign" class of residents and thus were not entitled to protections within the United States. Therefore, the rhetoric of African colonization powerfully wove together the threads of settlement and citizenship by both legitimizing white Americans' exclusive claim to settle North America and suggesting that a similar process of settlement in Africa was African Americans' only path to self-determination.

Colonizationist Citizenship

Within the first decades of its existence, the African colonization movement made a powerful case to white audiences that African Americans were inadequate as settler citizens within the United States while simultaneously arguing that they could become productive citizens by settling in Liberia. Prior to the creation of Liberia, white colonizationists had forged a consensus for building an African colony by repudiating the idea that African Americans could participate in settling North America alongside whites. However, the entire trajectory of the subsequent colonization movement was predicated on the notion that African Americans were ideally suited to settle and realize their potential for self-government in Africa. To understand this outcome, it is necessary to explore how both colonizationists and their black critics debated the relationship between settlement and citizenship. Discussions about African colonization consistently invoked the question of citizenship: to whom its privileges belonged, where it could be asserted, and under what circumstances it should be promoted. African Americans became concerned that the logic endorsed by the African colonization movement was, in fact, a thinly veiled assault on their right to be settler citizens in the United States. African Americans who made claims to citizenship in the United States did so by rejecting African colonization and settling within the colonized lands of North America. In so doing, they were joining white settlers in asserting their rights to U.S. territory, all the while remaining painfully aware that white Americans might choose to remove them as violently as they had with Native peoples.

The earliest black protests against the colonization movement called attention to the tenuous position of African Americans as settler citizens. Only a few weeks after the ACS was formed, an anonymous group of African

Americans from Washington, D.C., published a "countermemorial" that attacked the organization's memorial for congressional action on colonization. Their statement warned: "The men who assume to themselves the power to decree that other men are miserable, whether they be so or not, will easily pass from *persuasion* to *force*."[4] From the movement's inception, free black communities recognized that colonizationists' purportedly benevolent intentions served to mask violence and coercion. Shortly after the counter-memorial's publication, several northern black communities organized to voice their opposition to the ACS in a series of public protests and statements. Their immediate and strident response would set the tone for future anticolonization protests in the coming decades.[5]

Few black critics denounced the early colonization movement more forcefully than David Walker. Walker was a Boston-based activist whose 1829 *Appeal to the Coloured People of the World* played a galvanizing role in the early abolitionist movement. He devoted a significant portion of his pamphlet to dismantling what he called the "colonizing trick." In large part, he did this by merely quoting the words of white colonizationists in order to show that while they claimed to support black citizenship in Liberia, they did so by explicitly demonizing African Americans in the United States. Walker identified the official ACS organ, the *African Repository*, as the primary purveyor of a rhetoric of violence that linked colonization with black anticitizenship: "from its commencement to the present day—see how we are through the medium of that periodical, abused and held up by the Americans, as the greatest nuisance to society, and throat-cutters in the world."[6]

Initially, most white antislavery activists judged Walker's incendiary pamphlet to be excessively radical; however, a growing segment of this community began to follow his lead by making similar critiques over the next few years. Speaking at the 1833 annual meeting of the New-England Anti-Slavery Society, the white abolitionist Amasa Walker argued that "those who contend that we ought to colonize the Blacks in Africa . . . maintain the principle, that that unfortunate class of our fellow creatures have not the rights of men; merely the right of existence, in such place and under such circumstances as we may see fit to assign them."[7] The emerging abolitionist critique had absorbed more than a decade of black protest, which had consistently argued that the colonizationist vision was fundamentally dishonest and harmful to black citizenship rights. The claim that the African colonization movement undermined black citizenship in the United States was no exaggeration. Indeed, a central theme running throughout the speeches and writings of the early colonization movement was that African Americans could not become full citizens of the United States. As Walker noted, many of the earliest issues of ACS's *African Repository* were explicitly aimed at attracting white elites who viewed free African Americans as a dangerous and troublesome segment of the population.

Nearly all colonizationist appeals presumed that African Americans' full participation in U.S. civil society was impossible, either because they were deemed to be racially inferior or because white racial prejudice was considered to be too intractable. In 1826 Charles Carroll Harper, the son of a prominent Federalist senator, made a speech to a crowd of white citizens in Baltimore that typified this sort of thinking. He argued that emancipated African Americans had become a "corrupt and degraded class" because they had been "shut out from the privileges of citizens, separated from us by the *insurmountable* barrier of color, they can *never* amalgamate with us, but must remain *for ever* a distinct and inferior race, repugnant to our republican feelings and dangerous to our republican institutions."[8] Colonizationists such as Harper believed that the presence of free African Americans inevitably threatened the foundations of the republic because they were destined to occupy a lower caste of U.S. society. According to this logic, racial diversity bred disharmony, and thus only a white republic could be a well-ordered republic.[9]

In the early American republic, the question of citizenship was intimately linked to the question of settlement. Both the United States and Liberia were settler states, and therefore citizenship was always framed within the politics of expansion and settlement within those territories. In the same speech, Harper also emphasized the degree to which African Americans should be considered unnatural settlers on U.S. soil. He informed his audience that "there are now at least five thousand free blacks in the city of Baltimore. We can make it in their interest to remove. Every thing urges them to go. By their departure, thousands of places will be opened for our fellow citizens who are in want of employment. Into these vacant places, will immediately rush a white and more wholesome species of population." He went on to say that white settlement would create an environment in which "industry will be encouraged" and the "city strengthened." Harper's support for black removal and his description of a "rush" of whites into "vacant places" illustrates how colonizationists often positioned African Americans as being akin to indigenous populations by preventing white settlement of territory and the establishment of stable republican institutions. In this way African Americans were not only deemed to be inadequate U.S. settlers; they were also characterized as impediments to creating settler citizen governments within the United States.[10]

Free African Americans were particularly cognizant of these connections amid raging debates about the removal of Indian nations during the 1820s and 1830s. In 1831 a group of black residents from New York City made this connection clear in a series of published resolutions that catalogued the myriad ways in which the colonization movement had worked to alienate African Americans from both U.S. society and U.S. soil. They emphasized that colonizationist logic helped banish African Americans not only from employment, education, and political participation, but also from territorial spaces claimed by the United States. Although their statement did not directly reference the analogous plight of North America's Indian nations, it is implied in their conclusion that "when they say that they will not move us without our consent, we doubt their sincerity. They cannot indeed use force; that is out of the question. But they harp so much on 'inferiority,' 'prejudice,' 'distinction,' and what not, that there will be no alternative but to fall in with their plans."[11] This analysis reflected growing despair among northern free black communities and concern that the popularity of African colonization would push them so far outside the bounds of U.S. settler citizenship that they would be forced to accept the idea that their only hope to acquire basic rights was by becoming settlers in territory located outside U.S. borders.

Colonizationists often reinforced this fear by positioning African Americans as the antithesis of U.S. settler citizens while simultaneously arguing that this characterization would be reversed when they reached Liberia, a region they deemed suitable for black settlement. African Americans could settle there, in Charles Harper's words, from "whence they originally came"; as a result, racial distinctions would cease to promote disharmony. Instead, racial homogeneity would encourage black settlers to civilize and merge with indigenous African peoples. This would enable emancipated slaves to become "a flourishing and enlightened people, and enjoy under our protection, the free institutions we have taught them to admire."[12]

This transformative vision of colonization reflected the fact that many white Americans self-consciously traced the emergence of their own republican institutions to Anglo-American settler communities that had been forged through the displacement of indigenous populations. Therefore, the transformation from settler to citizen became an extremely common colonizationist claim precisely because it had been foundational to U.S. political imagination; the connection between settler and citizen was so strong that expulsion from one category necessarily required alienation from the other. Because these categories were so linked, the colonizationist assertion that African Americans could become settlers in Africa meant they also had the potential to become citizens there. Black settlers and white ACS officials recognized that enshrining black citizenship in Liberia would depend on the ability to control, defend, and expand land claims through treaties, alliances, and violence with the surrounding indigenous populations in Africa. However, the colonization movement's dominant narrative of Liberian settlement routinely obscured or eliminated the presence of indigenous Africans. Furthermore, colonizationists often built their case on the idea that African Americans were returning to their "native" home, thereby asserting the idea that black settlers possessed an inherent right to African soil. This sort of claim simultaneously situated African Americans as both settlers *and* natives even though indigenous West Africans clearly recognized this process as settler colonization. For the most part, the indigenous people did not see African Americans as a returned population of African "natives" but rather as the outside colonizers they were. As a result, they often referred to them as either "Americans" or even "white."[13]

From the earliest days of the colonization movement, many of its supporters emphasized the connection between settlement and self-government. An editorial published shortly after the ACS was founded summarized this position: "The African Colonization scheme . . . is one of the best foreign projects in which we can engage because it has its basis on what men can do for themselves, and not what we can do for them." To illustrate this point, the writer argued that the migration of people and the colonization of new lands were fundamental to forging national self-consciousness throughout world history. The author noted that "nations which settle in any country, appear to have an opportunity to proceed in the whole length of human greatness." Drawing a clear connection between U.S. and Liberian settlement, the editorialist argued that "it is in this way perhaps we are to redeem the honour of Africa, as we have that of America."[14]

While most colonization supporters did not frame the issue in such broadly philosophical terms, many shared the basic idea that Liberia would replicate the United States' model of settlement in Africa. White colonizationists consistently emphasized this point by connecting Liberia to the British settler colonies in the Chesapeake and New England, both of which, by the early nineteenth century, were central to the U.S. national narrative. Colonizationist speeches frequently compared the difficulties faced by these colonies to highlight the relative progress that Liberia had already made. By the time that Henry Clay addressed the ACS as its president in 1848, such parallels had become well-worn tropes of colonizationist arguments. Clay noted that "Jamestown and Plymouth both languished for years . . . yet now, what land is there on the broad surface of the habitable globe, what sea spreads out

its waste of waters, that has not been penetrated and traversed by the enterprise, the skill, and the courage of our New England brethren?" He noted
that in only twenty-five years Liberia had grown into an independent nation
and "immense numbers of the natives are crowding into the colony to obtain
the benefits of education, of civilization, and of Christianity."[15] Colonizationists presumed that African Americans would follow a path parallel to that
of early British colonists, but with the crucial distinction that this journey
toward settler independence was being fostered, rather than opposed, by a
benevolent U.S. empire.

Although ACS leaders such as Clay proposed that African Americans
would thrive if they became settler citizens on the African continent, black
critics argued that the true problem was that they were excluded from the
benefits of being both settlers and citizens within North America. In an 1831
editorial published by the *Liberator*, an anonymous "colored Philadelphian"
highlighted this hypocrisy by noting, "If they [colonizationists] would spend
half the time and money that they do, in educating the colored population
and giving them lands to cultivate here, and secure to them all the rights and
immunities of freemen, instead of sending them to Africa, it would be found,
in a short time, that they would be made as good citizens as the whites."[16]

This writer emphasized that not only were African Americans being
excluded from the benefits of education and political citizenship, but they
were also denied the opportunity to access land, the central mechanism by
which the U.S. settler state cultivated the idea that democratic opportunity
was linked to the displacement of indigenous people. In pointing out the
United States' failure to provide these opportunities to African Americans, the
writer highlighted the absurdity of expending vast resources on settling new
land in Africa and building political institutions there when the United States
had already built a republic that simply needed to integrate its black residents
as citizens and settlers. For this reason, many free black communities rejected
colonization on the grounds that it attached citizenship rights to an uncertain
future as settlers in a distant land while simultaneously undermining their
ability to realize the benefits of settlement within the United States.

Colonization Riots

Throughout the 1820s, African colonizationists built their case firmly on the
idea that Liberia was the only legitimate place where African Americans
could settle and thus enjoy citizenship rights. Although the colonization
movement claimed to encourage African Americans' consent in this process,

most black communities had, in fact, forcefully repudiated this prospect from its inception. Therefore, the colonization-linked mob violence in the late 1820s and early 1830s reflected both willful defiance of more than a decade of black protests and implicit endorsement of colonizationist rhetoric. Thus, there is a parallel between the way that white settlers used colonizationist ideas to invalidate African Americans' claim to settler citizenship within U.S. territory and the way they used purportedly benevolent removal policies to support violence against Native American communities. If settlement of the U.S. frontier fundamentally concerned access to indigenous peoples' land and resources, the colonization-inspired riots were more concerned with stigmatizing black settlers who occupied physical and symbolic space within the nation. Anti-Indian violence drew a clear line *between* settler and native, but antiblack violence distinguished *among* those settlers who possessed a legitimate claim to colonize territory and those who did not. As explored in earlier chapters, the conceptual separation of African colonization from the colonization of North America functioned to maintain the integrity of the white settler state, but the way that colonizationism became increasingly tied to excluding African Americans from settlement and citizenship clearly elaborates on this distinction.

Colonization riots occurred during an era in which white men increasingly defined their political identity around unrestrained access to both the elective franchise and expropriated indigenous lands. With the decline of property requirements for voting, most states had endorsed universal white male suffrage by the 1820s. At the same time, white men had long connected their independence with their ability to settle on the territory seized from Indian nations. The colonization movement presented Liberia as a settler republic that promised similar outcomes for black men. It offered the opportunity for both land and citizenship, yet it was crucially located outside of the United States' settler empire. Thus, for many northern black communities, both colonizationism and the mob attacks it helped inspire would come to define both the rhetorical and physical battlegrounds where the right to even exist on U.S. soil would have to be defended.

While this dynamic continued to play out in long-settled parts of the North, the recently colonized midwestern frontier would become a key battleground within this struggle. In that region, settlers had been rapidly creating territorial and state governments through the colonization processes established by the Northwest Ordinance of the 1780s. Over the next half century, settlers displaced Indian nations through a series of violent military conflicts, coerced treaties, "civilization" programs, and removal policies. In so doing, they were not only attempting to establish their political authority in the region but were also anxious to control the racial composition of the settler population, particularly because free African Americans could theoretically choose to settle on "free soil" within their borders. The fact that these were recent, sparsely populated, and often transient settler societies meant that any significant influx of black migrants appeared to be a threat to the foundations of a fragile white body politic. This would become increasingly clear by the 1840s when black migration was routinely depicted as bringing a foreign and alien population that contributed to an "immigration" problem. This reflected the sense in which settlers had come to naturalize their very recent political authority in the region by physically and symbolically eliminating local indigenous populations as well as distinguishing themselves as the true "native" population in contrast to black settlers.[17]

Therefore, to white settlers, Native Americans and African Americans reflected distinct yet overlapping threats: Native peoples were a receding external challenge from outside the settler population, while black migrants posed the ongoing threat of racial heterogeneity and internal disharmony among settlers. For example, when Indiana governor James Ray Brown addressed his state's general assembly in 1829, he drew clear parallels between the black and Indian populations of the state, arguing for the removal of both groups. Brown warned that a "non-productive" population of former slaves "is pouring in upon us ... living without visible means, or labor—most of whom are paupers on society" and suggested that colonization in Africa might be a practical remedy to the state's "problem." Brown echoed the common colonizationist rhetoric that free black populations were degenerate, dependent, and corrupt and set black migrants apart as a wholly distinct class of the state's settler population. Immediately following this section of his speech, he launched into a similar characterization of the state's Native populations and complained of their "growing indolence" and "increasing dependence" and suggested that if they were not removed beyond the Mississippi River "their national property will be carved up into individual rights."[18] Brown's speech highlights how whites often viewed both groups as obstacles to the establishment of stable white settler governments. In subsequent decades, settlers would increasingly advocate for African colonization out of concern over the prospect of increased black migration to the Midwest.

During the 1820s and 1830s Ohio became one of the first states of this region where colonizationist sentiment, racial violence, and exclusionary laws converged in a potent mix. As the first state carved out of the Northwest Territory in 1802, Ohio would come to be defined by its status as both an early western frontier and a border between northern free states and southern slave states. In response to significant numbers of emancipated and escaped slaves beginning to settle in the state shortly after Ohio was admitted to the union, the state government passed a series of laws aimed at constraining black settlement. So-called "black laws" passed in 1804 and 1807 required African Americans to post bond and provide proof of their free status when entering the state. Although such laws served to stigmatize the state's black population, they were generally unsuccessful in curbing black settlement. By some estimates, the black population had grown by more than 100 percent during the 1820s. By the mid-1820s the perception of many of Ohio's white settlers that the state's black population was increasing rapidly helped build support for the state's growing African colonization movement.[19]

As a growing frontier city separated from slave territory by the Ohio River, Cincinnati exemplified many of the racial anxieties evident in midwestern settler societies. While the city experienced only modest black settlement before 1820, by 1829 the city's directory listed "blacks and mulattos" at roughly 10 percent of the city's residents.[20] For the most part, Ohio did not enforce its "black laws," and many prominent white Cincinnatians were concerned that the city's growing black community would become a haven for freed and escaped slaves. Increasingly, white citizens began to demand action from the city and petitioned the Cincinnati City Council in 1828 and 1829 to take actions that would stem the tide of black migration.[21] In 1829 the *Cincinnati Daily Gazette* proclaimed that if steps were not taken to discourage black settlement, "we shall be overwhelmed by an emigration at once wretched in its character and destructive in its consequences."[22]

The African colonization movement helped fuel Cincinnati's growing public actions against black settlers. Although Ohio boasted only one ACS auxiliary in 1825, this number rose to forty-five branches of the organization throughout the state in the next five years as Ohio audiences enthusiastically endorsed ACS ideology. The Cincinnati Colonization Society was founded in 1826, and although the official membership of the organization numbered fewer than 150 persons, it boasted some of the city's most respected leaders. The prominent status of colonization supporters ensured that the idea would receive ample discussion in the city's newspapers and city council debates, particularly pertaining to the question of black settlement within municipal limits.[23]

As Cincinnati's white leaders increasingly portrayed black settlers as a festering problem, colonizationist ideas reinforced the notion that African Americans were unwanted "immigrants" or "aliens." The Ohio State Colonization Society's inaugural report in 1827 argued that the colonization movement was essential to the growth of the state because "the object [of this society] is to remove from us that unfortunate race of men, who are now, as aliens on their native soil.—A people who do not, but in a small degree, participate in privileges and immunities of the community—and who, from causes in their nature inevitable and reasons insuperable; never can be admitted to the full enjoyment of those rights as fellow-citizens."[24] Of course, Ohio was not "native soil" for the vast majority of its residents, including black settlers. In fact, Ohio state laws explicitly cultivated the notion that African Americans settlers were an "alien" population while recent white settlers possessed a "native" right to the state's territory. Colonizationist ideas conveniently justified this distinction precisely at a moment when white settlers were increasingly defining black settlers as an immigration threat. City officials in Cincinnati attempted to revive the enforcement of Ohio's early "black laws" and use them to exclude black settlers definitively from citizenship and residency in the state. For two decades these laws had been widely ignored, but in 1829 city officials demanded that all African Americans register their free status and pay the required bond to remain in the state or else they would be forced to leave the city.[25]

Many white Cincinnatians believed that the city should go even further by actively removing the city's black population, potentially with the use of force. Although city officials agreed with this basic goal, they objected to forced removal as an infringement on African Americans' basic ability to reside within the state. During Cincinnati's citywide debate over removing its black residents, a colonization supporter published a newspaper article demanding that it "is the time for the Colonization Societies 'to be up and doing.'" The letter, later republished by the *African Repository,* argued that Cincinnati's colonizationists "consider this class of people a serious evil among us" and supported the use of existing laws to "make arrangements for their final removal" because "the only remedy afforded is to colonize them in their mother country."[26] The fact that these calls for removal emerged alongside the renewed calls to enforce Ohio's "black laws" illustrates how African colonization essentially provided a ready-made justification for the shift in public discourse over race in the state.

In the face of gathering forces for removal, several of Cincinnati's black residents had formulated a colonization plan of their own. They created a group called the Board of Coloured People in Cincinnati for the Purpose of Colonization. This hastily established organization negotiated with the Canadian Land Company for thirty thousand acres on the Sabel River in British Upper Canada.[27] In the aftermath of the mob attacks, the leaders of this plan pushed forward, and a significant portion of the city's black population, by some estimates more than one thousand people, left to settle in the Canadian colony. There is considerable evidence to suggest that this group's desire to leave Cincinnati and construct a colony in Canada was not only forced by the situation on the ground in Ohio but was also, in fact, the culmination of the community's long-standing efforts to realize self-determination. While some black Cincinnatians had previously investigated the prospect of immigrating to Canada, plans were clearly accelerated by the ultimatums issued by the Cincinnati city government. The group's choice to use "colonization" in its name was likely calibrated to appease the city's white population, who were already supportive of African colonization. The organization's strategy to align itself with colonizationism was initially successful, and the city extended its deadline for leaving after black leaders created the Colonization Board and indicated their willingness to immigrate to Canada.[28]

In June 1829 the Cincinnati City Council posted a public declaration stating that black residents who were unable to meet the state's residency requirements would have to vacate the city within thirty days. The council later extended this deadline into early September, but prior to this expiration date, some three hundred white residents, discontented with the pace of removal, decided to take matters into their own hands. For nearly a week in late August, white rioters terrorized the Fourth Ward, the city's largest black neighborhood, destroying a number of buildings and attacking individuals. The rioting subsided after a few whites were wounded and killed by African Americans who rose in defense of their community.[29]

According to the few existing accounts of these events, a considerable portion of the city's rioters were unskilled white workers who believed that removing black competitors would boost their own wages. An editorial published shortly after the August riot suggested that these laborers were central to the violence and tacitly supported some form of colonization: "[The workers are] animated by the prospect of high wages, which the sudden removal of fifteen hundred laborers from the city might occasion."[30] A few years before the riot, a Cincinnati colonizationist had predicted such grievances could lead to widespread ACS support in the city because African Americans were "a great and manifest drawback on the prosperity of this city" as they made "it difficult for the laboring poor white people to obtain employment."[31] While white workers were socially far removed from the elite members of the ACS, colonizationists often presented the idea in ways that appealed to racial solidarity across class lines based on the notion that black settlement undermined the opportunities for all white settlers.

David Walker's *Appeal*, written shortly after Cincinnati's 1829 removal campaign and riots, keenly assessed what was at stake in these events. In particular, he questioned the exclusive settler claims made by whites in the state, arguing that "America is more our country, than it is the whites— we have enriched it with our *blood and tears*," and turned this into a call for defiant resistance to the notion that African Americans should forsake their claim to U.S. settlement in exchange for settling Africa: "Will any of us leave our homes and go to Africa? I hope not. Let them commence their attack upon us as they did on our brethren in Ohio, driving and beating us from our country, and my soul for theirs, they will have enough of it." In contrast to the implicit weakness of accepting a status as a second-class settler citizen in Liberia, Walker grounded black claims to citizenship in the United States with a robust rebuke of colonizationism: "Let no man of us budge one step, and let slave-holders come to beat us from our country."[32] Walker recognized that the events in southern Ohio portended a convergence between African colonization, exclusionary public policy, and violent denials of citizenship.

While the Cincinnati removal campaign was one of the first examples of colonization-inspired violence, in the next few years there would be equally dramatic events in the far more established parts of the eastern United States. These conflicts would similarly link colonizationism to a politics aimed at delegitimizing African Americans as settlers and citizens. This linkage was particularly evident in the riots in New York and Philadelphia, separated by a matter of weeks from each other during the summer of 1834. Both cases featured the distinct influence of a political context saturated by the rhetoric and logic of colonizationist sentiment.

In the months leading up to the riots in these cities, colonizationists played a prominent role in fostering racial tensions. In New York this was marked by the rise of anti-abolitionism. The organizational woes of the ACS multiplied as the abolitionist movement attracted members in the early 1830s. From 1832 to 1833, ACS donations fell by one-third, prompting serious concern within the organization about the attacks by William Lloyd Garrison and his followers. In New York City this trend was evident when Arthur Tappan, one of the most prominent leaders within the New York Anti-Slavery Society, renounced the colonization movement in 1833. In the year preceding the 1834 riots, the city's prominent procolonization newspapers, the *New York Courier and Enquirer* and *New York Gazette,* had trumpeted their continuing support for the movement by encouraging violence and intimidation at abolitionist meetings.[33]

In New York, James Watson Webb, the procolonizationist editor of the *Courier and Enquirer*, was principally responsible for mobilizing anti-abolitionist sentiments into antiblack violence. In the months and weeks leading up to the July violence, he published several articles claiming that the city had been overrun by "negro mobs" who were inspired by abolitionism. On the first day of rioting, Webb's paper warned that if African Americans in the city continued to align themselves with abolitionists, "the consequences to them will be most serious."[34] Perhaps the colonizationist influence on rioters was most clear when, in one of the instigating events of the riot at New York's Chatham Street Chapel, a mob broke into a scheduled abolitionist meeting site and chanted vows to support African colonization. This was followed by a week of escalating violence and open attacks on both white abolitionists and black neighborhoods throughout the city.[35]

Edward Abdy, a visiting English abolitionist who had observed the outbreak of violence in New York, noted that the Philadelphia riots a month later were "similar, in their origin and objects, to what had previously occurred at New York . . . the end aimed at, being the expulsion of the blacks." However, unlike in New York, the initial disturbances that led to the riots in Philadelphia did not directly result from disputes within the antislavery community. In Philadelphia a personal conflict between groups of black and white men at an amusement park led white mobs to carry out premeditated attacks on black neighborhoods. Over the course of three nights, white rioters killed two African American men and destroyed thousands of dollars' worth of black-owned properties.[36]

Procolonization editors in Philadelphia played a much smaller role than in New York, but they printed similarly inflammatory articles that helped stoke the passions of rioters. The Pennsylvania Abolition Society (PAS) issued a report documenting that in the days leading up to the riots, several colonizationists made public speeches that disparaged the city's black population. The *Commercial Intelligencer* and the *Philadelphia Inquirer* echoed the sentiments in these articles and, in the opinion of the PAS, sought to "feed the fiendish prejudice against the colored man." On the day when full-fledged riots broke out, one of the city's procolonization papers published an article voicing grievances from the city's white workers: "Among the evils to which our good citizens are subjected, there is not more universally complained of, than of the conduct of the black porters who infest our markets." The article asked: "[Can] our citizens . . . be protected from their assaults? Is there no way in which the rudeness and violence of these ruffians can be prevented?" Another white observer of the riot recommended African colonization as a solution to such problems after characterizing two black neighborhoods as displaying "instances of loathsome disease, exhibitions of nudity or something near to it, intemperance, profanity, vice and wretchedness, in all the most disgusting forms."[37]

Pennsylvania's ACS auxiliary commonly alluded to the "immorality" of the state's free black population. Shortly after the riot, Job Tyson, a prominent Philadelphia colonizationist, made a speech emphasizing the purported criminality of the city's black residents using evidence that black representation in the state's prison system was far higher than their proportion of the population. Tyson also objected to the fact that the state formally considered "freemen of colour" to be "free citizens" because they are "yet very low in the scale of moral virtue." In advocating colonization as a solution, he cited James Mechlin, a former colonial governor of Liberia, who claimed that the "morals of the colonists" were "much better than those of the people of the United States" where "you will find more drunkards, more profane swearers and Sabbath-breakers."[38] While characterizing African Americans as unfit to settle in Philadelphia, colonizationists such as Tyson argued that the process of forging a new settlement in Africa would transform the black anticitizens into exemplars of temperance, productivity, and civic virtue in Liberia.

Despite the apparent influence of colonizationist rhetoric on white rioters, it is worth drawing some distinction between participants in the New York and Philadelphia riots and the generally more cautious members of the ACS. There is no evidence that active members of the organization directly encouraged rioters with their words or actions. When they did speak on the subject of the riots, leaders of the colonization movement generally distanced themselves from the obvious racial animus that motivated the violence.[39] Nevertheless, it suggests a broader constituency for colonizationism than simply those political and religious leaders who founded and supported the movement. Indeed, at a moment in the early 1830s when elite support for the ACS was beginning to founder, these riots show how colonizationism could migrate out from the narrow confines of the organization's explicit agenda and filter into public consciousness as a free-floating set of ideas that worked to undermine the notion that African Americans had any right to settle in the United States.

In particular, the violence in these riots featured an exterminationist undercurrent designed to demonstrate that African Americans should not be considered part of the legitimate settler community of the United States but instead, like the Native Americans, were a population to be removed or eliminated. The white abolitionist Elizur Wright made reference to this sentiment in recounting to a friend the experience of an African American man from New York who was told by a colonization supporter that the agitation of abolitionists would lead to the destruction of black residents if they did not go to Liberia.[40] Edward Abdy wrote that the attacks on "the churches and houses of the colored people" in the New York riot "gave convincing proofs that the friends of the Colonization Society are not always the friends of those whose welfare it professes to promote."[41]

Both riots demonstrated that class resentments among white workers were fueled by the concern that some African Americans had already achieved a degree of status as respectable citizens. Leonard Richards's analysis of the New York riots has shown that its participants included many people of lower to middling economic status, primarily mechanics and young journeyman artisans, but not necessarily common laborers who directly competed with African Americans for work.[42] Despite this reality, at the time many observers anecdotally noted that class resentments were a significant factor in the riots. The labor activist and editor of *Workingman's Advocate*, George Henry Evans, was particularly frustrated with worker participation in what he called the "colonization riots" because he believed they were expressing class-based grievances through misdirected mob actions that often aligned them with the city's elites.[43]

By all accounts, the Philadelphia mobs were composed of young unskilled workers, a fact endorsed by the city's official report on the riot. Edward Abdy noted how class resentments were bound up with the colonizationist sentiment among some rioters: "The mob consisted chiefly of young men—many of them tradesmen. One of the sufferers, a man of wealth and great respectability, was told afterwards by a white that he would not have been molested if he had not, by refusing to influence the black community in Philadelphia to go to Liberia, prevented others from leaving the country."[44] In this case, it was the conspicuous success of black men, combined with their refusal to settle in Liberia, that earned the wrath of white crowds. Although rioters were often spurred on by colonizationist claims of black "degradation," this episode illustrates that they could also be motivated by evidence of black class ascension.[45]

In Philadelphia, such attacks were offset by the fact that a segment of that city's black community exhibited uncommon prosperity for the era. One of Philadelphia's most prominent black gentlemen, James Forten, was so respected that the mayor of the city honored his request for police protection in a black neighborhood during the riot. Forten's long-standing opposition to colonizationism illustrates how the African colonization movement became implicated in the broader politics of citizenship and social class in the city. Before the riot, he had been a driving force behind organizing opposition to Pennsylvania's recently passed law that outlawed black migration into the state. When the legislation was being debated, he led a group of black Philadelphians to oppose the law by explicitly confronting the colonizationist logic behind the settlement restrictions: "I have since lived and labored in a useful employment, have acquired property, and have paid taxes in this city. Here I have dwelt until I am nearly sixty years of age . . . yet some ingenious gentlemen have recently discovered that I am still an African; that a continent three thousand miles, and more, from the place where I was born, is my native country. And I am advised to go home."[46]

Like other black critics of colonization, Forten rejected the idea that he should become a settler in Liberia because it was his "native country." In fact, he was arguing that his birth and accomplishments in the United States gave him right to claim "native" status in the same way that other settlers of European descent now claimed to be "natives" on the lands of displaced indigenous peoples. With a history of opposition by the black community in Philadelphia to the growth of colonization-inspired rhetoric, it is not surprising that Forten's fifteen-year-old son, as well as several other visibly wealthier members of the black community, were targeted by rioters. Within this context, it is difficult to untangle whether such attacks were motivated more by Forten's relative wealth and social status, his high-profile opposition to African colonization, or his defiant claims to U.S. citizenship.[47]

A few years earlier, in a speech before Philadelphia's free black community, the abolitionist William Lloyd Garrison made a similar point when he deconstructed the racist assumptions around the nativist strain of colonizationist rhetoric. Garrison stated: "[The colonizationists] generally agree in publishing the misstatement, that you are strangers and foreigners. Surely they know better. They know that, as a body, you are no more natives of Africa, than they themselves are natives of Great Britain. Yet they repeat the absurd charge; and they do so, in order to cover their anti-republican crusade." He highlighted this contradiction by pointing out that if all "foreigners" were forced to leave North American soil, we would have "a most alarming deduction from our population." He heightened the absurdity by imagining a "philanthropic and religious crusade" in which "the Dutch, the French, the Swiss, the Irish, among us" were removed "to New Holland, to enlighten and civilize her cannibals."[48] Although Garrison did not question the fundamental assumptions of settler citizenship in the United States, he did emphasize what would become a common refrain among abolitionists in coming decades: that the colonization movement was fundamentally defined by antiblack and antirepublican sentiments.

While the riots in New York and Philadelphia highlighted how colonizationism could mobilize racial violence and deportationist sentiment, they also functioned similarly in smaller rural communities where the dynamics of black settlement had even greater potential to threaten whites' fragile sense of settler sovereignty. A few days after the events in Philadelphia, a similar riot broke out in Columbia, Pennsylvania, a town of just over two thousand residents, demonstrating that smaller black communities outside urban areas could be just as successfully inspired by colonizationist rhetoric. The violence there followed the pattern of the earlier urban riots that summer, beginning on August 16, when some white residents went into the black neighborhood of Columbia and began to destroy property for unknown reasons. Whites participated in random violence there for the next two nights, culminating on August 19, when a mob of more than fifty people gathered to terrorize the community after a rumor spread that a black resident of the neighborhood had shot a white man. After this series of events, many of Columbia's black inhabitants fled into hiding outside of town for several days until tensions subsided.[49]

Columbia's residents were certainly aware of the recent colonizationist-inspired violence in New York and Philadelphia, but they had also been exposed to the movement's political impact for several years in their community.[50] In 1830 white citizens formed their own local auxiliary of the ACS in Columbia, and the town's only newspaper, the *Columbia Spy*, featured numerous articles supporting the colonization movement and reporting on the progress of the Liberian colony.[51] One editorial in the *Columbia Spy* pointed to the town's increasing black population to demonstrate why colonization was necessary: "With some few gratifying exceptions what are they but an amalgamation of ignorance and wretchedness. . . . Nearly all from their vicious and idle habits acquired in slavery, are incapable of maintaining their families. Their few pennies, the produce of their toil and sweat are taken from them and a jug of rum is given in return.—Thus they spend the summer and county jail or poor-house affords them an asylum in the winter."[52] While such commentary positioned African Americans as a malevolent alien presence within the town, the black community responded forcefully to the way that whites were using colonizationist rhetoric to undermine their right to settle in the region.

In the years prior to the riot, leaders from Columbia's black community organized against the increasing influence of the colonization movement by protesting when the local ACS auxiliary was founded there.[53] In a statement distributed around town, they bluntly condemned colonizationism: "We will resist all attempts to send us to the burning shores of Africa. We verily believe that if by an extraordinary perversion of nature, every man and woman, in one night, should become white, the colonization society would fall like lightning to the earth." In this statement, Columbia's black residents argued that the colonization movement was driven by a desire to maintain the privileges of white citizenship, and they resolved "that we will not be duped out of our rights as freemen, by [Liberian] colonists, nor by any other combination of men. All the encomiums pronounced upon Liberia can never form the least temptation to induce us to leave our native soil, to emigrate to a strange land." In claiming Columbia as "native soil," the city's black community asserted its right to settle in the region and rejected the colonizationist notion that they should be naturally considered either natives or settlers in a "strange land." Moreover, black Columbians challenged colonizationists' false "encomiums" on republican citizenship in Liberia by noting that such disingenuous claims actually undermined African Americans' "rights as freemen" in the United States.[54]

African Americans in Columbia were virtually alone in their rejection of colonizationism within the town, but their history of protest serves as a crucial background to the violence during the summer of 1834. While the *Columbia Spy* denounced rioters' unlawful actions, its editors claimed sympathy for their endorsement of African colonization and the removal of the entire black community from the town. Newspaper accounts of the events revealed the extent to which colonizationist discourse influenced reactions to the riot. A *Columbia Spy* editorial claimed that "a reflecting mind" must be "impressed with the necessity of colonizing the blacks and getting them from among us," suggesting that "the two races never can, [and] never ought to be amalgamated, and the spectacle of two distinct nations living commingled together under the same government, entirely disconnected one from another and the one necessarily inferior to the other, is one which has never yet been exhibited upon the globe."[55] Following other colonizationists' interpretations, the *Spy* rejected the idea that African Americans could continue to settle alongside whites in Columbia and that they would only be elevated to citizens by realizing their status as a "distinct nation" once settled in Africa.[56]

A few days after the riots, Columbia's town hall housed a meeting for "working men and others favourable to their cause." While those attending the meeting officially denounced the rioters' unlawful actions, like the *Spy* they implicitly supported their aims. The meeting drafted a statement that predicted doom for white workers if the pattern of black settlement in the city was not halted and reversed through African colonization: "As the negroes now pursue occupations once the sole province of the whites, may we not in course of time expect to see them engaged in every branch of mechanical business, and their known disposition to work for almost any price may well excite our fears, that mechanics at no distant period will scarcely be able to procure a mere subsistence."[57]

The white working men of Columbia also defined their protest against black residents as one in opposition to "amalgamation," which they believed would threaten the value of their labor and their status as white citizens: "The cause of the late disgraceful riots throughout every part of the country may be traced to the efforts of those who would wish the poor whites to amalgamate with the black." They warned that "the poor whites may gradually sink into the degraded condition of the negroes—that, like them, they may be slaves and tools, and that the blacks are to witness their disgusting servility to their employers and their unbearable insolence to the working class." As in the previous riots, Columbia's white workers expressed the idea that proximity to black workers and the prospect of "amalgamation" reflected a specific class-based threat to the value of their labor power and status as independent citizens. In order to protect against such a possibility, workers concluded that "the Colonization Society ought to be supported by all the citizens favorable to the removal of the blacks from this country."[58]

While such calls to remove African Americans from the town were rhetorically linked to the colonization movement, some white residents of the city also attempted to rid the town of its black population by buying the property of some of the town's more prosperous black residents. As in Philadelphia and New York, white workers in Columbia felt threatened by both competition with black laborers and conspicuous examples of black prosperity, such as Steven Smith, a successful lumber and coal dealer who was forced to confront mobs in defense of his property. In the aftermath of the riots, local white businessmen banded together to force out the town's most prosperous black residents, including Smith. The *Spy* reported that the "[citizens of the town] recommend the subject to the attention of capitalists; having no doubt that, independent of every other consideration, the lots in question would be a profitable investment of their funds, and that if a commencement were once made nearly all of the colored freeholders of the borough would sell as fast as funds could be raised to meet the purchases." Efforts to remove both black workers and black owners of capital from the town illustrate how the colonizationist rhetoric of removal could unite whites together across class lines. However, it also shows that the vicious rhetoric used to describe

the "degraded" nature of black residents was complicated by the success of
Columbia's black men of wealth, who were urged to leave not with threats
of removal but with property buyouts. Although some black businessmen
attempted to liquidate their assets, on the whole the removal campaign failed,
and it seems that black residents did not depart from Columbia in significant
numbers.[59]

None of the riots during this era succeeded in entirely removing black
communities from urban areas, yet they did successfully link African colonization to the notion that African Americans had no right to settle or become
citizens within U.S. territory. The African colonization movement had always
implied this idea, but rioters made this concept starkly concrete when they
used it to violently discourage African Americans from settling within northern cities. Widespread colonizationist arguments identified black populations as foreign and illegitimate and provided justification for targeted acts
of terror by making the expulsion of black communities appear to be a log-
ical and achievable goal. In doing so, the colonization riot offered a venue
for whites to express multiple grievances, including fears of racial mixing,
resentment about black class ascendency, and anxieties from job competition. The public spectacle of the riot also illustrates how colonizationist
ideas had a much broader base of support that extended beyond the small
coterie of reformers who composed the ranks of ACS auxiliaries. Although
the national colonization movement suffered decline in both resources and
members throughout the 1830s and 1840s, the ideas it advanced had proven
to be both popular and malleable to white audiences. While the formal
leadership of the colonization movement was composed of political elites,
middle-class reformers, and evangelical leaders, the riots demonstrated that
colonizationism could also mobilize a broader cross-section of northern
populations against African Americans by identifying them as the antithesis
of U.S. settlers and U.S citizens.

Constituting Settler Citizens

Within the context of the antislavery movement, these riots characterized
the transition into an era of diminished prospects and organizational disarray for the African colonization movement. During this period, the ACS
endured federal political defeat, growing abolitionist attacks, and diminished
membership and fundraising. However, the riots also illustrated the way that
colonizationist ideas would continue to thrive as a popular justification for

black exclusion from settler citizenship in the United States. If the riots of the early 1830s exemplified how colonizationist ideas could be successfully translated into deportationist sentiments aimed at removing black populations, in subsequent years state constitutional conventions demonstrated how African colonization could be used within formal political processes to unite white citizens around rejecting black citizenship and settlement within state borders.

In the early nineteenth century, U.S. states convened to write new constitutions with relative frequency. By the late 1830s many of the former British colonies in the East had already rewritten their constitutions at least once since the Revolutionary era, and shortly thereafter several western territories would embark on their first or second efforts to craft state constitutions. As nonslaveholding states wrote new or revised constitutions during this period, colonizationist ideas played a central role as convention delegates increasingly debated the place of African Americans as both citizens and settlers within their states.

Pennsylvania's effort to revise its constitution in 1837 exemplified how African colonization would shape subsequent political debates about black citizenship and settlement. Pennsylvania's initial 1776 constitution included some of the broadest suffrage provisions of the Revolutionary era, allowing nearly all adult men to vote, including African Americans.[60] In practice, the state's white majority had often informally restricted black residents' access to their nominal voting rights, but on paper these rights had remained intact through the state's first constitutional revision in 1790. This history made it particularly significant that Pennsylvania's 1837–38 convention would become a central battleground in the effort to formalize black disenfranchisement in the North. Pennsylvania delegates focused their discussion of black citizenship primarily on extensive debate over whether the word "white" should be inserted in the state constitution before the word "freeman" in order to definitively outlaw black voting.[61]

Some convention delegates directly referenced the African colonization movement in order to justify creating such a racial definition for voting rights in Pennsylvania. For instance, Charles Brown framed his support for the change in colonizationist terms when he suggested that "the negro is free to select a country for his residence where he can enjoy the same political privileges which white citizens possess here." Brown urged his fellow delegates to change the constitutional language in order to send a clear message to potential black settlers in the state: we do not wish you to come here; it is not in our interest, nor to yours, that you should inhabit the same soil, mingle in the same social circles, and we will not invite you here. We will place a few barriers between you and us. We will offer you a premium to go elsewhere, for this is not your home." However, Brown believed this strong language should be accompanied by "inducements to leave us, and go to a climate and country, in which they would be comfortable and happy, and not be degraded as they are now."[62] By using African colonization to discourage black settlers from entering the state, Brown converged with rioters in his state who, only a few years earlier, had opted for violence rather than legal remedies to achieve similar ends.

Brown advocated African colonization in order to preserve the privileges of white citizens, yet unlike most rioters, he attempted to do so while specifically admitting that African Americans had the potential to become self-governing citizens as settlers outside of U.S. borders. Brown claimed that he "had no prejudices against the negro on account of color," noting that he knew "negroes living in the county of Philadelphia, who were fully as competent to exercise the right of voting as any man in the city or county of Philadelphia." Despite this, he simultaneously wondered if "any man [would] place the poorest white man, who goes to the polls with the highest, and deposits his vote as fearlessly, on the same footing with the negro? . . . Did any one entertain the belief that the negro should be raised to the level of the poorest man who was fit to enjoy and exercise the rights of sovereignty?" Thus, Brown acknowledged that although African Americans were capable of citizenship, he believed that their "sovereignty" must be exercised outside of the United States.[63]

The convention's debate over voting rights foregrounded the question of black political sovereignty. Some delegates argued that African colonization would provide a way to demonstrate that African Americans were indeed worthy of citizenship rights. Walter Forward, a delegate who supported making whiteness an explicit requirement for voting, claimed that if African colonization proved that "the colored population were entirely capable of self-government, that slavery would be yielded up, and better feelings and better principles will universally prevail throughout this extensive country."[64]

Another delegate, George Woodward, echoed these sentiments in a speech to the convention: "We may love the virtues which they [African Americans] display, and we may sympathize in their sufferings, and alleviate their wants, but white men will not consent to the self debasement, which political and social equality with them would imply." Woodward argued that "by giving the black the right of suffrage, an everlasting obstacle is thrown in the way of colonization—it will chain them to us. . . . Undoubtedly they deserve civil and religious freedom. . . . Let them go with our political principles and establish governments after our model, which may protect them, and exert salutary effects on their fellow Africans, now ignorant of all the blessings of civilization." While Woodward implied that black voting rights threatened white citizenship in the United States, he nevertheless argued that when black settlers reproduced a version of this republican citizenship in Liberia, it would make them a "great, free and prosperous people."[65]

Convention delegates, like those involved in the riots a few years earlier, employed colonizationist logic to address the question of whether African Americans should be considered illegitimate settlers within the state. The ideas of the African colonization movement reinforced emerging nativist sentiments by branding would-be black settlers as implicitly foreign and apart from white settlers, who were positioning themselves as the true "native Americans" by displacing indigenous peoples. William Darlington attempted to pass a resolution that would have restricted both free African Americans and all other "foreigners" who sought to settle in the state, a measure aimed, in part, at stemming the growing tide of Irish immigration.[66] He was opposed by Thomas Earle, who argued that this nativist sentiment sprang from a growing concern that Pennsylvania would cease "to be a white population" and was driven by "particular classes of citizens" that had "feelings" against both Irish and African American residents. Earle noted that these racial anxieties and a firm commitment to maintaining white republicanism animated such efforts to restrict settlers; however, he argued that such claims had no basis in the state's actual demographics, noting that, in fact, the state benefited from the role they served within the division of labor: "There is no doubt that, in all our intercourse with both the Irish and the coloured emigrant, we get the best of the bargain. They submit themselves to do menial service, and we get the profit."[67]

Earle's comments laid bare an underlying concern that animated the convention's extensive discussion of black voting rights: whether a "white" majority would remain firmly in control of both the physical territory and the representative government of the state. This is revealed by the way that the terms of the debate worked to make African Americans seem more foreign while making Irish immigrants appear less than fully white. In the convention, John Cummin lamented such an implication for Irish immigrants, arguing that "they came as freemen, to make use of their industry as their means of support . . . [and] to associate such a people with the blacks, was an insult not to be endured."[68] Throughout the debate, most delegates, like Cummin, presumed that Irish immigrants could be integrated into a white settler citizenry despite the implication that such an antiforeign law might call into question their whiteness. Notably, delegates did not mount a similar argument in favor of admitting African Americans to the state because they possessed an inherent "native" right to settle on U.S. soil.

In the end, the convention succeeded in passing provisions to restrict black settlement and limit voting rights to "white freemen." The debates that resulted in their passage bore the imprint of the same colonizationist discourse that had helped incite riots in the state a few years earlier. The Pennsylvania convention demonstrated the growing racialization of citizenship in a state that was still anxious about the composition of its settler population. The terms of this debate would echo through the mid-1840s to the early 1850s as a string of states held constitutional conventions in the more recently colonized territory of the Midwest. While some of these states, such as Illinois (1847), Michigan (1850), Ohio (1851), and Indiana (1851), were revising their constitutions for the first time, other more recently created states, such as Iowa (1844) and Wisconsin (1848), were writing their first state constitutions. As in Pennsylvania, the debates in these conventions attest to the relationship between colonizationist ideas and the erosion of black rights throughout the North. The conventions held within the states of the Upper Midwest only occasionally addressed the topic of African colonization, but in the several states closest to slaveholding regions, delegates frequently made reference to it in their debates. In particular, delegates used colonizationist arguments for delegitimizing the rights of African Americans in the United States by highlighting their ability to become citizens in the newly independent black Republic of Liberia.

Midwestern convention delegates anxiously addressed these questions because the nearby slave states had made it increasingly difficult for free African Americans to exist within their borders. For instance, in 1849 Kentucky passed laws that forced free black residents to leave the state on penalty of hard labor in the state penitentiary. During Indiana's constitutional convention, one delegate referenced these laws when he argued that "the action of an adjoining State [Kentucky], has rendered it necessary that the State of Indiana should defend herself from the accumulation of the negro race within her borders." Another delegate concurred: "Self-defence, sir, is the first law of our nature. . . . We are surrounded by slave states and consequently have and are always liable to have a constant immigration from those States both of fugitive slaves and of free persons of color."[69]

Often employing this narrative of self-defense, several states contemplated severe restrictions on black settlement by linking it to African colonization. At the Illinois convention, Benjamin Bond supported a resolution that would prohibit further black settlement by arguing that migrants should not be allowed into the state "unless we go the full length of admitting the negro to a participation of all the privileges of freemen. . . . Will we do it? For my own part I answer, nay. Nature has drawn a line between them and ourselves."[70] Later in the convention, Bond justified such sentiments by arguing that "the only true project in my opinion by which we can be entirely freed from this nuisance, is by sending the blacks to some other country, under the guidance of a benevolent institution like the Colonization Society."[71] While Bond acknowledged that African Americans deserved to settle and enjoy full citizenship rights somewhere, settlement within U.S. borders was unacceptable, and only the prospect of African colonization could make this possible.

At the Indiana convention, George Gordon argued that African colonization would ultimately serve to restrict black settlement and produce the desired all-white settler population. "If we prohibit the further immigration and settlement of Negroes in our State, and at the same time make provision for the gradual colonization of such Negroes and their descendants as may be in our State at the time of the adoption of this Constitution, the time will come when there will not be a Negro within the limits of our State."[72] Gordon concluded that "exclusion and colonization are inseparable; and I will not vote for the one without a fair prospect that the other will be adopted." Another Indiana delegate approved of this demographic argument for settler exclusion and even backed it up with numbers: "If you hope to rid the State of the number of negroes in it in twenty years, then the appropriation should be $20,000 or $30,000."[73] Casting African Americans as a foreign element within Indiana's population allowed the issue to be framed in terms of protecting the political sovereignty of the state's white settlers.

Like those attending the Pennsylvania convention, even those midwestern delegates who opposed explicit restrictions on black settlement accepted the colonizationist terms of the debate by regularly characterizing African Americans as a "foreign" population. Arguing against the antiblack settlement provisions, Indiana delegate Milton Gregg explicitly made this connection when he noted that "if the poor negro, whose presence has all at once become so hateful to us, had migrated to this country of his own free will and accord, and if we still found him voluntarily forsaking his own foreign home, to seek an asylum in this boasted land of liberty and free government, we might with more propriety close our doors against him, and bid him go back to the shores of Africa from whence he came."[74] While Gregg was not opposed to racial restrictions on settlement within the state, he distinguished between the measures that could be taken against foreign immigrants and native-born migrants. In doing so, those who sought to effectively deport

African Americans were able to treat them as foreigners for whom Liberia could be considered their "native" country rather than the United States.

Other opponents of exclusionary laws posed their arguments against restricting black settlement within a distinctly colonizationist framework. At the Illinois convention, Jessie Norton argued that "this resolution is unequal, unjust and opposed to the first principles of free government. These colored people came to this country not of their own accord, we brought them here, they cannot get away; it is said to colonize them, how? They cannot colonize themselves." Alluding to the then ongoing war between the United States and Mexico, he observed, "Our armies are now fighting at the south and the probability is that we will extend the area of our freedom, and that States are to come into the Union with people of every stripe and color, and can they come in without full and equal rights?"[75] In raising this question, Norton went even further to imply that an exclusionary conception of citizenship was incompatible with U.S. expansion, suggesting that the notion of racial republics in both Liberia and the United States would ultimately prove untenable. However, such voices were clearly in the minority within the midwestern conventions. Most delegates represented constituencies that had come to believe that African Americans had no legitimate claim to settle or become citizens within the United States. As whites increasingly regarded African Americans to be unlawful "foreign" residents, they believed that they could only realize their civil and political rights by settling in Liberia.

Aside from the question of whether black migrants should be allowed to reside within state borders, convention delegates extensively addressed the interrelated question of black citizenship rights. Edward Ryan, a delegate to Wisconsin's convention, connected black citizenship directly to the question of settlement, arguing that the "extension of the right of suffrage would cause our state to be overrun with runaway slaves" and that "the system of colonization" was the "proper mode of effecting the object aimed at by those friendly to the negro race."[76] Following Pennsylvania's convention, several midwestern states extensively debated whether "white" should be used in their constitutions as a qualification for voting rights. At the Michigan convention, Joseph Bagg rejected any suggestion that black residents were entitled to citizenship rights, contending that this would be the first step on the road to "amalgamation." Despite his unwillingness to allow African Americans to become citizens as U.S. settlers, Bagg believed that the "hand of Providence" had delivered them to North America for "a great purpose" so that they could eventually acquire and disseminate U.S. institutions in Africa. He predicted that when African Americans "shall be raised to a certain state, in comparison with our

Figure 4. The official seal of the Republic of Liberia, adopted in
1847. Adopted at the 1847 constitutional convention, Liberia's
seal highlights the symbols of settler republicanism by featuring
a sailing ship, a plow and spade, and the national motto "THE
LOVE OF LIBERTY BROUGHT US HERE." Wikimedia.org.

own, [they] will go back to Liberia—to Africa—to find the source of the Nile,
which has never been found by those barbarous tribes."[77]

In a similar discussion of black suffrage in Indiana, Alexander Stevenson
argued that any debate over black citizenship rights was inherently futile. He
reminded his fellow delegates that the state should "colonize them in Africa
where they are surrounded only by their equals, governed by a man of their
own color and race, and allowed a free participation in all the institutions
and privileges of society and government." John Parvin, a delegate to one of

Iowa's constitutional conventions, also supported making "white" a requirement for voting in his state, but he argued that he did not support this kind of law because he felt African Americans were incapable of citizenship, stating that he judged "a man by his head and his heart," not by "the color of his skin." Accordingly, Parvin argued that while citizenship should remain restricted to white residents in Iowa, "we owe them [African Americans] a debt which we should repay by educating them, and colonizing them in their own country."[78]

Very few convention delegates seriously considered granting suffrage, or any other citizenship rights, to African Americans; instead, they debated the best strategies for protecting the white settler population and enshrining white citizenship. Referencing a referendum on black suffrage, Indiana delegate Robert Dale Owen stated, "No man who knows anything about public affairs in Indiana, will maintain for a moment, that the proposition to grant to Negroes the right of suffrage, can obtain amongst the people more than a very small minority." He went on to state, "They can never obtain political rights here. They can never obtain social rights here. And for these reasons, I think we ought not to have them amongst us."[79]

Although many convention delegates adamantly supported excluding African Americans from becoming settlers or citizens within their states, some insisted that they at least deserved access to these rights. At the Illinois convention, Daniel Pinckney explicitly argued that removing the black population from the state should be accompanied by securing rights for them elsewhere. Pinckney stated, "If any man proposes to keep these unfortunate persons from our State by just and humane measures, I shall not object. I am in favor of removing them not only from this State, but from all the States, that they may in some other place enjoy human rights and privileges. . . . I therefore concur with the gentlemen in giving the Colonization Society great praise."[80] In this way, delegates used the colonizationist vision of racial republicanism to reconcile the inherently exclusive nature of U.S. citizenship with its purported claims to universalism. One Ohio delegate, William Sawyer, clearly expressed this tension when he stated that the Declaration of Independence meant that "all men were born free and equal, and possessed of certain inalienable rights," but he admitted this must be understood through a lens of racial separation. Referencing Liberia, Sawyer stated his belief that "a negro had a right to hold office" and "a right to sit as President in a convention, but not at *this* convention—he had a right to sit as a judge, to serve as a juror, to be a witness, to vote as an elector, and, in short, to have a right to possess and control everything that he had. But, every man in his own place, and in his own order." For Sawyer, African Americans did not belong to the political community of U.S. settlers and therefore needed to settle their own nation in order to access and enshrine these rights.[81]

All of the midwestern conventions of this era successfully passed constitutions that either maintained or expanded restrictions on black citizenship and settlement. Indiana's constitution explicitly attached these restrictions to African colonization measures. The state's 1851 constitution included a section that stated, "No Negro or mulatto shall come into, or settle in the State, after the adoption of this Constitution," which also required that fines collected for violation of this law would be used to fund African colonization and help establish a state board of colonization.[82] Shortly after the new constitution passed approval from Indiana's voters, the state's governor, Joseph Wright, announced that "Indiana, by her recent vote, not only decided in favor of *exclusion* of Negroes and Mulattos, but likewise for the *colonization* of those among us. . . . She [Indiana] desires the gradual separation of the two races; that this separation is called for by all the principles of CHRISTIANITY, HUMANITY and FREEDOM."[83]

Colonizationist ideas and rhetoric played such a prominent role in midwestern constitutional conventions because many state legislatures had already begun to connect colonization to restrictions on black settlement and citizenship. In some ways, the Midwest represented the heart of colonizationist rebirth during this era, in part because it was characterized by less populated societies where the issues of settlement and citizenship posed obvious questions about the future composition of the body politic within each state. In mid-1851 the *African Repository* remarked on the recent support for colonization in the region by optimistically claiming, "We have seen the finger of Providence pointing to Colonization as the only way of escape. And we are glad to see, that in the same States, where the evils are most felt, Legislatures are beginning to look at the subject in earnest."[84] Appealing to the U.S. House of Representatives, S. W. Parker, an Indiana congressman, attempted to build on his state's constitution to revive congressional support for African colonization. He pointed to the resounding success of his state's recent convention: "The people of my state have just been making a new constitution, and by a majority of some *ninety thousand*, have declared that no foreign black man shall ever again set his foot upon the soil of Indiana, and that the scheme of colonization is their remedy for the evil of our existing black population."[85] Indiana's *Lafayette Daily Courier* urged black populations to leave because "they never can and never will be placed upon an equality with the white population in this country" and promised that "in Liberia the colored man enjoys all the rights and privileges which the whites enjoy in this country, and which constitute the basis of human enjoyment."[86] For many midwestern whites, such statements encapsulated the overarching idea that African colonization was essential to maintaining the United States' white settler citizenry, a notion that found purchase in the laws passed during this era.

Following the lead of other midwestern states, Ohio politicians renewed public interest in African colonization, a movement that had declined in prominence since its earlier peak during the era of Cincinnati's riots in the 1820s and 1830s. In the early 1850s David Christy, Ohio's primary ACS agent, helped devise a plan called "Ohio in Africa," which would create a state-funded colony affiliated with the Republic of Liberia.[87] After several politicians supported the plan and wealthy Cincinnatians donated money to help get it started, the Liberian government initially set aside land intended for this purpose. In an effort to secure firm guarantees of state support for the idea, Christy presented the plan to both the Ohio general assembly and the state's 1850 constitutional convention. While the general assembly demonstrated sufficient interest to pass a resolution encouraging free African Americans in the state to leave for Liberia, Ohio's political leaders were ultimately not willing, as their neighbors in Indiana would do in their 1851 constitution, to guarantee state appropriations.[88]

Nevertheless, Ohio politicians and activists continued to push for a state colonization policy. In 1852 state senator Alonzo Cushing introduced a bill into the Ohio general assembly that aimed to expand restrictions on black settlement and support the Liberian colonization plan on the grounds that "the voters of the State of Ohio, by the adoption of the new Constitution, have decided against the admission of people of color to the right of citizenship in the State." The bill proposed to ban all black settlers from entering the state after January 1, 1854, on the grounds that "a portion of the colored people have determined to secure themselves equal rights elsewhere [in the Republic of Liberia]."[89]

While this bill failed, Ohio colonization supporters continued to press the issue throughout the decade. In the late 1850s Ohio state representative Robert Christy revived another bill that paired the exclusion of settlers with state endorsement for colonization. Speaking on behalf of the bill, Christy worried that the recent wave of exclusionary measures in nearby states would invite a flood of black settlers into Ohio, which he feared would become a "receptacle for all the itinerant negroes of the Union." He noted that "Illinois is exceedingly severe in her legislation; she imparts heavy fee upon any of them that come into the state. . . . Indiana in her constitution of 1852, has engrafted a

policy scarcely less severe. But she, likewise, provides a fund for their colonization in Africa. Iowa and Wisconsin have forbidden citizenship to free colored people since 1850." Referring to the wave of settlement unleashed by the
California gold rush, he noted that this caused "thousands of white Americans [to] forsake home and peace and without hesitation encounter the toil
and hardship of the prairie [and] the knife of the murderous savage. . . . Let
us then unite to inspire the black man with similar enterprise." While he
invoked fear at the prospect of black settlement in Ohio, he also presented
Liberia as a solution rooted in a parallel logic of U.S. settler colonization.[90]

By the early 1850s colonizationism had such a profound influence on state
laws aimed at restricting citizenship and settlement that it caused many African Americans to reassert their strong opposition to the movement, even as
the recently independent Republic of Liberia had begun to attract some interest among potential black settlers. In March 1853 a group of black residents in
Syracuse, New York, called a meeting to oppose the resurgence of colonizationism, which they characterized as driven by "the most intense hatred of the
colored race, clad in the garb of pretended philanthropy." They argued that
"the expulsion[s] of colored citizens" from several midwestern states were
"kindred manifestations of a passion fit only for demons to indulge in."[91] An
editorial in Frederick Douglass's newspaper published around the same time
argued that "the enemies of mankind have long labored to make Liberian
Colonization a political question. . . . It has arrived at that point; and hereafter we may expect it to mingle lustily with the plans of parties and statesmen." Pointing to the simultaneous resurgence of colonization proposals and
black exclusion laws, the article asked, "How happens it that these enemies
of the black man and the human race, have so simultaneously started up, to
fasten this infernal scheme upon this country?"[92] In refuting the resurgence
of African colonization, black critics pointed out how the movement's logic
had worked to criminalize black settlement and civic participation within
nominally free states.

*   *   *

The riots of the late 1820s and early 1830s, as well as the state legislative actions
of subsequent decades, attest to the durability and flexibility of colonizationist rhetoric even as the ACS generally faced declining fortunes. White mobs
targeted black residents of northern cities and referenced African colonization in order to reinforce these public spectacles of terror designed to assault

the physical presence of African Americans. Colonizationism undergirded this violence by portraying African Americans as a foreign and alien population with no legitimate right to settle in the United States. During the late 1840s and early 1850s, colonization supporters expanded on these ideas to argue that African Americans had some claim to rights, but those claims could never be realized within U.S. borders.

It was no coincidence that African colonization proposals thrived at a time when the United States was actively displacing indigenous communities from their lands. Many whites recognized that individual acts of physical violence and the collective power of state governments could complement each other as well as stigmatize and remove African Americans from their settler communities. However, the colonizationist rhetoric of removal functioned somewhat differently when directed at black populations. White colonizationists portrayed African Americans as an obstacle not to the settlement of lands but to creating racial and political cohesion among settlers. Therefore, both urban riots and constitutional conventions served to define who was a legitimate settler within U.S. territory and who could claim the political rights of citizenship that defined the sovereignty of that settler community. Bound by their common identity as settler citizens, a cross-class constituency of whites endorsed colonizationist ideas to assert their basic right to reside in the United States, but they did not necessarily subscribe to the benevolent reform agenda advanced by elite colonizationist leaders.

In support of African colonization, white settlers used the language of "native," "foreign," or "alien" to define their ability to make political claims for both themselves and the African Americans they wished to displace. Claiming a native right to colonized lands was one of the central ways in which settlers naturalized their presumed sovereignty over that space.

Within the framework of colonizationism, African Americans became alien immigrants on U.S. soil and native Africans on Liberian soil, despite the fact that they had not been born there. White colonization supporters cast African Americans as natural settlers in Liberia with an obligation to return to their "native" continent, where they would presumably foster a racially homogenous political community. Because African Americans had only native rights to colonize Liberia and no native right to colonize U.S. soil, white colonizationists argued that they should belong to a settler republic in Africa rather than North America.

At the moment in which residents of midwestern states deployed a colonizationist framework to naturalize such distinctions between rights to "native soil" in both North America and Africa, politicians in this region

were advancing a parallel conception of "free soil," an idea that would ani-
mate politics through the U.S. Civil War. While free-soil ideology was explicitly concerned with preserving U.S. territory from the spread of slavery, it was
also an ideology of white settler colonialism. In western regions where Native
Americans had been recently dispossessed of their land, the settler state was
relatively small and fragile. In those places, Free-Soilism explicitly advanced
the idea that it was maintaining territory for exclusive settlement of whites
by preventing the migration of African Americans, either as slaves or free
men. By the late 1850s this linkage would become even clearer as colonizationists began to shift their attention to Central America, where they argued
that African Americans could become black homesteaders in the tropics,
mirroring the same process as white homesteaders in the temperate regions
of North America. If the demise of the postrevolutionary plans for black colonies in the West had been driven by whites' rejection of African Americans'
place within an expanding settler empire, their subsequent refusal to recognize African Americans as legitimate migrants helped consolidate this vision
by linking black political rights to settlement outside U.S. borders.

CHAPTER 5

The United States of Africa

In an editorial published in 1847, Hilary Teage, an African American settler in Liberia, reflected on the encroachment of Europeans on the western coast of Africa. Just as Teage's own colony was poised to declare itself an independent republic, he mockingly wished potential colonizers success in securing territory on the coast but warned them that eventually "we or some of our brethren will surely possess them." He suggested that "sacrifice of money and life" would soon dissuade Europeans from colonizing the continent and implied that his nation was the beginning of an Africa governed solely by people of African descent. Teage urged them to "yield the direction of affairs" and allow "the hands of intelligent colored men" to transform their colonies "from a European dependence into an African Government."[1] The *Daily National Intelligencer* republished the article in the United States and remarked that in the colony a "germ" of "future growth is planted" because Liberia's settlers "have imbibed the rudiments of civilization and Christianity; and they now go back to the country from which they came to infuse some touch of Caucasian energy into the torpid body of old Africa which may arouse her from the sleep of ages."[2]

Teage's insistence on the inevitable proliferation of black-led governments in Africa reappropriated the notion that nationhood should align with racial identity and echoed the sentiments of colonizationists in United States, who rejected African Americans as citizens within a white republic. Despite the abstract parity between an emerging black nation-state in Africa and white nationhood in the United States, Teage's U.S. commentator was quick to identify "Caucasian energy," rather than black self-determination, at the root of Liberian success. Not surprisingly, African American audiences in the United States largely rejected the disingenuous portrayal of an independent Liberia because it simply reasserted the hierarchies of race by reproducing the features of U.S. nationalism within a purportedly benevolent imperial context.

Nevertheless, many black settlers and their U.S. supporters shared a similar vision for Africa that drew from the ideology of U.S. expansionism. In his
article, Teage asserted a familiar model of settler colonialism that positioned
Liberia against the empires of Europe by holding up the former colony as
the embodiment of U.S. republican ideals and a seed for settler expansion
in Africa. Over the course of the early nineteenth century, the United States
developed this idea into the ethos behind its program of national expansion.
Although quick to distance itself from the methods of European empires,
Americans nonetheless employed similar tactics to enhance the nation's
security against rivals within the Western Hemisphere and to acquire territory through displacement of indigenous populations. Within this logic of
expansion, many whites explicitly excluded African Americans from U.S. settler citizenship based on the idea that they could only realize political sovereignty by becoming Liberian settlers.[3]

During the high tide of manifest destiny, colonizationists pointed to
Liberia as a variation on the expansionist ethos of the era. While the proponents of colonization had long imagined that black colonists would, in the
words of the historian Nicholas Guyatt, "create their own versions" of the
United States, by the late 1840s both the expansionist mood of the era and
Liberia's newfound status as an established republic elevated the stakes of this
argument.[4] In so doing, they suggested a different way of envisioning U.S.
power abroad. Up to this point, the United States' strategies of expansion had
focused on North America and typically promoted direct territorial, strategic, or economic goals, as evidenced by the nation's war with Mexico. However, Liberia had no such clear-cut appeal. For this reason, and because of
the complicated domestic politics of colonization, the U.S. government continued to be ambivalent about the prospect of establishing Liberia as a commercial or military outpost. Most supporters of African colonization did not
advocate that the United States should directly control or manage this territory. Instead, they suggested vaguely that the new Liberian republic could
serve the United States best by reproducing its political values. Therefore,
the debate over Liberian independence was clearly informed by the broader
rhetoric of U.S. expansionism, even if the colonization movement's supporters were unclear about exactly how the new nation might further the United
States' interests.[5]

Discussions addressing the advent of Liberia's independence offer an
important window into how the United States imagined itself in the world
during the mid-nineteenth century. The independence of Liberia received
considerable attention within northern newspapers, speeches, and literature.[6]

Most white observers focused on details such as the nation's Declaration of Independence, its republican form of government, and its U.S.-modeled flag to validate the theory that such a colony, under the United States' tutelage, could become a sovereign and self-governing nation. While African colonization had played a prominent role in national debates about race and slavery since the early nineteenth century, the independence of Liberia reframed the ACS's campaign for the colony.[7] The fact that colonizationists could now promote Liberia as an independent and self-governing nation helped support white northerners' efforts to exclude free African Americans from settlement and citizenship within their borders. From their perspective, a viable black settler republic in Africa confirmed the United States' commitment to white settler republicanism within its borders.

These discussions about Liberian independence suggest the importance of placing the United States' racialized conceptions of democracy and nationalism in a global context. The fact that many white observers in non-slaveholding northern states championed a black republican government in Liberia runs counter to prevailing understandings of the increasing disenfranchisement of free African Americans throughout the early nineteenth century. Most historians link these escalating efforts to situate free African Americans outside the bounds of U.S. citizenship to the expansion of universal suffrage through the abolition of property requirements for voting during this era.[8] The discussions of African colonization in state constitutional conventions and legislatures often employed the rhetoric of colonizationism to justify black exclusion, but they also reveal a more complicated advocacy for black citizenship rights in Liberia.[9] Rather than dismissing black capability for participation in civil society outright, supporters of colonization endorsed a vision of race-based nationhood in which a black settler republic in Liberia would mirror the white settler republic in the United States. The obvious asymmetry of power between these two nations on the world stage ironically allowed some whites to support black self-determination and disenfranchisement at the same time.

From Settler Colony to Settler Republic

The ACS was on the rise throughout the 1820s, but by the mid-1830s the strength of the colonization movement began to decline following relentless attacks by abolitionists, divisions between its northern and southern factions, and mounting financial problems.[10] However, a resurgence of interest in the movement took place in the late 1840s and early 1850s, fueled by sectional tensions over the spread of slavery and growing fears in the North about migration of black populations. During this period, white politicians in Congress, in individual state governments, and in national political parties once more took up the discussion of colonization seriously. At the same time, African Americans' growing despair about their prospects in the United States, particularly following the Fugitive Slave Act of 1850, moved some black audiences to reconsider a movement they had decisively opposed since its inception. In large part, this shift in attitudes coincided with the prospect of Liberian independence, which helped breathe new life into a movement that many had written off by the early 1840s. Indeed, during the ten years following independence, the number of colonists who immigrated to Liberia was nearly five times higher than it had been in the previous decade.[11]

The white architects of the African colonization movement had always prefigured Liberia's eventual sovereignty by presenting the historical arc of the nascent nation as parallel to that of the United States. Colonizationists courted public support successfully, in part, because they claimed to promote a colony that was destined to become an independent and self-governing nation. It was in this spirit that they frequently invoked comparisons between Liberia and the early British colonies in North America; however, unlike these antecedents, colonizationists explicitly claimed that the African settlement would not develop into a formal colonial possession of the United States.[12] This was evident in a pamphlet from the early 1830s claiming that the "establishment of a *single colony*" should not be the "*limit* of American enterprise" but that it would be the "first in a series of future colonies," which would expand "like our own Republic, by the union of many confederate States, into one great and free Commonwealth."[13]

Many colonizationists believed that the process of Liberian colonization would result in a settler citizenry that could ultimately realize its political independence. Even before settlers in this country had moved to declare themselves independent, some white colonizationists argued that the colony had already demonstrated a greater capacity for self-government than other settler republics in the Americas. In 1840 the *African Repository* printed a letter written by a white colonizationist from New Orleans who believed that Liberia was poised to "grow into a great nation" and suggested "the idea of declaring Liberia free and independent." The writer went on to claim, "It is already a better Government than Texas; more independent than Mexico; and far superior to the nameless, worthless republics of South America."[14] When Liberia eventually declared its independence, less than a decade later,

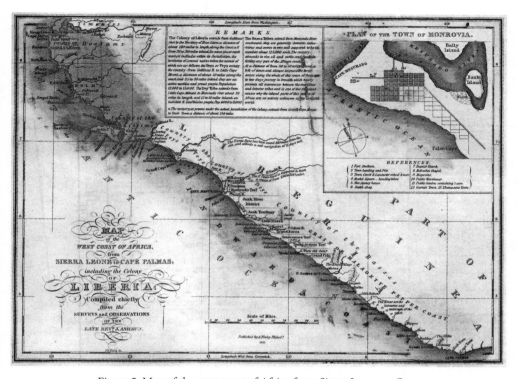

Figure 5. Map of the west coast of Africa from Sierra Leone to Cape
Palmas, including the colony of Liberia, by A. Finley, 1830. This map
was one of the most detailed early portrayals of Liberia. The scope of
the map reflects the settler ambitions of colonists. While these coastal
settlements form only a small sliver of the territory represented here,
the map depicts much of the land that colonists would claim as part
of Liberia. Library of Congress Geography and Map Division.

colonizationists used similar superlatives to position Liberia as a unique, and
uniquely American, expression of republican government.

Despite colonizationists' grand ambitions for the colony, ACS officials
had been slow to make good on their promise that Liberia would eventually become a self-governing nation. For the first two decades of the colony's
existence, white colonial agents from the United States controlled much of
its actual administration. Black migrants' resentment about the leadership
of the colony persisted for the next two decades as their expectations of settler citizenship confronted the reality of white colonial governance. Settlers

who had migrated to Liberia expecting greater political power first voiced their discontent in the mid-1820s, only a few years after the colony had been established. As a result, Jehudi Ashmun, a white colonial agent, was forced to return to the United States after black settlers protested that he was unjustly rationing supplies from the colonial store and distributing lots of land within the colony. Although ACS officials were able to restore order before the colony broke into open rebellion, the continuing tensions between black settlers and white officials eventually persuaded the ACS Board of Managers to write a new constitution for the colony in 1839. This document mandated a settler-elected Commonwealth Legislative Council and eventually the appointment of Liberia's first black governor, Joseph Roberts, even though the colony still remained largely under the direct control of the ACS.[15]

Following this change in governance structure, Liberia's ultimate path to independence ostensibly began over a dispute about trading rights between Europeans and the African populations bordering the colony. During Liberia's first two decades, settlers continuously clashed with the surrounding indigenous groups over the colony's territorial limits and claims to authority within the region.[16] While colonizationists in the United States frequently claimed that African Americans were merely African "natives" returning to their ancestral home, they simultaneously positioned them as settlers who were expected to displace, civilize, and absorb indigenous Africans into their society. Like the U.S. settler state, the Liberian colony acquired land by using the threat of force to enact treaties in which settlers and indigenous populations had very different understandings about what such agreements entailed. As a result, the region's inhabitants had little respect for the colony's fragile control over a narrow swath of West African coast, and this instability led to conflicts with European traders who frequently ignored Liberian laws and tariffs in their transactions with Africans.[17]

After several traders tested the legitimacy of Liberia's political standing, the British government began to communicate with the United States to clarify whether it claimed any authority over matters in the colony. In an 1843 letter the U.S. diplomat Edward Everett wrote to the British Earl of Aberdeen and argued that "extra-continental possessions" were not extended the protections "to which colonies are entitled from the mother country by which they are established." While denying that the United States had any sort of formal colonial relationship with Liberia, Everett warned that British encroachments on this "independent political community" would be a "fatal blow to its very existence."[18] President John Tyler's administration also solicited advice from ACS agent Ralph Gurley, who explained that "the

Government of the United States has never assumed any control over the government of the colony; and since Liberia has entered into no political relations with Europeans or other civilized countries, it would seem entitled, politically, to the character of an independent State."[19]

In 1844 a British naval officer wrote to Liberia's governor, Joseph Roberts, to argue that his nation's traders should be allowed to operate freely in the colony because it did not possess "the rights in question, those of imposing custom duties, and limiting the trade of foreigners by restrictions, are sovereign rights, which can only be lawfully exercised by sovereign and independent states, within their own recognized borders and dominions." The officer also added, "I need not remind your Excellency that this description does not yet apply to 'Liberia' which is not recognized as a subsisting state, even by the Government of the country from which its settlers have emigrated."[20] The escalating British crisis over sovereignty made news in the United States, and some began to call for Liberia to declare itself an independent nation.[21] The prominent New York newspaper the *Commercial Advertiser* suggested that Britain should not infringe on the colony's right to existence, and by extension U.S. interests in the region. The editor of the *Emancipator and Weekly Chronicle*, a northeastern antislavery paper, agreed with this sentiment, taking it a step further by suggesting that the United States' "government [should] acknowledge the nationality of Liberia, as it has of Texas, and as it has not of Haiti, and then our government will have just as much right to interfere to preserve the separate *independence* of Liberia, as Great Britain has to interfere to preserve the *separate* independence of Texas."[22]

Although some Americans viewed Liberia as a parallel structure to the Texas settler colony, commercially minded politicians had already begun to investigate the potential for Liberia to forge a new form of U.S. colonialism. In the early 1840s the Commerce Committee in the U.S. House of Representatives examined the possibility of making Liberia a formal colony of the United States. A report issued to the committee argued that the United States had a compelling interest in pursuing a direct colonial relationship with Liberia in order to facilitate overseas U.S. expansion. In the 1842 report the committee's chair, Rep. John Pendleton Kennedy, outlined a vision for potential U.S. colonial governance in Africa, arguing that "the idea of an American colony is a new one. It is manifestly worthy of the highest consideration. The committees see nothing in our Constitution to forbid it. We have establishments of this nature but somewhat anomalous in the character of their dependence on our Government, in the Indian tribes which have been placed beyond the limits of the States, on purchased territory of the Union."[23]

Building on the notion that the United States' colonial administration of Native American territory had laid the groundwork for adapting Liberia into a formal U.S. colony, Kennedy argued that a more decentralized colonial management structure in Liberia would be preferable to the complicated and costly management of "domestic dependent" Indian nations. While Kennedy suggested a more formal colonial relationship, he retained the colonizationist devotion to racial republicanism and suggested that such a colony might remain politically independent from the United States while serving U.S. national interests as both a home for black migrants and a sphere of commercial influence in the region.

Despite this plan's potential to resolve the United States' increasingly complicated diplomatic situation in Liberia, the notion of formally adopting it as the United States' colony received little support. This was likely because most supporters of colonization had long held a different vision for the settlement. Shortly after the House Commerce Committee published its report, the *African Repository* printed a response to the efforts on Capitol Hill, asserting that Liberia should become a "great and virtuous republic" that would facilitate a large presence for the United States in the region: "Let the American Government become the ally and protector of these colonies. Let them assist them to complete the purchase of those portions of territory, the title of which has not yet been acquired from the natives. Let them avail themselves of the advantages which these colonies present, for prosecuting that valuable commerce, which is now opening to the world."[24]

This exchange ostensibly addresses the proper political relationship between Liberia and the United States, but it also highlights how different conceptions of colonizationism reveal subtle debates over the scope of U.S. imperialism. While Representative Kennedy claimed that the prospect of an "American colony" was "new," he notably referenced the United States' history of settler displacement and control over indigenous populations as potential precedent. In some ways, it was a suggestion more in line with the early North American colonization plans that conceived of black colonies as an extension of U.S. settler expansion. By now proposing to extend this form of colonial control over West African territory, Kennedy went against the decades-long effort by most colonization supporters and government officials to keep Liberia relatively separate from the United States' settler empire, even as the colony sometimes relied directly on U.S. financial and naval support. The ACS response, evident in the *African Repository* article, does not dispute that the United States could exploit the colony for broader imperial objectives. However, it emphasizes a move away from settler empire as the primary framework for U.S. expansion. The article argued that the United States could still enjoy the imperial advantages of its connection to an independent, republican Liberia without needing to alter its fundamental relationship to the colony. In the late 1850s colonizationists would revive this line of argumentation when proposing Central and South American colonies, which many Americans perceived to be even more strategically important than West Africa and would serve a similar function in the region.

Responding to the implications of this broader diplomatic debate, Joseph Tracy, a key official in the Massachusetts branch of the ACS, asserted that Liberia, as a commonwealth, already had the features of a sovereign nation and should be treated accordingly. In an April 1845 article in the *African Repository* he argued, "It should be universally known and admitted that the Commonwealth of Liberia is a sovereign State, having its own constitution, government, and laws, and rightfully claiming all the powers, prerogatives, and privileges essential to sovereignty." Alluding to the complicated relationship between the United States and Liberia, the author continued to argue that "no acknowledgement by other nations is necessary to *confer* the rights of sovereignty. On the contrary, sovereignty must exist, and manifest itself, before it can be acknowledged." Tracy dismissed any suggestion that Liberia needed to declare its independence from the ACS because he claimed that it was "wholly unnecessary to sunder the relation of the commonwealth to the Colonization Society, as some have proposed, for the purpose of establishing or perfecting its sovereignty."[25]

At the same time Tracy publicly denied the necessity of Liberian independence, he privately consulted with Simon Greenleaf, a professor at Harvard Law School, to pursue a method for legally detaching the colony from the ACS. In April 1845 Tracy wrote to Greenleaf and noted that the growing diplomatic disputes with European empires had created a crisis around the question of Liberian sovereignty, remarking that "there is a strong presumption in the minds of many of our friends, that for this purpose, the Commonwealth of Liberia must be made wholly independent of the Colonization Society." From Tracy's perspective, the central issue in any potential transition of governance was whether the ACS could "keep our hold on public confidence, when we can no longer be responsible for the character of the laws of Liberia, or for their administration." In response to these issues, Tracy asked Greenleaf to study the question and "show us, in the light of the principles of jurisprudence and international law what ought to be done."[26] As Tracy's letter to Greenleaf acknowledged, the issue of public confidence in colonization threatened the movement because the appearance of ACS control and

white colonial leadership in Liberia had helped bolster the settlement's legitimacy. Although the prospect of Liberia's eventual independence loomed
large in colonizationist rhetoric, white ACS officials had worked to temper
any potential concern among U.S. audiences that African Americans were
governing the colony without oversight from white authorities.

While representatives of Britain, the United States, and the ACS disputed
Liberia's legal status in the mid-1840s, black settlers in the colony seized on
this disagreement to articulate a growing nationalist ethos. The 1839 shift
toward a legislative commonwealth structure had marginally increased settler participation within the colonial government, but the crisis with Britain
had revealed how little currency the colony's claims to sovereignty had on the
world stage. During the dispute, a vocal group of settlers, led by the colony's
primary newspaper, the *Liberia Herald*, reframed the legalistic discussion of
sovereignty and commercial rights by insisting on the historical significance
of building a self-governing black nation-state. In a December 1846 speech
Hilary Teage, then the editor of the newspaper, argued, "Fellow Citizens! We
stand now on ground never occupied by a people before—However insignificant we may regard ourselves, the eyes of Europe and America are upon
us, as a germ destined to burst from its enclosure in the earth. . . . Rise fellow
citizens! Rise to a clear and full perception of your tremendous responsibil-
ities. . . . You are to give the answer, whether the African race is doomed to
interminable degradation."[27]

Echoing this theme, Governor Roberts, in a January 1847 speech before
the Legislative Council of Liberia, argued that if Liberian colonists accepted
the British characterization that they were merely a "private company of
traders, or settlers" they would, in the eyes of the world, be "without a country or a home;—outcasts upon the world, and persecuted in every clime."[28]
Although a practical legal dispute had initiated these discussions of independence, the settler elite quickly amplified the stakes of this conflict by situating
Liberia as a pioneering black nation with a right to self-determination.

As black colonists took steps toward asserting greater political control
of Liberia, ACS officials in the United States attempted to manage the independence movement from afar. The ACS secretary, William McLain, echoed
Joseph Tracy's concerns about public confidence when he wrote to Governor
Roberts about the society's desire for a smooth transition in "carrying on the
work of Colonization under the new regime." He called on Roberts, as both
the most powerful black settler and the principal representative of the ACS
in Liberia, to ensure that "no hasty change be made either in the men now in
office in Liberia, or the policy now in present advancement." Fearing a future

of diminished ACS control over the colony, McLain ominously warned, "The time of change is always a time of danger, all political revolutions need to be guarded and guided with the profoundest wisdom and discretion."[29] Following up on these concerns, the ACS passed along Professor Greenleaf's initial draft of a constitution a few months later in a letter to Roberts. If black settlers were determined to pursue independence, the ACS was not about to lose a stake in how it unfolded.[30]

ACS members presumed that by proposing the outline for a new constitution, they could continue to shape Liberia's future. Most of the settlers expected that the ACS would continue to support the colony, but many privately bristled at the organization's attempts to insert itself directly into the independence process. The momentum for independence came out of the shift in legal relations between the ACS and the colony as well as black settlers' increasing desire to exert more control over Liberian affairs. The settler elites who were most directly involved in pushing for independence maintained an amicable relationship with the ACS and did not pursue this goal in open defiance against the organization. Nevertheless, the differing approaches of black settlers and ACS officials to the process of independence highlight underlying tensions about the meaning of independent Liberian nationhood to each group.

Although the ACS implicitly endorsed the effort for Liberian independence, its members were uneasy about any loss of control and the effect on public perceptions of an independent nation governed solely by African American settlers. During the annual meeting of the ACS Board of Directors in 1847, several members expressed their unease about the transition to independence. Concerned that "this Society and its general rights in Liberia, should be in some form recognized in the Constitution," the Board of Directors recommended "that commissioners on the part of Liberia should come here and have a full and free conference with us before a constitution is framed."[31] They also suggested that the ACS should retain all of its rights to property in the colony as well as the ability to renegotiate future relations with Liberia. Again, the ACS asked Simon Greenleaf to draw up additional constitutional provisions that would allow the organization to preserve its property interests in the new legal context of an independent Liberia.

Shortly thereafter, William McLain passed along the new Greenleaf-penned constitutional provisions in a letter to Joseph Roberts. McLain condemned the "unkind and uncalled for" things some settlers had been saying in the newspapers. He demanded that Roberts set the record straight in the Liberian press by explaining "all that has been done in Liberia and in this country touching the Independence of the Commonwealth and bringing prominently to view the fact that the Society has never urged the Commonwealth to declare its independence, but that we should be perfectly satisfied that you continue as you are."[32] McLain's letter reflected ACS members' growing concern that the independence process was leading Liberian settlers to disrespect the organization's historical role in founding and building the colony. Despite ACS protests, Joseph Roberts did not follow this advice and publicly declined to defend the organization in the Liberian press. Roberts, a consummate politician, was astutely aware of the political implications of directly aligning himself with the ACS in the midst of an increasingly nationalistic independence movement.

In July 1847 twelve settler-elected delegates held a convention in Monrovia where they produced their own Liberian constitution that was largely free from ACS interference. Three months later, the male settler population ratified the constitution with a popular vote, and Liberia declared itself to be legally independent of the ACS. The document followed the same gendered boundaries and settler framework for citizenship as the U.S. Constitution. The constitutional process excluded both women and most indigenous Africans within the colony. Despite the passage of a constitution, the settlers' new republican government held an extremely tenuous claim to political authority. The Republic of Liberia controlled only a few coastal settlements. In fact, neighboring indigenous groups, such as the Bassa, Vai, Kru, Gola, and Grebo, still exercised considerable autonomy within the region and largely rejected the legitimacy of the settler state.[33] In addition, nearly half of the settler population, primarily from Bassa, Montserrado, and Sinoe Counties, abstained from the constitutional vote to protest the colony's domination by the coastal mercantile elite.[34] With dissenting colonists largely absent from the early national formation, Liberia maintained its settler-merchant leadership by electing Joseph Roberts, the sitting ACS-selected governor of the colony, to become the republic's first president.

Although this fractured political situation gave the new government little standing in the region, Liberian nationalists had transformed the question of the colony's sovereignty from a relatively narrow diplomatic dispute into an expression of racial self-determination through nationhood. Liberia's Declaration of Independence, issued alongside its constitution in 1847, reflected this rhetoric by focusing its grievances on the United States rather than the ACS. The document denounced the United States for excluding African Americans "from participation in government" and the "rights and privileges of man," and it criticized the nation's racial basis for citizenship that rejected black citizens in favor of "strangers from other lands, of a different color than ours."[35] This rebuke of white republicanism was also evident in some sections of the constitution, one of which declared that only "Negroes or persons of Negro descent shall be eligible to citizenship in this Republic," while another limited property ownership only to citizens of the nation, effectively barring whites from purchasing land.[36] ACS leadership opposed both of these provisions and again enlisted Simon Greenleaf to write alternative language, which delegates would ultimately reject during the course of the convention. Although the framers of the constitution appeared to be aiming these sections at preventing the persistence of ACS control after independence, symbolically they were pointedly reversing the United States' racially exclusive citizenship rights as also referenced in the Liberian Declaration of Independence. By legally enshrining these principles in its constitution, Liberia went even further than the United States to establish its identity as a racial republic.

Most existing evidence indicates that Liberian settlers were principally responsible for formulating their own constitution. However, following independence, when narrating their version of the constitutional process, ACS officials exaggerated the importance of the role played by Simon Greenleaf. A year after independence, Elliott Cresson, a key ACS official, wrote to Greenleaf that with "the independence of the young Republic having been happily achieved," they owed him a "deep debt of gratitude for your admirable chart of their future course." This ACS-centric narrative of the convention prevailed, in part, because the only surviving account of its proceedings came from fragments of a journal kept by James Lugenbeel, a white ACS agent and medical doctor who had lived in the colony for several years. Lugenbeel painted a harshly critical portrait of the settler delegates, implying that a constitutional convention was beyond their legal or political capabilities. In his journal he recorded that one of the delegates claimed authorship of a constitutional draft that was "almost an *exact copy* of the Constitution which was sent out, as a model, by Professor Greenleaf." Lugenbeel found it even more troubling when the same delegate suggested that "the people of Liberia do not require the assistance of 'white people' to enable them to make a Constitution for the government of themselves." He went on to say that he found these remarks to be "really sickening, coming as they do from so ignorant a man." Although the settlers rejected many of the ACS's suggestions and had an integral role in writing their own constitution, Lugenbeel's racially tinged assessment of the delegates' abilities shaped his conclusion that they were underplaying their debt to Greenleaf's constitution. His reaction revealed what the ACS had largely assumed since the beginning of the constitutional process: black settlers were largely incapable of authoring their own framework for a political community in Liberia.[37]

Interpreting Independence

Conflicts between white ACS officials and black settlers over the meaning, and even the necessity, of independence had punctuated Liberia's fraught process of formally declaring itself a republic. However, in the aftermath of independence, white observers in the United States often diminished settlers' agency in the process. Instead, they presented a largely positive portrait of Liberian independence that celebrated the ways that the nation emulated U.S. institutions and typified U.S. global expansion. A year after independence, Samuel Benedict, a recently appointed Liberian Supreme Court justice, recorded his astonishment at the positive reception of his nation's independence in the United States: "We did not think at the time that our own feeble labors could have been so generally sanctioned."[38] Indeed, during a period when most whites were deeply skeptical about African Americans' capacity for self-government, they offered a notable degree of support for Liberian independence. Although the ACS ultimately had little success in controlling how independence progressed in Liberia, the organization quickly shifted its focus toward shaping the perceptions of the event by U.S. audiences and ensuring the continuity of "public confidence" in African colonization. They downplayed behind-the-scenes constitutional disputes and the colonists' harsh indictments of U.S. racism and stressed how the colony had emulated the symbols and governing structure of the United States. In doing so, the ACS presented Liberian independence as an event that was fundamentally unthreatening to the racial order in the United States, reassuring Americans that Liberia would become a crucial, if inherently unequal, international partner.

On the eve of independence, the ACS issued its annual report, which predicted that Liberian independence would be a "demonstration" to "show to the world that *their race* is capable of *self-government*" by acquiring "a respectable standing among the nations of the earth." The report emphasized that Liberia could show that it was a "free and happy republic, composed and governed entirely by colored men," which would allow them to stand "upon an equality, as to rights, privileges and prospects, with any other man in the world."[39] In arguing for the historical singularity of Liberia's republican claims, colonizationists often situated the new nation as a product of the United States' exceptional national narrative. They reasserted Americans' long-standing denial of the revolutionary black republic in Haiti and contrasted Liberia with the ongoing liberal revolutions that were simultaneously unfolding in Europe. In an 1848 meeting of the New York Colonization Society, one speaker announced that he "looked with more interest on [Liberia] ... the only black republic that had ever been established in the world" than "the mighty changes going on in Europe." He predicted that "every despotic nation in Europe will perish before Liberia" because its citizens had "learned the principles of liberty in the United States."[40]

Observers in the United States had a long tradition of viewing other nation-building projects around the world through the lens of its own history. As an example of U.S. exceptionalism, Americans, who commented on the revolutionary violence of European events in 1848, often contrasted these to an imagined past in which the origins of the United States had been orderly. This had been a consistent theme in U.S. discourse dating back to the nation's tortured relationships with the French revolution and the even more threatening Haitian revolution. While many Americans had expressed support for independence movements in Latin America and Greece during the 1820s, their enthusiasm was always tempered by others who believed that the United States must lead through its exceptional example rather than by direct intervention in foreign revolutionary conflicts. Nevertheless, while most American observations of nation-building elsewhere vacillated between admiration and condemnation, discussions of Liberian independence optimistically situated the event as a new expression of American exceptionalism in a proxy nation overseas.[41]

While some colonization supporters were concerned that European revolutionaries received more attention than the new republic in Africa, the ACS campaigned to frame independence as an extension of U.S. ideals and a historic demonstration of black self-government. This effort dovetailed with coverage of the event in several regional and national newspapers. The influential *Niles' National Register* closely followed the events leading to independence in a series of articles published in 1847. Shortly after Liberia announced its independence, the paper printed a story that depicted a peaceful transition of power and focused on the United States' role in inspiring the nation's Declaration of Independence, constitution, structure of government, and flag. The article observed, "Everything connected with the organization of the government seems to have been conducted with admirable order.... A flag was presented to the president by the ladies of Monrovia, on which occasion the military were out in great force."[42] Other national press reports connected the nation's adoption of the symbols of U.S. nationalism to a broader expansionist agenda for both the United States and Liberia. The *Journal of Commerce* proclaimed that an independent Liberia was "one of the most remarkable phenomena of modern times" and predicted that the "infant Republic shall expand its fame and extend its influence over the whole African continent, becoming alike the asylum and the glory of the free colored man."[43]

The *New York Sun* situated Liberian independence within the growing scope of U.S. global power by calling the nation a "triumph" of the United States' "benevolence and missionary zeal, the counter part of that glorious achievement [of Hawaiian missionaries] in the Pacific Ocean." The *Sun* rejoiced at the broadened horizons of U.S. expansion: "Within the brief period of twenty five years, American missionaries and benevolence have founded the kingdom of the Sandwich Islands on this hemisphere, and laid a sure, and we hope lasting, foundation for the Republic of the United States of Africa on the eastern hemisphere."[44] Such commentaries connected far-flung and rather distinct processes of colonization within Liberia and Hawaii and framed them within a vision of the United States' broader missionary enterprise. This conception dovetailed with the notion that Liberia remained independent yet part of a broader project of the United States' fledgling Christian global empire.[45]

The coverage of Liberia's independence in regional northern newspapers followed the national press reports. While acknowledging the global significance of the achievement, it nevertheless emphasized the triumph of U.S. political values abroad rather than heralding black participation in creating a new political community. Reports often focused on the American origins of Liberia's constitution, and several newspapers claimed that the document was copied directly from the state and federal governments of the United States. A typical news bulletin noted that "the new Constitution is very much after our own model—a President, Vice President, Senate and House."[46] A Massachusetts newspaper announced that the "Republic of Liberia now takes its place among the independent nations of the earth" and justified this claim by quoting large sections of the constitution to demonstrate the United States' direct imprint on the colonists' achievement.[47] The *Hartford Daily Courant* noted that Liberia's independence "places her claims upon new ground. It is for an Independent Republic we plead, and the more glorious for being composed of colored men." It also predicted that the "strictly republican" foundation would become a "vast republic of confederate states, perhaps like our own" and called the nation "one of the most auspicious enterprises of the present century."[48] Some papers simply published details about Liberia's government officials or the nation's U.S.-modeled flag. In foregrounding the United

Figure 6. Cover of pamphlet, *Liberia, 1847–1893*, published
in 1893. American Colonization Society Papers, Library
of Congress. This pamphlet cover, intended to highlight
the independent Liberian government in the 1890s, shows
the U.S.-modeled flag, a symbol of U.S. republicanism,
a fact noted by many Americans who observed the
nation's independence in the late 1840s and early 1850s.

States' inspiration within Liberia's narrative, newspaper accounts attributed little credit for independence to black settlers, who were generally depicted as mere vessels for transporting U.S. institutions to Africa.[49]

Although most coverage focused on the abstracted details of Liberian nationhood that paralleled the United States' own history, the newspapers' celebration of the world's most recently created republic also had a clear racial subtext. The U.S. press generally interpreted independence as a symbolic test of the United States' political ideals and racially exclusive nationalism rather than as an affirmative act of black self-determination. In these descriptions, newspaper accounts attributed very little agency to the settlers themselves and suggested, as James Lugenbeel had, that delegates had dutifully copied U.S. institutions while offering minimal input of their own. One report ignored the settler activism that had motivated the independence movement and misleadingly asserted that Liberia had declared itself a republic "at the suggestion and by the advice of the American Colonization Society." The same article suggested that an independent Liberia could effectively represent U.S. interests by becoming "a people respectable and influential for good" in West Africa, but the author also considered Liberian nationhood as a trial of whether "colored men are capable of maintaining among the nations of the world a free, independent and enlightened government."[50] Another article pointed out that "the proudest slaveholder, should he pay a visit to Liberia, would be constrained to treat the colored man as his equal" because "the tables are turned in a country as regards political rights, none but colored men being entitled to citizenship."[51] One newspaper made this point even more bluntly in a short headline and news bulletin: "TURN ABOUT IS FAIR PLAY. The constitution of the new Republic of Liberia declares that no white man shall be a voter in that Republic."[52] Such commentary directly responded to the racial limits of Liberian citizenship by implying that the nation acted as a mirror to the same policies in the United States.

The early press coverage of Liberian independence reveals how colonizationists could amplify the event's meaning by linking it to the United States' rhetoric of republican nationhood, racial nationalism, and settler expansionism. Despite their initial wariness over how political sovereignty would play out in the new republic, some white colonizationists looked on independence as an opportunity to rebrand the African colonization movement by highlighting how Liberia was ultimately validating many of its long-held claims. In the years following independence, the ACS emphasized its own role in creating the nation rather than the actions of black settlers. Even before Liberia became formally independent, some ACS members recognized how they might more effectively sell African colonization to the public by employing this sort of rhetoric. In 1846 Dr. S. M. E. Goheen, a missionary and physician who had worked in Liberia, appealed to white colonizationists to support a path to independence, arguing that "free persons of color, it is well known, have been so prejudiced against the Colonization Society as to refuse to go to Liberia under any circumstances." In contrast, Goheen claimed that independence from the ACS would remove the obstacle "which deprived Liberia of a class of citizens who alone can make it what it should be."[53] The idea that African Americans would be more likely to support a free and independent Republic of Liberia came to play an increasingly large role in the case for colonization during the coming decade.

By the time the ACS recognized that independence was likely inevitable, the organization had already begun to emphasize this way of framing the event to the broader public. An 1847 ACS report argued that "many would go to Liberia" if it rose to "a respectable standing among the nations of the earth."[54] Following independence, the *African Repository* directed its energy toward demonstrating the viability of the newly independent republic to both white and black supporters. One article asserted, "Interest, pride, ambition, self-love, self-respect, benevolence, faith, hope and charity, all combine to lead them to Liberia, as the home for themselves and their children, and the field for the most perfect development and display of their powers, and the most extensive and intense usefulness!"[55] Such appeals focused more clearly on the historical significance of an independent black republic in an effort to generate support from both black and white audiences.

After Liberian independence, African colonizationists often emphasized the event as the triumphant culmination of a U.S.-modeled settler narrative. While colonizationists had long depicted the Liberian colony as reproducing the early British colonies and their role in the U.S. origin story, they now completed this narrative with independence and the ultimate realization of republican nationhood. A few years after independence, the *African Repository* published an article titled "Analogy Between the Anglo-American and the Liberian," which predicted that "the year 1820 is destined to be ever memorable in the annals of Africa. It will be regarded by the black man as the year 1620 is by the descendants of the Puritans; and Sherbro will be his Plymouth. . . . May we not hope that the analogy will continue and that Liberia will become the United States of Africa?"[56] While Liberia had always invited comparisons to earlier North American settler colonies, after independence colonizationists increasingly promoted Liberia as a realization of the claim that republican virtues could flourish abroad under U.S. tutelage.

Colonizationists also used this analogy to highlight the similarity of the displacement of indigenous people by Liberian settlers to the United States' colonization of North America. In 1849 one ACS member argued that "at least 15,000 natives have already become subject to their [Liberia's] influence," claiming that their "grade of civilization is about equal to that of the Indian in his wildest states." He contended that the indigenous populations had "adopted a civilized costume and habits, and are ardently seeking to ele-vate themselves to a level with the colonists." Like the United States, Liberia's success as a settler colony depended on its particular form of republican gov-ernance: "There is not a [former] Spanish colony at this day, where civil and religious rights are as well understood, and as firmly established, as in the infant Republic of Liberia. The little colony maintains democratic institutions in peace and in security, administers justice, and levies taxes, maintains a prodigious ascendency among the surrounding tribes, who regard her with admiration and wonder, without a standing army, and without tumult or dis-order."[57] Although whites had increasingly deemed African Americans unfit to settle on indigenous lands claimed by the United States, colonizationists believed they had succeeded in doing so in Liberia.

The ACS strategy of promoting Liberian independence was particularly successful in those midwestern states where white politicians used coloniza-tionism to argue that African Americans were rightfully destined to become settler citizens of Liberia and not of the United States. In 1851 the Ohio state legislature passed a resolution that supported the recognition of Liberia, not-ing, "Intelligent colored men in the United States, who might be eminently useful in Africa, are unwilling to emigrate to Liberia until its independence shall be acknowledged by the government of the United States."[58] A few years later, the same state's legislature considered a bill that would build on its recent constitution in which black citizenship rights were already diminished by preventing "the further settlement of blacks and mulatto persons in this State" and imprisoning nonresidents in county jails. This bill was grounded in the dynamics of settler citizenship, but it also looked outward by noting that "the Republic of Liberia declared its independence as a sovereign nation more than five years since, and has been acknowledged as such by France, England, Belgium, Prussia, and Brazil," recommending the United States do likewise.[59] At the same moment when northern white politicians were explic-itly pushing African Americans farther outside the bounds of U.S. settler cit-izenship, they argued that a colony of black settlers must be recognized as a legitimate nation on the world stage. Many whites saw that the promises of independent nationhood and political sovereignty in Liberia were crucial because they worked to undermine black citizenship in the United States.

While ACS members, politicians, and the press promoted Liberian inde-pendence for a variety of reasons, a small group of white women, Helen Knight, Harriet Beecher Stowe, and Sarah Hale, also promoted Liberian independence in their long-form narrative writings. Literary scholars have examined the ways in which these women's books reflect gendered ideologies of race and empire, but they are also of interest because they illustrate many of the common themes evident within public discourse about the meaning of postcolonial Liberia.[60]

The first of the three books to be published was Helen Knight's *The New Republic* (1850), one of the earliest extensive accounts of Liberian independence produced for public consumption. Knight was a New England–based writer who had been involved in a variety of religious and benevolent reform efforts. While ostensibly presenting a straightforward history of Liberia, Knight wrote the book in a narrative fashion aimed clearly at educating a broad audience who were only vaguely familiar with the colony's development and recent independence. One section of the book was even reprinted in some newspapers, under the title "The New Republic—A Thrilling Sketch." Its title and style were similar to a popular genre of sensationalist stories that dramatized the events of the Mexican-American War.[61] Interestingly, this excerpt did not include scenes from Liberia's recent history but told a story of the colony's 1821 founding featuring war hero U.S. naval officer Robert Stockton, who had recently become famous for his role in the war with Mexico. Knight presented a much-mythologized story of Stockton's efforts to secure a location for the colony by forcing a local indigenous leader to sign a land treaty at gunpoint. The story concluded with a nationalistic scene in which "the American Flag was hoisted on Cape Mesurado—Three cheers for the American flag" and the "little band" was congratulated for "laying the foundation of that new Republic, which is to bless and benefit Africa, with the light of its Christianized civilization."[62] With such a scene, Knight built on the recent public interest in Liberian independence by framing it within a familiar settler narrative of indigenous dispossession and populating it with the iconic hero of a recent expansionist war.

Although the first several chapters of *The New Republic* concern the settlers' early problems establishing the colony, the book eventually moves on to recent Liberian history. It focuses its attention on many of the symbols of U.S. nationhood that had dominated recent public discussion about the nation, publishing its entire Declaration of Independence and offering detailed descriptions of Liberia's flag and constitution. The last chapter in Knight's book focuses on Liberia's efforts to secure diplomatic recognition from France, England, and Belgium, and after successfully doing so proclaiming, "Behold, then, Liberia! a free, independent, recognized sovereignty among the civilized nations of the world." The text concludes with a plea for U.S. audiences to recognize the importance of supporting a nation that was based on U.S. political ideals: "Liberia is the child of our own institutions, bearing our likeness, breathing our spirit, and bestowing our privileges. . . . May this American Republic stretch out its own strong arm, and with honest pride and fearless independence, give her a just and honorable *recognition* among the sovereignties of the world."[63] While Knight explicitly aimed to garner support for Liberian recognition, her book fit neatly into the themes already present in media coverage of the event by asking readers to connect the stories of U.S. and Liberian settler nationalism.

Two years after *The New Republic* was published, Harriet Beecher Stowe's famous antislavery novel *Uncle Tom's Cabin* appeared, containing a controversial section in which one of the main characters, George Harris, leaves the United States to settle in Liberia near the end of the novel. Harris is a resourceful and defiant slave who escapes to Canada and eventually to France, where he receives a university degree. Ultimately, he decides to take his family to Liberia after concluding that his talents would be wasted if he returned to the United States. With the George Harris character, Stowe depicted precisely the type of individual that white colonizationists imagined would make a productive settler citizen in an independent Liberia. In a letter to his friends and family, Harris writes of his reasons for choosing to finally settle in Liberia: "On the shores of Africa I see a republic,—a republic formed of picked men, who, by energy and self-educating force, have, in many cases, individually, raised themselves above a condition of slavery. Having gone through a preparatory stage of feebleness, this republic has, at last, become an acknowledged nation on the face of the earth,—acknowledged by both France and England. There it is my wish to go, and find myself a people."[64] In having the novel's most educated black character leave the United States, Stowe reflected the widespread notion that Liberian independence had made the nation suitable for fostering black citizenship.

In 1853 Sarah Hale, the editor of the popular women's periodical *Godey's Lady's Book*, wrote a book titled *Liberia or Mr. Peyton's Experiments*, which she conceived partially as a response to Stowe's famous novel published a year earlier. Unlike Stowe, Hale depicted the institution of slavery as a largely benevolent institution. The story centers on a kind and paternalistic Virginia planter, the titular Mr. Peyton, and his quest to secure favorable terms of freedom for his slaves. The "experiments" alluded to in the subtitle refer to Peyton's endeavors to establish new lives for his former slaves as they attempt to become landowners in the rural South and laborers in the urban North. Both efforts fail miserably, and Mr. Peyton's slaves ultimately leave the United States for the recently established Republic of Liberia. Once the main protagonists make it to Liberia, the character-driven narrative largely falls away, and Hale uses the last three chapters to explain Liberia's significance as an independent nation.[65]

Despite Hale's national prominence as a female editor, her novel made far less an impact than *Uncle Tom's Cabin* did. Indeed, the abolitionist press almost purposefully ignored the book, even as they afforded considerable attention and debate to Stowe's relatively brief passage on Liberia. In concert with other writings at the time, Hale's novel depicted Liberia as a nation exclusively modeled on American ideals. In a scene where Mr. Peyton meets with President Joseph Roberts, he calls the leader a "fair specimen of a Liberian" and hopes that "the time will come when from that little spot the laws and principles will go forth that will control all Africa." In Liberia Hale's characters tour the country and see how its institutions exemplify a well-established basis for republican nationhood. They witness a prosperous and bustling national capital in Monrovia, a thriving black-run newspaper, a successful system of agriculture, and a functioning democratic government. Hale concluded the book with an extensive appendix in which she reproduced the Liberian Declaration of Independence, constitution, flag, and testimonials from African Americans who supported colonization.[66]

Despite these authors' differing motivations, all three books reflected the shift in public discourse about African colonization following Liberian independence. Both Knight and Hale were concerned with promoting the idea of an independent Liberia, but their books had slightly different emphases. *The New Republic* consciously targeted white middle-class readers and paid scant attention to the perspectives of black settlers. In framing Liberia's story for a white audience, Knight was placing it within a larger narrative of the United States' expansionist nationalism, as evident in her account of the colony's founding by a U.S. naval officer. By emphasizing such anecdotes, she hoped to serve her apparent agenda of promoting Liberia's campaign for diplomatic recognition. With *Liberia or Mr. Peyton's Experiments*, Hale similarly hoped to garner support for the new nation, but her black main characters and testimonials from black writers demonstrate that she may also have been concerned with motivating an educated free black readership to imagine themselves as participants in building a new republic. Although Harriet Beecher Stowe's brief Liberian plot thread was not central to *Uncle Tom's Cabin*, it had the greatest national impact of the three books. The novel generated considerable debate because abolitionists had forged their core identity in opposition to African colonization. Nevertheless, it is significant that Stowe, an ambivalent supporter of Liberia, decided to resolve the George Harris story line through a colonization plot within a thoroughly antislavery novel. Seemingly seduced by widespread and grandiose claims about Liberia's significance, Stowe looked past her own skepticism about the movement in order to invest Harris with a hopeful nationalist outlook on the new republic.[67]

The Contested Meaning of a Black Republic

Although many white northerners enthusiastically praised the declaration of an independent Liberia, African Americans expressed a far more ambivalent attitude toward the newly formed nation. Most free black communities had steadfastly denounced the ACS since its inception in the first decades of the nineteenth century. However, during the late 1840s and early 1850s, the advent of Liberian independence helped fracture African Americans' nearly unified opposition to colonizationism. Although some black audiences were motivated to reconsider Liberia after its independence, they were also concerned that the prospects for ending slavery and expanding black rights in the United States were worsening following the passage of the Fugitive Slave Act in 1850.[68] This legislation fundamentally threatened the livelihood of all black communities in the United States by giving the federal government tremendous power to help capture enslaved people. Many African Americans believed that this law demonstrated that the United States was willing to maintain and even expand the institution of slavery and that their only hope for securing freedom was to leave the nation altogether. As a result, several black leaders promoted emigration plans to various locations in Canada, the Caribbean, and Central America on the basis that African Americans required a national territory that would enshrine and protect their rights. Within this context, the Republic of Liberia also represented a place where some African Americans could imagine a redemptive nationality that would counteract the exclusionary racial republicanism of the United States.[69]

Of course, this was not the first time that African Americans had looked abroad for the prospect of redemptive black nation. In the first decades following the American Revolution, several black leaders looked toward Africa, culminating in Paul Cuffe's frustrated attempts to cultivate commercial and cultural ties to Africa through the British colony of Sierra Leone. However, the co-optation of African emigration by white colonizationists heightened black leaders' skepticism toward all such plans and turned some away from any association with "African" identity more generally.[70] At the same, African Americans had also closely watched the Republic of Haiti as well as the progress of British emancipation in the Caribbean. While Haiti's volatile internal politics often complicated black identification with the nation, it remained far more attractive to many African Americans than Liberia, both as a resonant symbol of black nationhood and as a potential destination for migration. Thus, black receptiveness to the Republic of Liberia was always shaped by the ways that the ACS had negatively framed black identification with Africa as well as the long shadow cast by the nation's more radical counterpart in Haiti.[71]

Echoing the popular discourse that followed the announcement of Liberia's independence, some black leaders, despite long-standing skepticism of colonization, also connected this event to the spread of U.S. republicanism. At the 1847 National Convention of Colored People, one black delegate declared, "[Liberia is] taking a stand among the independent nations of the earth," appealing to the nationalist pride of his audience by encouraging them to "share in the glory and honor of the Liberians, in building their villages and cities, constructing their canals, [and in] raising their ships."[72] Edward Wilmot Blyden, an African American clergyman who moved to Liberia shortly after independence, recounted some general impressions that he had overheard about the nation among black residents of a boardinghouse in New York: "They see in Liberia colored men rising to the most dignified stations that white men can fill in this country. They see them projecting, and governing themselves by wise and prudent laws,—acknowledged as a Republic by some of the most potent and enlightened nations of Europe." While Blyden noted their considerable interest in the prospect of Liberian nationhood, he lamented that, nevertheless, most African Americans he spoke to "prefer to fight it out here." He chastised black communities in the United States and wondered whether they lacked the collective racial will to help realize Liberia's imperial destiny on the African continent: "If the colored people in this country had half the energy and enterprising spirit of the Anglo-Saxon race, how soon would the Republic of Liberia include within its limits the dark regions of Ashantee and Dahomey."[73] Although Blyden encouraged African Americans to think of themselves as having a parallel destiny to white settler colonists in North America, other black leaders echoed white observers who viewed Liberian independence as part of U.S. global expansion. At the Free Colored People's Convention in 1852, James A. Handy attributed Liberia's success to the "genius of American enterprise," which he claimed was "unbolting the massive door and securing the commerce of China and Japan" and leading to "the redemption of Africa." He urged the convention to endorse "the infant republic of Liberia" because it was already "acknowledged by England, France, Russia and Prussia—four of the greatest powers on earth."[74]

During the period after Liberian independence, aspiring black emigrants sent an unprecedented volume of letters to the ACS, many of which reflect a similar investment in Liberia's nationalist symbolism. Even though these letters touched on a variety of concerns, including how to obtain transport to the nation, the costs of emigration, and the prospects for land and work in Liberia, the writers clearly crafted them with an audience of ACS officials in mind. As a result, these letters drew on some of the themes of nationhood that some black leaders and the press promoted, including the necessity of building a republican government in which citizens were allowed to reach their full potential through institutions modeled after those in the United States.[75]

Some aspiring emigrants saw themselves as part of a grand narrative of the United States' progress and used such terms as "freedom," "liberty," "citizenship," and "rights" in conjunction with symbols of U.S. nationalism. One writer claimed: "I have [tried] a great [many places in these United States] and I find that . . . Liberia is the [only] place" that "colored men" can "[enjoy] the rights of man."[76] Others were more suspicious of these ideals and believed they would never receive the blessings of citizenship while they remained in the United States. One letter denounced the "mock freedom for the [colored] man in the United States," arguing that Liberia was the most viable alternative for those "who have not lost all love for liberty and mental elevation."[77] Another writer argued that he could do much more good in Liberia because on "this side of the Atlantic" he was not recognized as a citizen. One man was pleased to hear that more African Americans had immigrated to Liberia because they "had seen that [the United States]" was not "[their] country of liberty and freedom," and that the way to achieve freedom was to "leave this land to [establish] a free government of [our] own."[78]

Despite their critiques of exclusionary U.S. citizenship, several prospective emigrants used the history of the United States as a model for the colony's trajectory. Following independence, the ACS began to produce copies of the Liberian flag and constitution for distribution to African Americans. Several aspiring emigrants' letters requested both of these articles, which they likely regarded as significant and tangible manifestations of black nationhood. One such black writer explicitly connected Liberia's settler-colonial narrative to the European colonization of North America and hoped that "by [our] industry it may be in time as richly covered with [cities,] farms and [commerce] as the grate United States of [America] which 300 years ago was an wilderness."[79] Whether absorbed through colonizationist discourse or broader U.S. nationalism, the settler narrative was important to some African Americans who saw colonization as an act of racial redemption.

This redemptive settler-colonial narrative was grounded in a gendered rhetoric of nationhood that was common to both white colonization supporters and aspiring black settlers.[80] Colonizationists often emphasized that the process of settlement could itself function as a transformative act of masculine deliverance. This framework was particularly prevalent following Liberian independence. For instance, an *African Repository* article from mid-1847 argued that "with the strength of manhood" Liberia is "about to enter a career of independence and freedom, which will give [it] a name, and, we doubt not, an honorable place among the nations of the world."[81] Another article, published shortly after independence, described Liberia's recent ratification of its constitution as an "act, by which a young community throws off the yoke of its tutelage, and asserts its character of political manhood."[82] African Americans often expressed their desire to construct a nation in Liberia using a similar rhetoric of masculinity. One aspiring migrant argued that the Republic of Liberia would allow "the African to be able to show to the whole world, that he can be a man."[83] Another contended that through the creation of a national state with military forces, colleges, schools, and doctors, African Americans would "cease to be 'hewers of wood and drawers of water,' and be men."[84] Some writers spoke of nation building in terms of a masculine labor, one claiming that he knew machinists, tailors, engineers, masons, blacksmiths, farmers, and ministers who wanted to "be useful citizens to that young [republic]" and another claiming that the black man must "till that [piece] of earth with his own hands and water it with the sweat of his brow. . . . He must plant the tree of liberty, and [build] a temple sacred to religion and [justice]."[85]

While some African Americans argued that Liberia offered the potential for masculine redemption, others questioned whether black masculinity must be necessarily tied to an assertion of black nationhood. This struggle is apparent in an 1851 public debate between two well-known black men, Frederick Douglass and Augustus Washington. Augustus Washington was a prominent daguerreotypist from Hartford, Connecticut, who immigrated to Liberia in 1851 after being inspired by its recent independence. Washington published a letter in the *New York Tribune* that praised the attention given to the "infant Republic of Liberia" by both "the enlightened nations" and "the press of both England and America." Echoing the sentiments of some letter writers to the ACS, Washington urged African Americans to immigrate to the new republic because he believed it was the only place "the colored people of this country" could find "a home on earth for the development of their manhood."[86] A few weeks after this letter was published, Frederick Douglass responded by scoffing at the recent uptick in black support for colonization and offering his own vision of black masculinity to support it: "When will our people learn that they have the power to crush this viper which is stinging our very life away? And still more, when will they have the energy, the nerve, and manliness, to use it?"[87] The *Christian Statesman*, a white pro-colonization paper, analyzed this exchange by praising Washington's initial letter, contending that in advising African Americans to "go to a country where they will at once be liberated from every political and social trammel" and become "the governing class," he has shown "a nobler sentiment of self-respect, and of respect for his race." In contrast, the paper noted, Douglass, who it said advised "his colored brethren to doggedly remain . . . without the shadow of a hope," does not display "an independent and manly spirit."[88] The conflict over these conceptions of masculinity highlights how the colonizationist claim that political statehood was the only proper basis for restoring black masculinity contradicted the abolitionist notion that manhood depended on rejecting the colonization movement's implicit acceptance of racially exclusive citizenship in the United States.[89]

Although some African Americans considered Liberian immigration to be an increasingly attractive option, the idea remained controversial within most northern free black communities. This was evident in the discussions within black newspapers and black political conventions of the era, as well as the publication of several books and pamphlets that tried to dissuade African Americans from settling in Liberia. For instance, African American residents of Indiana responded negatively when William Findlay, a black man from the state, published an appeal "to the colored people of Indiana" claiming that for African Americans "to be *truly* independent," they needed to travel to Liberia to "enjoy rights and privileges *as broad* and *as liberal* as those enjoyed by the citizens of the United States."[90] To most African Americans in the state, Findlay's argument that settling in Liberia was the only way to acquire political privileges rang false in a state where white colonizationists were using the same logic to deny African Americans the right to settle and become citizens. A group of black residents from Fort Wayne, Indiana, chastised black colonizationists such as Findlay, portraying them as traitors to their race. At an 1849 meeting they stated, "We feel insulted when asked to emigrate to Liberia; and when a colored man becomes the tool of such [a] society, or on his own responsibility advocates Colonization, we look upon him as recreant to the best good of his race."[91]

Although many black colonizationists had based their appeals on Liberia's connection to the institutions and logic of U.S. settler republicanism,
several black critics countered this perspective by framing independence as
a manipulative exercise in political theater. They criticized the false assumption of equivalency between the two nations. A delegate to a black convention in Ohio pointed out the absurdity of comparing officeholders in Liberia
to their counterparts in the United States. He wryly encouraged his audience
to "go to Liberia [to] become President, Senator, Judge or what not. Come
to this country and see how the founders of this scheme will treat you."[92]
Shortly after Liberia's independence, the Colored National Convention condemned colonization as the most "deceptive and hypocritical" of the "oppres-
sive schemes" enacted within the United States because it was " 'clothed with
the livery of heaven to serve the devil in,' with President Roberts, a colored
man, for its leader."[93] A report from a New York convention cautioned that
"all kinds of chicanery and stratagem will be employed to allure the people
[to the colony]. . . . The independence of its inhabitants; the enjoyments and
privileges of its citizens, will be pictured forth in glowing colors, to deceive
you." While white audiences responded positively to the image of Liberia as
an example of transplanted U.S. institutions, many African Americans were
skeptical of the way that such nationalist symbolism was employed to promote the significance of independence.[94]

This conflict over the meaning of the Republic of Liberia within black
communities was particularly evident in the public disputes concerning
how *Uncle Tom's Cabin* depicted colonization. Edward Blyden approved of
Stowe's nod to incipient Liberian independence in her novel and wrote a
public letter, published in antislavery newspapers, in which he claimed to
be "very agreeably surprised" that the novel depicted "an intelligent colored
man in America" who expressed "a desire for an 'African nationality' " and
"[intended] to emigrate to Liberia." Blyden believed that this was "the position which every intelligent colored man should take."[95] This stance illustrates
that Stowe's George Harris character was echoing celebratory white discourse
about Liberian independence at the same time he affirmed ideas about "African nationality" that were already circulating within northern black communities. In contrast, the New York Anti-Slavery Society condemned the "evil"
consequences of the novel's promotion of Liberia and hoped "something
would be done to counteract the Colonization influence" of the book. Backlash to this section of the novel prompted Stowe to distance herself from the
colonization movement in public letters addressed to the abolitionist community in which she expressed regret for including the passage in the book.

Figure 7. Liberian Senate by Robert K. Griffin, ca. 1856. This
watercolor painting provides a rare early depiction of the Liberian
legislature during the first decade of the nation's independence.
Marian S. Carson Collection, Library of Congress.

Stowe claimed that she did not write the section to promote a colonizationist
agenda but because she believed the establishment of Liberia was a "fixed
fact" that afforded an opportunity "of sustaining a republican government of
free people of color."[96]

Shortly after the publication of *Uncle Tom's Cabin*, the black abolitionist
Martin Delany wrote a scathing critique of the book in a public letter addressed
to one of Stowe's defenders, Frederick Douglass. In this letter, which was published in the newspaper edited by Douglass, Delany questioned the sincerity
of Stowe's support for black nationhood, noting that she "sneers at Hayti—the
only truly free and independent civilized black nation . . . on the face of the

earth—at the same time holding up the little dependent colonization settlement of Liberia in high estimation." Delany concluded that the only explanation for the distinction she made between these two black republics was that "one is independent of, and the other subservient to, white men's power." Frederick Douglass published Delany's letter, followed by his own response to it, in which he argued that he would not "allow the sentiments put in the brief letter of George Harris, at the close of *Uncle Tom's Cabin*, to vitiate forever Mrs. Stowe's power to do us good." While Douglass had long opposed African colonization, he made a distinction between supporting the movement and supporting the Republic of Liberia. Noting that the ACS had "systematically, and almost universally, sought to spread their hopelessness among the free colored people," he nevertheless argued that "we are *far* from saying this of many who speak and wish well to Liberia."[97] The intensity of the debate over *Uncle Tom's Cabin* reflected the fact that arguments for colonization based on Liberia's national status had made some headway within black communities that had previously been nearly unanimous in their rejection of the idea.

By identifying Stowe's disparate treatment of Haiti and Liberia, Delany reflected a shift in black critiques of the colonization movement from primarily questioning the motives of its white supporters toward examining the actions of an independent Liberia alongside other visions of black nationhood on the world stage. In the late 1840s and early 1850s, Liberian independence was situated within the emerging debates about emigration and colonization within black communities. By the early 1850s Delany had become a prominent advocate of creating black settlements in the Caribbean and Latin America. In marked contrast to his dim view of Liberian sovereignty, he imagined that such colonies would become nations where African Americans could pursue a destiny independent from the United States.[98]

Shortly after Liberia's independence, in an article published in the *North Star*, Delany decried the parallels being drawn between Liberian and U.S. nationalism to promote the new republic. In particular, he commented on the way that white colonizationists disingenuously heaped praise on Liberia's president, Joseph Roberts, noting that Henry Clay, "that venerable slave-breeder and pre-eminent negro-dreader," had pronounced Roberts "to be equal to the most eminent executives and statesmen in our country." Delany also criticized Roberts because he submitted an "official report" to the ACS regarding his diplomatic tours through Europe despite acting as "the Minister of Liberia, an independent nation!" He pointed out that Roberts was "clothed in paraphernalia of a nation's representative and armed with the proud panoply of a freeman's rights," yet he was still required to report "his official doings

[to] a private white man in the United States."[99] A few years later, Delany summarized his critique in his most widely published pamphlet: "Liberia is not an Independent Republic: in fact, *it is not* an independent nation at all; but a poor *miserable mockery*—a *burlesque* on a government."[100] Delany, as well as other black critics of Liberia, hinged their criticism on the fact that the public campaigns for the republic situated it as a product of U.S. republican ideals even while the nation undermined its independence by remaining subordinate to the United States' interests.

Around the same time, William Nesbit, a disenchanted black traveler to Liberia, published a book that sought to expose the new nation's thin veneer of legitimacy. Nesbit claimed: "They assume to be [a] republic, to have copied their forms and laws from the United States" and give "color" to this assertion by "pretend[ing] to have vested their power and authority in executive, legislative, judicial, and all other departments, cabinets and bureaus known in the government of nations." However, he contended that most of the nation's power was located in the executive branch, controlled by President Roberts, who he claimed was "but a tool in the hands of the Colonization Society."[101] While Liberia's contested path to independence demonstrates that Americans in the ACS had far less control than critics such as Nesbit and Delany might have supposed, their acerbic commentary indicates that some African Americans were unwilling to accept a highly dubious rhetoric that positioned democracy in Liberia and the United States on equal footing. In the end, they believed that the two nations remained structured by a dependent colonial relationship even after independence.

Several participants in black political conventions also expanded on this theme by questioning the value of Liberia's sovereignty when the nation's prospects were considered within the broader imperial interests of United States. One convention issued a report condemning the Republic of Liberia's attempt to gain formal diplomatic recognition through promises of dramatic trading concessions to the United States. The report contended that Liberia is "willing, in substance, to bow slavishly to the worst sense, feelings, and views of the American government" by offering the United States "any business it might desire transacted in Africa. . . . Was there ever such a treaty formed and ratified in the history of civilized nations?"[102] The convention concluded that the United States would continue to threaten the integrity of Liberia's sovereignty through a persistent colonial relationship that was rooted in the inherent power disparity between the nations.

Two years later, another black convention's report denounced Liberia's alignment with the imperial projects of the United States and Europe. After reminding convention delegates of the numerous injustices committed by Dutch and British colonizers in Africa, the report predicted, with startling pre- science, that "Africa is destined to be the theatre of bloody conflict, between her native sons, and intruding foreigners, black and white, for a century yet to come. The British in the South and North, the French in the south-east and the Americans on the west, speculating in lands, cheating and warring, afford little promise of a political millennium for the land of Ham." The report pointed out that "the Liberians themselves, with their government backing them, are pursuing precisely, the same policy, that other colonizers have for the last hundred years in Africa: They boast that they have made their arms so often felt, that 'no combination of the natives can be induced to fight them.' "[103] Such a critique pointed out that, despite claims to the contrary, the Liberian settler state was not so distinct from the destructive models of European colo- nialism it purported to transcend. This raised the fundamental question of whether African Americans should fashion themselves after white Americans and become settler colonizers or whether they should recognize a common interest with the colonized indigenous peoples of Africa. While few African Americans explicitly suggested this sort of framework for envisioning pan- African solidarity, most rejected the idea that Liberia would allow them to reproduce the United States' settler republic in Africa successfully.

*   *   *

Several years after declaring independence, the Republic of Liberia was still not officially recognized by the United States. For some black critics this was a confirmation of their prediction that the new nation would be both disrespected and manipulated by a growing U.S. empire. A newspaper pub- lished by black expatriates in Canada argued that the refusal to recognize Liberia revealed the hollowness of a rhetoric that promoted a government modeled after the United States: "The colonizationists of the United States have unquestionably the control of the United States Government; how hap- pens it that they have not recognized the independence of Liberia? Why have they never recognized the independence of any black government in any part of the world? The treatment of colonizationists towards black citizens of the United States, towards Liberia, and towards other black governments, is a true key to real colonizationism."[104] Indeed, many of the nation's most pow- erful politicians, including several presidents, had been public supporters of the colonization movement. Nevertheless, congressional actions on behalf of diplomatic recognition for Liberia were consistently defeated throughout the 1850s. The simple explanation for the failure of these efforts was the solid block of southern congressmen who believed that recognizing an independent black nation fundamentally undermined the institution of slavery by publicly acknowledging African Americans' capacity for self-government.

However, this failure to recognize Liberia diplomatically also highlights the profound tension between the promise that it would become the United States' peer in a world of independent nations and the reality that it seemed doomed to perpetual status as a subordinate, second-class republic. Since the inception of the colonization movement, this tension had always been present in its logic; however, the prospect of independence magnified it. In contrast to the meanings that colonizationists and white U.S. audiences attached to the colony's new political status, the disputes over the authorship of the constitution demonstrated that the true meaning of "independence" was deeply contested. In the end, Liberia's constitutional convention did not produce a document radically at odds with the wishes of the colonizationists, and the change in regimes was relatively seamless, despite the settlers' apparent dissatisfaction with continuing ACS paternalism. Ultimately, the Republic of Liberia succeeded in superficially emulating U.S. institutions through a nonrevolutionary process that resonated with white audiences in the United States. Those who followed the details of early nationhood consistently emphasized that independence was both a distinct break from a colonial relationship and a validation of the United States' exceptional ability to shape the world in its image. To many white observers in the United States this was an appealing message whose flexibility would prove to be its enduring strength. As Americans increasingly looked toward Central America in the late 1850s and early 1860s, they would again reimagine colonizationism in order to serve the United States' increasingly global strategic interests.

CHAPTER 6

Reimagining Colonization in the Americas

In 1844 Robert J. Walker, a U.S. senator from Mississippi, became a central figure in the debate over U.S. expansion when he published a widely disseminated letter that urged the United States to annex the independent Republic of Texas and prevent the prospect of immediate abolition. Annexation, in his opinion, would instead lead to a "gradual and progressive" end to slavery in which African Americans would be diffused "through Texas into Mexico, and Central and Southern America, where nine-tenths of their present population are already of the colored races."[1] Furthermore, his particular vision highlighted the popular notion that the United States needed to secure further territory in the Americas or else the British empire would come to dominate the region. These arguments played a critical part in rallying support for the annexation of Texas, helping push the United States toward war with Mexico, and laying the groundwork for the expansionist ethos of manifest destiny.[2]

While Walker is largely known for his role in fomenting the Mexican-American War, he is less remembered as a Civil War–era colonizationist. Nearly two decades later, in 1862, Walker published an article commending President Lincoln's federal colonization policy. Earlier that year, Lincoln had helped pass a law to fund colonies for African Americans. At the same time, his administration had initiated contact with diplomats and businessmen in Central American countries about the possibility of planting settlements in that region. In his article Walker heaped effusive praise on the success of the "great republic" of Liberia for carrying "our language, laws, religion, and free institutions" to Africa and particularly endorsed the president's efforts to apply the Liberian model to the Americas. Using his stature as an prominent advocate of U.S. expansion, Walker emphasized the commercial and geopolitical benefits of planting colonies that would be situated on "one of the great interoceanic routes," remarking that "it is a great object to secure the control of this isthmus by a friendly race, born on our soil, and the selection [of that location] corresponds with the views expressed in my Texas letter of 1844."[3] The proposed settlements fulfilled Walker's expressed desire to "diffuse" former slaves throughout the Americas by employing the colonizationist notion that African Americans could serve as ambassadors for U.S. interests in the Western Hemisphere.

Walker's famous 1844 letter intervened in a set of debates about U.S. expansion that concerned the crucial question of how the United States would maintain its integrity as a white settler state while managing an increasingly vast multiracial empire. Although Walker argued that his prior justification for Texas annexation converged neatly with President Lincoln's proposed colonization program, in many ways this rhetorical appeal obscures more than it reveals about historical tensions between colonization proposals and U.S. territorial expansionism. In the late 1850s and early 1860s, many Republican politicians believed that they could resolve these tensions by transplanting elements of Liberian colonization to Central America and, in the process, perhaps forge an alternative framework for U.S. imperialism.[4]

Republican politicians explicitly designed the proposed Central American colonies as a rejoinder to slaveholders' widespread plans to colonize parts of the Americas, known popularly as "filibusters." Scholars have often placed these filibustering schemes at the center of mid-nineteenth-century debates about U.S. expansionism, but they have been more reluctant to elevate the plans for black colonies to the same stature.[5] These proposals deserve more careful consideration because while they grew from the logic of U.S. settler colonialism, they also suggested different practices of expansion that emphasized the spread of U.S. institutions more than its acquisition of territory. The notion that Liberia would become a "United States of Africa" served as an example of how racial republicanism might become the basis for expanding U.S. power around the globe. As the United States' sectional crisis helped restore this idea to mainstream political discourse, colonizationists presented the racial republic as a means to advance U.S. economic and strategic interests within the Western Hemisphere.

Manifesting Racial Destinies

In the late 1840s both the advent of Liberian independence and the United States' war with Mexico helped recast the place of colonizationism within the politics of U.S. empire. In 1847 a Virginia newspaper celebrated Liberia's recent independence by repeating the common mistaken claim that its constitution was "copied from the State Constitutions of the U. States," but then it went on to make a less typical observation when it asked "those whose daily task is to malign our country" to reflect on "the monument of wisdom and benevolence she has quietly rented upon that benighted continent [in Liberia], while pursuing her own magnificent 'destiny' at home [in Mexico]."[6] By invoking the United States' ongoing war with Mexico and referencing the ideology of manifest destiny to justify it, the article made a claim for American greatness based on the continuity between Liberian colonization and U.S. territorial expansionism in North America. Other contemporary observers also recognized the connection between these events but instead cast them in opposition to each other. The *National Intelligencer*, a long-standing advocate of African colonization, noted that "we doubt whether the prospects of Colonization are, just now, much brightened by our national operations in another quarter: our benevolent plans can hardly proceed at once on all sides; and African colonization must probably yield to Mexican. Our 'manifest destiny' calls us in another direction; to havoc, not restoration; to spreading desolation over an unhappy land, not making the waste bloom and blossom like the rose; to trampling on the weak, not raising up the afflicted and depressed."[7] This comparison suggests an increasingly important way in which colonizationism could be framed as a benevolent model of U.S. expansion in contrast to militaristic wars of territorial expansion, such as the one being conducted against Mexico. While such direct comparisons between Liberia and Mexico were relatively rare at the time, they offer a glimpse of how colonizationism would come to be repositioned amid the United States' self-conscious debate over the strategies and limitations of empire building in the age of manifest destiny.

Following the Mexican-American War, a key question in this debate was whether the United States should seek to solidify its hemispheric position militarily and expand farther into Central America and the Caribbean basin. A group of ardent expansionist politicians, known as the "All Mexico" faction, had bristled at the unwillingness of U.S. officials to push for acquiring more territory from Mexico at the conclusion of the war. In subsequent years, similarly frustrated U.S. expansionists turned to private military campaigns or filibusters as a means of realizing their territorial and strategic ambitions for the United States. Several filibusters, such as those attempted within the Mexican states of Sonora, Baja California, and Monterrey, aimed to expand farther into territory not claimed during the war, while some attempted to capitalize on persistent U.S. interest in acquiring Cuba. Others stretched even farther still by looking to seize territory in parts of Central America. An American, William Walker, planned and led several such expeditions, the most infamous of which succeeded in briefly asserting military control over the government of civil war–torn Nicaragua. During Walker's brief period of rule he declared himself president and reinstated the institution of slavery before his forces were driven out of power. Even though Walker's invasion was one of the very few proposed expeditions that actually came to fruition, their proliferation within U.S. culture testified to the southern elites' widespread belief that expanding slavery throughout the Americas was essential to the continued survival of that institution in the United States.[8]

All of these expansionist plans faced the vexed question of how white supremacy could ultimately be reconciled with republicanism in a growing multiracial empire. The historian Thomas Hietala characterized the dilemma facing expansionists as tensions between two principle objectives, namely, the desire "to acquire land in order to augment the nation's wealth, power, and security" and the drive "to ensure racial and cultural homogeneity within their expanding empire." Hietala noted that, with the addition of Texas, Oregon, and California, expansionists' "demand for territory could be accommodated with their desire for ethnic and racial purity," but "at other times, as in the All Mexico movement or proposals to acquire Cuba or Yucatan, the two impulses clashed and inhibited them." Since the founding of the republic, the United States had successfully employed strategies of state-sponsored violence, forced relocation, and political displacement to construct a white settler state in places where the volume and strength of incoming migrants could quickly overwhelm local nonwhite populations. However, as the United States looked farther afield within the hemisphere, it faced much larger populations of African, indigenous, and mestizo peoples, most of whom were theoretically represented by republican governments that the United States recognized.[9]

For many expansionists who supported filibusters, the answer was to displace local governments, which they routinely characterized as illegitimate, despotic, and corrupted by monarchism, Catholicism, and racial amalgamation. Such sentiments had helped fuel the Mexican-American War, yet the most zealous expansionists had been frustrated when postwar treaty negotiations resulted in the cession of only the sparsely populated northern regions of Mexico, rather than most or all of its southern portions. However, opponents of expansionism argued that political incorporation of such a large nonwhite population would be untenable. In particular, they echoed the concerns of many Americans about the Treaty of Guadalupe Hidalgo, which offered the prior inhabitants of newly acquired Mexican territories the promise of full U.S. citizenship rights.[10] Filibusters tried to address these issues by proposing a regime of racial and political domination like the one William Walker forced on Nicaragua. In his brief tenure as president, Walker attempted to Anglicize the population through the imposition of the English language, encourage white American immigration to overwhelm the indigenous and mestizo majority, and, most importantly, establish a plantation economy by reinstating African slavery. Proponents of filibusters envisioned a society that would be dominated by white American settlers and built on the bedrock institution of racial slavery.

In contrast to filibuster schemes, the plans for black colonies offered the possibility of expanding U.S. power presumably without requiring large-scale military interventions, the annexation of territory, the extension of slavery, or the threat of racial mixture. Like Liberia, these colonies were portrayed as places where settlers would model the principles of U.S. republicanism and commerce for local populations, thus drawing them more closely into the United States' imperial orbit. The suggestion that black populations could be displaced into proxy nations that would complement the United States' geopolitical interests merged colonizationism with the ideology of manifest destiny and offered a new strategy for the United States' informal domination of the Americas.[11]

Formed in 1854, the ascendant Republican Party would come to play a central role in promoting this new wave of colonization proposals. The Republicans developed their plans separately from previous efforts led by proto-black nationalists such as Henry Highland Garnet and Martin Delany who aimed to encourage black immigration to Central America.[12] During the late 1850s Francis "Frank" Blair, Jr., a congressional representative from Missouri, would become the most prominent advocate for Central American colonies on the national stage. In subsequent years Blair would help persuade several Republican senators and governors to adopt this cause. Ultimately, Abraham Lincoln and the Republican-controlled Congress would go on to support a version of his ideas during the Civil War. Blair hailed from a prominent, well-connected family, and both his father, Francis, Sr., and his brother, Montgomery, were important players in Republican Party politics. Like many conservative and moderate Republicans, Frank Blair supported colonization proposals not only because he wanted to halt the spread of slavery but also because he was intensely opposed to granting African Americans any form of political equality within the United States. He believed that the ACS had failed to achieve its goals in Liberia and hoped to shift colonizationist sentiment toward a more expansive and, in his view, more practical set of objectives in Latin America. From an early stage, Blair's even more influential father, a founding member of the Republican Party, helped develop and advance these ideas. Throughout the late 1850s Frank Blair, Jr., provided the public face for colonizationism, while Francis Blair, Sr., used his influence behind the scenes to sway key supporters.[13]

The confluence of Central American travel writing, entrepreneurial boosterism, and official diplomacy explains, in part, why the Blairs and their fellow politicians rapidly embraced this new colonizationist agenda. Travel writing was part of a larger trend in mid-nineteenth-century U.S. print culture in which travelers published their experiences as books, pamphlets, and popular articles claiming "expert" knowledge about various parts of the Americas. Although these writers often presented themselves as neutral observers, many framed their writings around expansionist designs to reshape the region toward U.S. interests.[14] Frank Blair became particularly interested in Central America through the popular writings of William Vincent Welles and E. G. Squier. Authors such as these helped garner a sympathetic audience for the new colonization plans among elite politicians who consumed this literature.[15]

E. George Squier was not only a journalist, amateur ethnographer, and speculative entrepreneur; he was also familiar with Central America having served as the United States chargé d'affaires during the late 1840s and early 1850s. His work exemplifies how the merging of descriptive travel writing with expansionist propaganda and commercial boosterism laid the groundwork for Central American colonization proposals. In the latter half of the 1850s, Squier became increasingly interested in how to develop Central America economically. He particularly advanced the Honduran Interoceanic Railway, one of many competing transportation schemes U.S. businessmen pursued throughout this era. While Squier's commercial plans ultimately failed, he promoted the project in concert with his ideas about regional transformation in articles published in U.S. periodicals and full-length monographs. Acting as an interlocutor for U.S. audiences, his writings interpreted Central America for a wide range of educated U.S. policy makers and businessmen.[16]

While Squier never directly advocated the creation of black colonies in Central America, he emphasized issues that would become prominent themes for Blair and other colonizationists of this era. Squier's writings argued that Central America was absolutely essential to the United States' future prosperity, but he claimed that extensive colonization by white settlers was out of the question because of the region's tropical climate, noting that "the Spanish half breeds and mestizos, and the native Indians live and thrive where white men die or live a wretched sickly existence." He was also firmly opposed to the

chaotic method of "tropical buccaneer wars" encouraged by "filibusterism."
At the same time, Squier was uncertain whether the region's current population, which he characterized as a "collection of negroes, mestizos, mulatoes
and renegades of all colors," could actually form a government there because
they lacked "political ideas, a sense of right, or notions of common humanity."[17] Republican colonization proposals absorbed the dire racial prognosis
of commentators such as Squier but attempted to recast it more positively.
Such proposals imagined that a more racially homogenous group of politically educated African Americans could effectively colonize and regenerate
the failed republicanism of this racially mixed region by infusing it with U.S.
institutions and commerce.[18]

Squier's writings not only attracted the interest of colonizationist politicians such as Blair but also appealed to commercially minded politicians
such as Robert Walker. Although Walker's support of Texas annexation and
his history of fervent expansionism would seem to make him a natural supporter of filibusters, during the 1850s he was far more interested in capturing
Central America through economic, rather than military, conquest. Walker
was among the investors who funded Squier's failed Honduran railway project, but he was equally interested in using former slaves to advance U.S. interests. Before he promoted President Lincoln's Central American colonization
policy, Walker, as James Polk's secretary of the treasury, lent his voice to the
1850 congressional debate about whether to federally fund a line of steamships carrying mail to Liberia. Although the steamship bill ultimately failed,
Walker's commercial case for the United States to develop its connections to
the recently independent Republic of Liberia and form a "new republican
empire on the shores of Africa" easily carried over to his interest in Central
American colonies a decade later.[19]

By the late 1850s the overlapping agendas of writers, businessmen, and
public officials such as E. G. Squier and Robert Walker had created a discourse
of political and economic speculation about Central America in which colonizationism could thrive as an alternative to the filibustering model. This
groundwork is evident in a *New York Tribune* editorial published six months
before Blair began to build public support for his colonization plans in Congress. The writer commented on a profilibustering article published in another
newspaper and agreed with its basic sentiment that "the negroes of the tropics are to play" a "very important part" in "the future of commerce and civilization" in Latin America because they were "perfectly well adapted to this
tropical climate." However, the writer disagreed with the idea that this future
involved enslaved African Americans because "if we did but know how to use

them and were willing to do so, [they would be] a most powerful and essential instrument toward extending ourselves, as it were—our ideas, our civilization, our commerce, industry and political institutions." According to the writer, they could successfully colonize Central America because they have become "black Americans just as we have become white Americans" by "adopt[ing] more and more our ideas, language, [and] habits" and taking "into their veins a constantly increasing portion of our Caucasian blood."[20] The editorial touched on many of the claims that would become foundational to colonization proposals in the next few years and illustrates how Central American racial commentary and economic boosterism easily lent themselves to colonizationist notions about spreading U.S. institutions abroad.

After more than a year of discussions with his father and other colleagues about a new Central American colonization policy, Blair took a public stand on the issue in early 1858.[21] He introduced a bill into Congress proposing that the United States acquire "territory either in the Central or South American states" for the purposes of colonizing African Americans. Blair argued that this plan would counteract the efforts of both southern slaveholders and British imperialists to dominate the region.[22] When Blair introduced the legislation, he had no illusions that it would actually pass in the immediate future. At the time, the president was James Buchanan, a Democrat largely opposed to colonizationism, and Congress featured an intractable southern faction who were opposed to any legislation that might cause an end to slavery. Nevertheless, Blair hoped his lengthy speech might serve as a platform for raising national awareness on the issue, and with this in mind he quickly turned it into a pamphlet to build public support.

Although Blair's bill made him the most prominent advocate of the plan, he was not the first congressman to raise the idea of sending U.S. settlers to Central America. A week before Blair introduced his colonization bill, Eli Thayer, a U.S. representative from Massachusetts, spoke in support of creating emigration companies to send Americans to the region. Like Blair, Thayer was a member of the Republican Party; however, unlike Blair, he was far more hostile to the institution of slavery and was most widely known for his role in organizing antislavery immigrants to settle in Kansas a few years earlier. Significantly, he spoke in support of Central American colonization during the debate on how the United States should address the unauthorized military interventions of William Walker in Nicaragua. Although Thayer condemned Walker, he noted that the discussion of filibusters had introduced "that great paramount, transcendent question, about which everybody is caring and nobody is speaking: 'How shall we Americanize Central America?'"

In Thayer's answer to this question, he framed it as a choice between Americanization through "conquest, by robbery, and violence" or "in accordance with the law of nations." He made a case for "organized emigration" of Americans into the region, similar to his prior expeditions, and compared it to the process by which settlers had recently colonized nearly "one State a year" in places such as Minnesota, Kansas, and Nebraska. Thayer claimed to be agnostic about whether such colonies might eventually be annexed to the United States, but he predicted that there was "no doubt we will have Central America," whether it be through creating affiliated republics populated by U.S. settlers or through the direct incorporation of the region as new U.S. territories.[23]

Although Thayer did not propose that these colonies should be composed of African American settlers, when Blair's plan was delivered to Congress a week later, there was a ready audience of politicians who were prepared to consider nonmilitaristic methods of "Americanization" in the Western Hemisphere. Thayer's support for large-scale emigration to Latin America dovetailed so well with Blair's efforts that he would later become associated with the Republican colonization proposals, even though he appears to have never publicly advocated for black colonies. Consequently, it is not surprising that two years after giving this speech, the New York Herald described the "free negro Central American colonization movement" as being "first broached by" both Frank Blair and Eli Thayer.[24]

After introducing the colonization bill in early 1858, Blair worked with his father to build support for the idea within national politics. This new colonization plan arrived at a time when the ACS had faded from view as a serious vehicle for the mass relocation of African Americans, even though many whites remained broadly supportive of its goals. Beyond this, Blair's plan was calibrated to address several interrelated issues that had been at the forefront of public discussion since the war between the United States and Mexico: the increasingly fraught question of whether slavery could be ended peaceably in the United States, the mounting anxiety about the racial consequences of U.S. expansion, and the widespread interest in exploiting Latin America economically. Blair's plan quickly found traction among politicians, businessmen, and newspaper editors, particularly in midwestern states where African colonization had recently played a significant role in legislative debates about black citizenship and settlement.

James Doolittle, a Republican senator from Wisconsin, would become Blair's most vocal political ally. Doolittle repeatedly discussed colonization proposals during Senate debates and sponsored a Senate resolution, which paralleled Blair's bill, calling on the president to begin negotiating with the

republics of Central America for potential sites. Although both Blair and
Doolittle introduced legislation on the topic, there was relatively little direct
discussion of their plans within either chamber of Congress. However, their
proposals did surface within the context of other issues concerning the future
course of U.S. expansionism, such as the filibustering campaigns of William
Walker, the questions of access to free-soil homesteads for white men raised
by Bleeding Kansas, and the contemplation of purchasing Cuba from Spain.[25]

Blair and Doolittle engaged in public and private advocacy campaigns
that helped convince several Republican senators and governors to join the
cause, including Sen. James Harlan and Gov. Samuel Kirkwood from Iowa;
Sen. Lyman Trumbull from Illinois; and Gov. William Dennison and Sen.
Benjamin Wade from Ohio. After Doolittle and Kirkwood wrote about the
growing support for colonization within their respective states, Frank Blair
enthusiastically reported to his father that "our plans are propagating and taking firm root in the minds of thinking men."[26] This outreach campaign led
some governors to pursue supportive state-level legislation in Illinois, Iowa,
and Ohio. Blair hoped that the cause could cross party lines, could somehow
be supported by both abolitionists and slaveholders, and would even broaden
support for the Republican Party in the South. Apparently aiming to attract
some moderate Democrats to the cause as well, the elder Blair reached out to
former Democratic president Martin Van Buren for his recollections of President Jackson's briefly discussed idea of supporting an African American colony in Mexico. Blair, Sr., believed that these historical references might help
"create a public opinion" in favor of his son's current efforts. Blair's plan also
attracted support from some abolitionists, such as Gerrit Smith and Theo-
dore Parker, who endorsed the idea despite the historical hostility between the
abolitionist and colonization movements. Frank Blair's brother, Montgomery,
optimistically claimed that Central American colonization plans could make
the Republican Party "as strong at the South as at the North" because it could
"define accurately our objects and disabuse the minds of the great body of the
southern people" of the idea "that the Republicans wish to set negroes free
among them to be their equals and consequently their rulers."[27]

Hemispheric Colonization

Without the institutional guidance of an organization like the ACS, the
Central American colonization proposals were primarily dominated by
those politicians who served as their most public advocates. Although Blair,

Doolittle, and other Republican senators and governors increasingly disseminated these ideas to their constituents, the debate over these colonies was far more top-down and narrow than earlier public discussions about African colonization. As a result, almost all recorded discussions about these ideas took place within congressional debates, public speeches, newspaper commentaries, or the private correspondence between politicians. Although these records reveal that proponents of Central American colonization had open-ended and vague ideas about the nature of the proposed settlements, the common themes of these proposals were firmly situated at the intersection between more than a half century of colonizationist thinking and the particular politics of U.S. expansionism during this period.

The tenacious persistence of colonizationist ideas helps explain why politicians and the public came to accept the new Central American proposals so rapidly. Liberia remained an inescapable frame of reference for the new wave of colonizationist politicians who oscillated between offering excessive praise for the republic and admitting that it had largely failed to achieve its goals. In Blair's initial congressional speech, he offered scant praise for Liberia and argued that despite the "best efforts of the best of men," the colony had been unable to successfully "spread civilization and religion over Africa." However, rather than dismiss it as a failed model of colonization, he blamed the African continent, which he declared "a desert, in which every effort to propagate the elements" of civilization had "proved failures."[28] Therefore, for Blair, the Central American colonies represented an opportunity to renew the squandered promise of Liberia in a region that would be apparently more hospitable to American ideals.

In pointing out Liberia's failures, Blair hoped to divert colonizationist energies toward a new region, but some of his allies continued to cite the republic as proof that Central American colonies could succeed. The prominent abolitionist Gerrit Smith wrote in support of Central American colonization by pointing out its Liberian precedent and noting that "for more than ten years Liberia has been a self governed community" with "the same liberty of speech and of the press, the same trial by jury, and the same representative institutions, and in the same perfection that we enjoy them."[29] James Harlan, a Republican senator from Iowa, supported Senator Doolittle's colonization plan by arguing that the United States should secure "a home and an abiding place" in Central America where black men could become citizens: "Let him there, as in the colony of Liberia, demonstrate to the world his capacity for self-government" where "[he could] build up for himself a country" that would be under "the temporary protection of the stars and stripes of the Union."[30] A *New York Evening Post* editorial expanded on these sentiments by arguing that the "sudden and violent changes of government which frequently occur in Hayti" were not necessarily "proof that the negro race are unfit to take care of themselves" but merely a reflection of the fact that "French slaves, if emancipated, will behave like Frenchmen" and "American slaves" would "behave like Americans." The writer went on to claim that "the government of Liberia" was "an instance of the success with which a community, when once put on the right track, follows out the principles of free government to their most fortunate conclusion." Ultimately, the writer argued that the "example of Liberia shows what we might expect, if Mr. Doolittle's project of colonizing some part of Central America with free blacks [succeeds] . . . a vigorous, orderly and even hardy generation of men."[31]

This sort of claim situated Liberian independence as the first act in a gendered racial drama that would be realized as a "vigorous" and "hardy" generation of black men settled and became citizens in Central American colonies. Employing a similar rhetoric, Frank Blair claimed that African Americans could "reinvigorate the feeble people of the Southern Republics." By representing the presumed failure of Latin American republicanism in the feminized terms, Blair drew on the colonizationist narrative of black masculine redemption and linked it to the redemption of republican manhood in the failed republics carved out of the Spanish empire. Employing tropes commonly used by Americans to demonize Latin America, Frank Blair viewed the Central American states as "feeble" or "corrupt" republics that had fallen into the hands of dictatorship by racially mixed rulers. The colonizationists contrasted their plans explicitly for Americanizing Latin America to slaveholder expansionism. Blair claimed that black settlers, capable of spreading U.S. republicanism, would act as a counterweight to the southern filibusters that would "subject those regions, in [William] Walker's own language, '*to military rule*'."[32] James Doolittle presented the colonization of the Americas by black settlers as being in opposition to the militarism of filibusters, arguing that "conquests are to be made by the victories of peace, rather than of arms." In countering the appeal of what historian Amy Greenberg has called the "martial manhood" symbolized by Walker's exploits, such appeals offered a gendered vision of expansionism that advanced a redemptive and mutually beneficial civic masculinity for both African Americans and the mestizo peoples of Latin America.[33]

Some colonizationists explained their proposals within the context of a "great battle of ideas" over imperial agendas for the Western Hemisphere. James Doolittle used such language when trying to convince Hannibal

Hamlin, then a Maine senator and soon to be Abraham Lincoln's running mate, by claiming that black colonies would "take away the temptation from the men of the South who lust after these countries" whose "grand project" was to "open the slave trade" and "seize all Central America" and control all the "cotton of the world."[34] Such rhetoric was compelling enough that it made its way into Ohio governor William Dennison's 1860 inaugural address in which he justified his advocacy for the colonization proposals in similar geo-political terms. He first outlined the evils of slaveholder expansionism in the tropics and then claimed that black colonies "would enable the United States to guaranty the liberty and independence of Mexico and Central America— give stability to their Republican Governments, and assume the high charac-ter on this continent, in very deed, which the Monroe doctrine announced as the duty of the nation."[35]

In connecting antifilibusterism to the Monroe Doctrine, Dennison, like other colonizationists, was positioning potential colonies as bulwarks against both slaveholder and European imperialism. Since the early 1840s, advocates of U.S. hemispheric expansion had often justified their policies by expressing growing concerns that British commercial dominance was actually an effort to colonize the region unofficially. Just as Anglophobia had helped drive the annexation of Texas, the conquest of Mexican territory, and the filibuster-ing campaigns, colonizationists now employed fear of British dominance to argue that black colonies would support the Monroe Doctrine vision of non-European intervention in the Americas.[36] Frank Blair argued that a "rivalry between England and the United States" was taking shape on the "shores of Central America" over how "to exert the command over that region; to peo-ple it, civilize it, give it peace; in a word, make it in some sort a dependency." He argued that Americans should seize this opportunity to assert the Western Hemisphere as the United States' domain because "Great Britain has her hands full in Christianizing, civilizing, and improving, for commercial usefulness, the old continents. She must leave to us the regeneration of the new one."[37]

By imagining that the proposed colonies would play an ongoing role in a regional imperial competition, colonizationists were explicitly investing them with far more strategic and commercial importance than they ever had given Liberia. In support of Doolittle's Senate plan, Gerrit Smith argued that while there was "no country in the world [that] has exhibited a union of liberty and law" more than Liberia, "the absence of trade and business renders Liberia anything but a desirable country to settle in."[38] Both Blair and Doolittle pushed the commercial angle consistently in their appeals, likely motivated by the fact that travel writers, businessmen, and filibusters had helped generate tremendous economic interest in Central America during the 1850s. Doolittle often argued that the area contained "the most productive regions of the whole earth," while Blair consistently claimed that colonies would "sustain free institutions under stable governments" that would inevitably help develop "the incredible riches of those regions" by opening "them to our commerce, and the commerce of the whole world."[39] While colonizationists occasionally employed these sorts of ostensibly altruistic free trade arguments, they consistently underscored the idea that these colonies would prevent other European powers from dominating the region, thus creating a tremendous advantage for the United States to tap into its unrealized potential. When Francis Blair, Sr., wrote to Pennsylvania senator Simon Cameron in order to convince him that the project was urgently important, he argued that the new colonies would "establish a foothold that might form a nucleus" and with "aid of our power" that part of the world could become "free yet subject to our influence."[40]

By suggesting that the contest for dominance in the Americas was a struggle between an established British empire and an ascendant U.S. empire, colonizationists began to sketch out an alternative framework for U.S. imperial presence in Central America. Since the United States' founding, the nation's expansion had been focused around the annexation of more territory that was directly incorporated into the settler state; however, the debates over the Mexican-American War and the postwar filibusters had increasingly begun to call into question this method of extending U.S. power. During the war with Mexico, some African colonizationists supporting the Whig antiwar position had directly contrasted the invasion of a sovereign Mexican republic through a militaristic war of expansion with the benevolent model of expansion exemplified by promoting the newly independent Liberian republic. A decade later, Central American colonizationists employed similar logic when presenting their plans as a distinct alternative to filibustering, laying the groundwork for an empire that theoretically required little or no military force, direct political oversight, or expectation of eventual annexation. Doolittle emphasized these arguments when writing to convince Hannibal Hamlin, claiming that this form of colonization was distinct from U.S. territorial expansion because it was "not for the purpose of annexing them as states, but to allow them to grow up into free states upon a footing of equality."[41] In public speeches Doolittle expanded on this sentiment by arguing that in avoiding military conquest "we shall gain all the benefits of annexation without the responsibility of governing millions of people differing in race, language, religion and customs from our own."[42] Frank Blair echoed this sentiment when he argued against the creation of an unwieldy and racially ungovernable empire, asserting that "we should avoid incorporating in the government the colored races of the South of us, but simply to extend our influence over them, so as to give them stability and make them subject to themselves and us."[43]

While Central American colonizationists seem to have been uniformly opposed to the direct annexation of these proposed colonies, they were keen to connect them rhetorically to the process of white settlers colonizing western territory within North America. Blair opened the lengthy speech on behalf of his original 1858 bill by arguing that his colonization plan, which featured racially segregated homesteading, could counteract slaveholders' efforts to simultaneously expand into Kansas and Central America. Other proponents of these colonies presented them as operating in direct parallel with white homesteaders who were then seizing territory from Native Americans and Mexican Americans in the West. In a debate over the admission of Oregon as a state, Preston King, a Republican senator from New York, harked back to the midwestern discussions of settler citizenship and African colonization from a few years earlier. King endorsed Oregon settlers' efforts to "have a homogenous white population, and to be free from the settlement of blacks among them" and then suggested that "the great body of the continent" be reserved for whites' "own race." He argued for an alternative homesteading process by which "the blacks" could establish a home in Central America "without interference with the whites."[44] Commenting in support of King's speech, the *New York Herald* framed it as a counterpoint to the white settler agenda of filibusters: "Gen. Walker has failed with his free white experiments, now why should not our free blacks be tried?"[45] King delivered this speech only a few months after Blair first introduced his colonization bill into Congress, suggesting that sympathetic politicians were ready to connect the new Central American colonization proposals to the questions of U.S. territorial colonization in North America. In the next few years, supporters of these colonies would often return to this concept of racial homesteading. Doolittle claimed, "We can give homes to our free colored men now treated as strangers and sojourners among us, in the territories of the tropics, as by a kindred policy we give home to our free white men in the Territories of the West."[46] In a similar vein, James Harlan advocated for Central American colonies in a speech about maintaining the white racial composition of "free soil" in U.S. territories while reserving a place "outside the United States within the tropics" where African Americans could "flourish and prosper."[47]

Such discussions linked colonizationism to the politics of Free Soilism, one of the foundational ideas of the Republican Party. For decades, free-soil ideology had developed within white settler communities as they incorporated themselves by excluding African Americans while tying their political fortunes to the settlement of a racially homogenous Liberian republic. By the late 1850s, colonizationist politicians were now shifting their focus back to the Western Hemisphere, after mostly abandoning it for nearly half a century in favor of the ACS agenda in Africa. As a result, colonizationists transitioned away from emphasizing the idea that Liberia was a symbolically important albeit far-removed reproduction of the U.S. settler republic toward explicitly arguing that African Americans and whites could be engaged in mutually reinforcing processes of colonization in the Americas. As in Liberia, these processes would complement each other by ensuring racially segregated settlement with the added benefits of fostering U.S. hemispheric dominance. This proved to be a powerful framework that served to revive the inchoate postrevolutionary notions about a segregated settler empire along with a more explicitly articulated agenda for racially separating these imagined political communities.[48]

The convergence between these visions of homesteading suggests that racial republicanism continued to play a foundational role in the new colonizationist plans of this era. Describing the convergence of race and politics in a letter to his brother, Frank Blair emphasized the "immense capacity for sustaining an industrious and hardy race of people, who will maintain our Republican government in all times to come."[49] Six months before Blair's colonization bill was introduced, a *New York Tribune* editorial speculated that "the great body of civilized negroes" within the United States are "a most powerful and essential instrument toward extending ourselves" into "all the American torrid zone."[50] This passing reference to the "American torrid zone" highlights the fact that the proposals for Central American colonies, like earlier appeals for African colonization, were often grounded in the claim that people of African descent were better suited to colonizing the region because they were biologically adapted to tropical climates. In particular, Frank Blair was obsessed with the way that climate connected to the "destiny of the races" in the Americas. Blair agreed with the popular conception of manifest destiny, which reserved North America for colonization by white Americans. However, he modified this notion by envisioning a parallel process by which the tropics would be governed by nonwhite races, a combination of African, Indian, and mestizo peoples, led by the influx of black colonists from the United States.[51] The stated goal of such separation was, as James Doolittle put it, to keep "our Anglo Saxon institutions as well as our Anglo Saxon blood pure and uncontaminated" while continuing to maintain a degree of control over the region.[52] If Doolittle's comments reveal how deeply racial thinking undergirded these proposals, they also highlighted how contradictory the implications of this type of thinking might be. By linking U.S. institutions to "Anglo Saxon blood," the question of how African Americans could be expected to reproduce those institutions in the racially mixed cultures of the tropics was unanswered.

For some supporters of these plans, the answer seemed to be that although popular racial thinking often characterized African Americans as the most inferior group, colonizationists presumed that they were, in fact, superior to most Latin Americans because of their supposed tutelage in U.S. political culture. Supporters often repeated the widespread belief that European intermixture with indigenous populations had led to a racial degeneracy that had doomed Latin American governments. Blair argued that the "African race" would constitute the basis for the "stable structure of free government" that would presumably reform the "insurrectionary disposition of the Indians and mestizos."[53] The *New York Tribune* pointed out that an "increasing portion of our Caucasian blood" made African Americans well suited for this task.[54] Gerrit Smith employed a similar argument when he claimed that African Americans should colonize "tropical regions" because "the triumph of Freedom in Kansas" against a proslavery government meant that "the great heart and centre of the North American Continent is to be colonized and occupied by the free Caucasian race." Echoing the concerns in the midwestern states from a decade earlier, Smith noted that "'Manifest destiny' points with unerring hand to the period when [North America] is to come under the direct control of the American Union and the question is daily growing in importance, by what class of our population shall it be colonized and occupied, and what institutions shall we plant on its fertile soil." He argued that colonizing Central America with a "laboring population" of "European origin" would be unsuitable, yet at the same time, the transplantation of a slave regime would be equally disastrous, leaving colonies of free African Americans to be the ideal solution.[55] While taking up the mantle of manifest destiny, Smith proposed that the dual colonization of the Americas by white and black settlers would ensure an end to slavery, separate the settlement processes by race, and encourage the spread of U.S. institutions and influence throughout the hemisphere without requiring direct political control.

The idea that the United States could institute a racially bifurcated vision of manifest destiny naturally raised the question of how black settlers would actually establish their versions of racial republicanism amid the existing populations and governments of Central America. Occasionally, colonizationists addressed this question of governance directly, particularly when they compared their plans to the military approach of filibusters. For instance, James Doolittle argued that, unlike William Walker, black colonists "will go, under our instrumentality, not to overturn the Government to which they emigrate."[56] However, other than drawing a sharp contrast between their plans and filibusters, most colonizationists preferred to vaguely speculate about how simply planting the colonies would somehow "transform" the region. They avoided confronting the reality of what it would mean to create colonies inside sovereign republics, an issue that would ultimately be central to their demise during the Civil War. Sometimes, colonizationists suggested that African Americans would serve as homesteaders creating their own separate settler states, while at other times they argued that Central America's mixed racial character would allow black migrants to "amalgamate" with local populations.[57] Regardless of the ambiguities and contradictions within these proposals, they presented an expansionist agenda that relied on and even harnessed sharp racial boundaries between white and nonwhite populations. These plans expanded on colonizationist racial republicanism to try to chart a course for U.S. expansion that was fundamentally organized around race but avoided making racial slavery or military conquest its central foundation.

Frank Blair, James Doolittle, and their many supporters championed a set of colonizationist ideas that were vague, provisional, and often incoherent. Nevertheless, a wide array of Republican politicians endorsed them, in part because they seemed to believe it was an issue that could resonate with the broader electorate. However, it is difficult to assess how the public truly judged these ideas. Like the earlier African colonization movement, the colonization plans of the late 1850s succeeded in attracting several high-profile supporters, but this did not lead to the creation of a formal organization to promote or coordinate these plans. For this reason, it was politicians themselves who instigated most of the public discussions of these ideas. Their goal was not to create a private movement to support the colony but rather to build political support among voters and other politicians for the idea that colonization could be a viable program for the federal government. At an early stage in promoting their plan, both Frank and his father Francis planned to extend their campaign to the broader public by soliciting favorable coverage of the idea from "newspapers and leading men."[58] This was apparently successful in Frank Blair's home state of Missouri, where dozens of favorable articles appeared in the state's leading newspaper, the *Missouri Democrat*.[59] The Blairs expanded the scope of this campaign by attracting interest from such figures as the influential Buffalo journalist William Dorsheimer, and the famous editor of the *New York Tribune*, Horace Greeley. As a result of Blair's congressional legislation and the active campaigning of both father and son, several newspaper articles extensively covered the topic in the last years of the 1850s.[60]

Frank Blair hoped that colonization would become a major campaign issue in the 1860 presidential election. Highlighting the commercial emphasis of his colonizationist pitch, he delivered speeches to several mercantile societies in growing midwestern cities such as Cincinnati and Saint Paul, as well as larger East Coast cities such as Boston and New York, to drum up support among important elite, business-oriented audiences.[61] Some of these speeches were then edited and published as pamphlets that were distributed to the public.[62] Blair used these speeches and publications to engage "the whole nation as an audience" by "bring[ing] out more strongly the commercial advantages of the colonization of our negroes in Central America."[63] After Illinois senator Lyman Trumbull made a series of speeches in support of the colonization proposals, Blair received several positive responses from the public, showing that it had the potential to be a winning issue for some voters. One of Trumbull's constituents claimed that the colonization plan "meets not only my views but of this part of the State I think it meets the views of all parties."[64] Another writer claimed widespread and solid support for colonization within his local area and asked Trumbull to continue speaking on the subject "especially to the people. We will sustain you." He argued, "It is the key of the whole question. The exclusion of slavery from the territories is only an incidental part of a general policy of which colonization is the corner stone."[65] Such responses reveal how state-level antiblack settlement efforts continued to exert influence on the logic of Free Soilism, a foundation on which Montgomery Blair believed Republicans could build colonization plans into an national issue. He claimed, "If our northern [governors] would come up boldly to the work and say that the policy of casting out free negroes" to somewhere they could have "political rights" would allow them to realize "their manhood," it "would rally the north as one man to our ranks."[66] Frank Blair optimistically asserted that he felt "satisfied that [the colonization plan] will make the best popular issue" on which the Republican Party could advance its national political goals, contending that there was not a line "of attack which cannot be defended before any class of people."[67]

By 1860 a group of key Republican politicians supported the colonization proposals, and many were eager to make them a more integral feature of party policy. After the prominent Ohio senator Benjamin Wade endorsed the idea of making Central American colonization one of the key Republican campaign issues in 1860, the *New York Herald* concurred with this approach, arguing that it would allow the Republicans to "be able successfully to parry the democratic electioneering clap trap that the republican programme comprehends the full recognition of 'negro equality.' "[68] At the Republican national convention several party members voiced their support for colonization proposals and nominated Abraham Lincoln, a longtime African colonizationist. Ultimately, the party did not formally elevate colonization policy to the status of an official plank within its 1860 platform, but this did not stop Republican politicians from promoting the idea over the course of the campaign.[69] Writing to a Wisconsin newspaper editor a few days after the convention, James Doolittle enthusiastically claimed that "our next President . . . will be elected on a colonization platform."[70] The particulars of party platform aside, the Republicans came to power in 1860 while offering the most explicit endorsement of a federal colonization policy since Henry Clay's failed efforts of the early 1830s. Therefore, the election marked a turning point for the fortunes of colonizationists, even as the course of the Civil War would sow the seeds of demise for colonization sentiment.

The Last Gasp of Colonizationism

Despite winning power in 1860, the Republicans' reluctance to make colonization a more central campaign theme deflated the optimism of some of its advocates. In a letter to his father, Frank Blair described support for the program to be "threadbare," but he held out hope that the growing secessionist movement might "incline men to listen."[71] As it turned out, Blair's suspicions proved to be prescient; within a year, Republicans would begin to revive the idea amid a backdrop of national civil war. Although the war proved to be a powerful catalyst for setting plans into motion, politicians continued to sell the colonization program on the grounds that it could advance a particular vision of U.S. expansion. When addressing colonizationism during this period, scholarly debates have tended to focus on Abraham Lincoln's political motivations and personal thinking about race, but historians have given less attention to how the policies themselves engaged with long-term debates about the scope and character of U.S. empire.[72] The Lincoln administration's colonization plans maintained continuity with those developed in the late 1850s by emphasizing the overlapping goals of racial separation and securing economic domination within the Western Hemisphere by fostering sympathetic republican governments. These proposals advanced a far more explicit imperial agenda than the African colonization movement while building on the long-held colonizationist notion that the United States could reproduce racial republicanism abroad.

The circumstances of war spurred the Republicans' unprecedented push to create the first true federal colonization policy since the aborted efforts in the early 1830s. In July 1861 President Lincoln adopted a policy of freeing slaves who had crossed over into Union lines. By late in the year, this had created a sizable group of freed slaves, defined as war "contraband," who were under federal supervision. Amid questions over the ultimate fate of these former slaves, President Lincoln publicly resurrected colonization plans in his December 1861 annual message to Congress. In this statement he suggested that Congress should appropriate money for purchasing territory for the purpose of colonizing both "contraband" former slaves as well as other free African Americans. On the surface, his immediate aim was to address the issue of the slaves who had come under federal control; however, his inclusion of free black populations in the proposed program suggests that he was already laying the groundwork for a more expansive federal colonization program.[73] This may have reflected Lincoln's desire to appeal to the Upper South by offering a method for potentially ending slavery in a way that would be acceptable to moderate leaders within the region. Lincoln could have also been motivated by his long-held admiration for colonizationism and his previously stated position that African Americans could never achieve political and social equality with whites in the United States.

Regardless of Lincoln's personal motivations, both his administration and Congress rapidly pursued a course of action that was directly in line with the new set of colonizationist arguments that Republicans had popularized in the preceding few years. Congress debated federal colonization policy as part of two bills introduced in 1862: one aimed at emancipating slaves in the District of Columbia, and another, the so-called Confiscation Act, that could punish treasonous Confederates with the emancipation of their contraband slaves. A significant number of congressional colonizationists advocated for voluntary rather than forced removal of emancipated slaves by framing the argument for colonization in the broader terms of U.S. expansionism that had been laid out before the onset of war. Supporters of a voluntary scenario presumed that former slaves would migrate to Central America in a way that would ensure both the mutual benefit of their colonies and the United States, a goal that might be undermined by employing harsh methods of deportation. Senators Lyman Trumbull and James Doolittle maintained their roles as primary advocates of colonies, but they would quickly be joined by a number of new adherents. One such supporter was James McDougall, a senator from California, who similarly argued for the colony on economic grounds, noting that he was not in favor of supporting colonization in Liberia, "a country to which we have scarcely any communication or business," but he did support one in Central America, which "is on the line of a large trade carried on by this Government with the Gulf of Mexico, and with Mexico."[74]

The final version of the Washington, D.C. emancipation bill included a colonization clause, but the scope of any broader program remained a contentious issue. Senators such as James McDougall, who had supported colonization of D.C. slaves partially on commercial grounds, believed that the more comprehensive colonization program outlined in the confiscation bill represented an overreach of federal power.[75] In response to such critics, colonizationist stalwarts such as James Doolittle claimed that these colonies could help promote a national agenda of global economic expansion and were therefore firmly within the purview of the federal government. In contrast to the vagueness of many earlier proposals, Doolittle outlined fairly specific plans for the proposed settlements and argued that the United States should negotiate treaties that would carve out legal space for the colonies in the existing nations of Central America.[76] These would allow settlers to maintain low duties for the products they exported with no tariffs for the importation of American products, thus, in essence, fully integrating the colonies into the United States' commercial empire. The question of colonial governance was left to negotiation between the black colonists and their host nations. By July 1862 the House and Senate had passed a reconciled version of the confiscation bill, which reflected the degree to which Congress had come to endorse this basic framework for the colonization program. The House report on the bill emphasized this point by spending much of its time dwelling on the commercial potential for Central American colonies and only minimally addressing the prospects of other potential settlement locations. The report also endorsed the key theme that black colonies served as a contrast to filibusters, which it claimed had attempted to "include [Central American republics] in an empire to be founded on the slavery of the colored races." Instead, it claimed that black colonies would "place the United States at the head of a grand confederacy of American republics" and "restore the good feeling and confidence" and "confer commercial advantage" without the "trouble and expense of armies to hold and protect" colonies that burdened the British empire.[77]

Although the bill's passage meant that Congress had now explicitly endorsed a notably imperialist framework for Central American colonizationism, legislators did so with the knowledge that President Lincoln had already been working for more than a year to lay the groundwork for such plans. Lincoln did not have the full support of his cabinet when he first began seriously discussing colonization proposals in the fall of 1861. Lincoln's secretary of state, William Seward, generally opposed the idea, while other cabinet members provisionally supported it on the basis of its potential geopolitical significance. For instance, Lincoln's secretary of the treasury, Salmon P. Chase, had never strongly supported colonization schemes but advised the president that he was in favor of the plan because it could mean "getting a foothold in Central America."[78] A similar attitude prevailed at the Department of the Interior, which was the federal agency Lincoln ultimately tasked with overseeing the colonization program. Neither of Lincoln's secretaries of the interior, Caleb Smith and John Usher, had previously expressed interest in colonization proposals but now became strong advocates for them primarily on economic and strategic grounds.[79]

Given the fact that the president, some of his advisers, and several members of Congress were interested in the prospect that colonies could secure an imperial advantage for the United States, it is not surprising that when the Lincoln administration began to pursue Central American colonization plans, they initially hoped to tap into the energies of American businessmen who were already planning or operating ventures throughout the region. This is best exemplified by the administration's ill-fated plan to create a colony in the Chiriquí province of Panama. While Lincoln would go on to consider a wide range of colonization proposals during his first years in office, Chiriquí is arguably the most important. This was not only one of the first proposals that Lincoln seriously entertained and devoted significant resources toward; it also spoke directly to the climate of U.S. business speculation, which had fostered the imperialist reinvention of colonizationism in recent years. Negotiations over Chiriquí began when Caleb Smith initiated discussions with Ambrose W. Thompson, an American entrepreneur, about the possibility of planting a black colony on territory to which he had acquired rights during the 1850s.[80] Thompson was a Philadelphia businessman who had become wealthy as a shipbuilder and trader, but his interest in Chiriquí coincided with the growth of U.S. attention to Panama as Americans sought more efficient routes to the West Coast following the California gold rush.[81] Thompson acquired claims to the Chiriquí territory when it was part of the politically volatile Republic of New Grenada. Over the course of decades of recurrent civil war, this territory would transition into becoming the Granadine Confederation in 1858, the United States of Colombia in 1863, and, by the end of the nineteenth century, the Republic of Colombia. U.S. negotiations over Thompson's tenuous land claim were further complicated by the fact that competing factions claimed diplomatic representation for the Colombian state for a period of time, and that part of the Chiriquí province was located on disputed territory bordering Costa Rica.[82]

Thompson's pursuit of a black colony in Chiriquí was a result of his previously failed efforts to convince the federal government to support his Central American commercial ventures. In 1854 he formed the Central American Mining Company in conjunction with several business partners, but shortly thereafter all but Thomson left the project. In 1857 he reorganized the company as the Chiriqui Improvement Company after securing a large land concession from the Republic of New Grenada. Thompson hoped to create a multifaceted business venture that would include serving as a carrier of U.S. mail for steamships, facilitating free travel across the land with the proposed railway, and aiding the U.S. navy by providing coaling stations. He attempted to raise capital for this company by securing contracts with the federal government, and in 1859 President James Buchanan initially agreed to pursue a $300,000 subsidy for the enterprise.[83] However, the deal fell apart when several congressmen and Buchanan's own attorney general voiced their concerns that Thompson did not have proper legal title to the land, had made inflated claims about the coal deposits and transit potential of the area, and lacked clear consent from the Republic of New Grenada.[84] In the summer of 1861 President Lincoln received a new proposal from Thompson that blended his earlier plans for economic development with the geopolitical objectives favored by Republican colonizationists. Although Thompson's proposal would attract considerable federal support and eventually economic resources, he was merely one among dozens of such merchants, land developers, and railroad or canal promoters who attempted to parlay their landholdings or political connections in Central America into federal contracts when they became aware of the government's colonization plans.[85]

To assess the feasibility of Thompson's proposal, Lincoln turned to one of the key architects behind the push for Central American colonization, Francis Blair, Sr. Not surprisingly, Blair heartily endorsed the Chiriquí colony and framed its significance in strategic terms, comparing it to Britain's use of commercial treaties to gain a foothold in its "East Indian Empire." While suggesting that black colonies could similarly help the United States build up its own global empire, Blair specifically endorsed the plan on the grounds that it would spread republicanism to the "whole barbarous region," predicting that "Chiriqui may be made the pivot on which to rest our lever to sway Central

America and secure for the free states on this Continent the control which is deemed necessary for the preservation of our Republican Institutions." On the advice of Blair and other Republican colleagues, the president pushed forward with the plan in late 1862, signing a contract that made provisions for founding a black colony on the territory and supplying coal to the U.S. Navy. He appointed Samuel Pomeroy, a U.S. senator from Kansas, to organize supplies and shipping vessels for the project.[86]

While Thompson's Chiriquí proposal progressed far enough to secure a federal contract, during this period the Lincoln administration entertained a wide range of proposals by U.S. entrepreneurs who had transportation, mining, or agricultural interests throughout the Americas. Although President Lincoln looked to recruit U.S. businessmen who were prepared to become partners in a colonization plan, he also asked William Seward to pursue regional support for colonies through diplomatic channels. During the year leading up to the passage of the colonization bills and negotiations over Chiriquí, President Lincoln dispatched various diplomats and members of his administration to engage in discussions with several Latin American governments. At this early stage, many of the governments proved to be remarkably receptive, and several leaders expressed the hope that black colonists might serve as a critical labor force in those portions of their nations that they wished to develop. Throughout late 1861 and early 1862 Montgomery Blair, then serving as Lincoln's postmaster general, corresponded with Matías Romero, a Mexican diplomat, about creating a colony somewhere on the Yucatán Peninsula.[87] During this same period, various U.S. diplomats were in contact with the presidents of Guatemala, Honduras, and Costa Rica about planting settlements within their national borders. Rafael Carrera, president of Guatemala, even raised the possibility that one of his personal land claims in the country could be used as a site for the colony.[88]

As President Lincoln negotiated with both Latin American governments and U.S. businessmen, he also attempted to secure support from black communities in the United States. In August 1862, a month after Congress passed the bill that laid the groundwork for a federal colonization program, Lincoln presented his preliminary plans to some African American leaders in a famous White House meeting. This event held crucial significance because northern black leaders had largely resisted colonization proposals for nearly a half century; therefore, their support would be critical to the success of any large-scale effort.[89] White supporters of Central American colonization believed that African Americans were more likely to embrace this destination than Liberia, a nation still tainted by its toxic association with the ACS. The

House of Representatives' report on the colonization bill cited the fact that during the prior decade, some black political conventions and black leaders had already endorsed colonies in Central America.[90]

With this in mind, Lincoln planned the meeting in an effort to mobilize this latent sentiment and build black support for the administration's colonization program. In the meeting, Lincoln argued that African Americans should not be "selfish" by remaining in the United States and should "sacrifice" for the mutual benefit of both races because it was impossible for whites and African Americans to live as equals in the United States. He also attempted to convince them that they were assured prosperity in Central America because "unlike Liberia it is on a great line of travel—it is a highway."[91] While this economic and strategic pitch had been successful in rallying white politicians to endorse the idea, Lincoln's invitation for African Americans to participate in a hemispheric U.S. empire was unable to attract widespread black support. In many ways this failure stemmed from the event being positioned more as a publicity campaign than a genuine effort to solicit input from black communities on the subject of colonization. Lincoln used a stenographer to records his words before the delegation, and shortly after the meeting they were distributed to the press and rapidly reproduced in the nation's newspapers. These officially sanctioned reports of the event attempted to amplify its significance by making the false claim that this was the first time Lincoln had met with any black leaders in the White House.[92]

The circumstances surrounding this meeting illustrate the complexity of black debates over emigrationism in the Civil War era. The mounting national crisis over slavery in the 1850s had caused several free African Americans to consider the possibility of leaving the United States, and the rapidly evolving conditions created by the war helped foster renewed interest, aided by the prospect of federal colonization policy. At the same time, most black abolitionists reemphasized the need to renounce emigrationism based on the prospect that war was opening the possibility of a more comprehensive emancipation within the United States. After President Lincoln made it known that he desired a meeting on the subject, some black residents of Washington, D.C., held a meeting to select a delegation. The group included five black ministers who were seemingly chosen for their stature within important local congregations. Far from being obviously receptive to the idea, some of these ministers were actually members of the Social Civil and Statistical Association (SCSA), an organization composed of elite black Washingtonians who made public arguments on behalf of black citizenship rights and vociferously argued against colonizationism.[93]

Despite the presence of such skeptical members, the fact that the local churches decided to send a delegation to a meeting on the subject of federal colonization policy demonstrates that there was, perhaps, a sizable minority of black residents who at least wanted to hear out the president's proposal. This seems to be borne out by the fact that in the months after the meeting, despite overwhelming negative publicity in the black public sphere, government colonization agents claimed that thousands of free African Americans had volunteered to emigrate to Chiriquí, an expedition that would ultimately never materialize.[94]

Although one leader of the delegation sent a private letter of support, as a body the group never issued a formal response to the president. Ultimately, the event became defined by both the public protests of northern black communities and the hostility of the abolitionist press. These tensions over the committee immediately became apparent as black residents of Washington, D.C., organized a protest meeting against the colonization plan shortly after Lincoln's words became public, and the organizers explicitly discouraged the presence of the black ministers at the meeting because, as reported by *Baltimore Sun*, they felt the delegation had "exceeded their instructions."[95] As details of the event became public, other black abolitionists criticized the idea that such a small local delegation would be presumed to represent the will of a large and diverse collection of northern black communities, let alone the millions of enslaved peoples in the South. When Frederick Douglass read the transcripts of the meeting, he used his prominent voice to renew his steadfast opposition to colonization proposals. Douglass's newspaper published a scathing condemnation of the proposal, noting the long-standing relationship between colonizationism and violence against black communities. Pointing to recent attacks in the North, it noted that "colonization gives life and vigor to popular prejudice, gives it an air of philosophy, piety and respectability, and the violence of the mob, gives the facts to sustain their pious negro hating theories."[96]

Outside of Washington, D.C., the sizable black communities of Philadelphia and New York City convened large meetings to denounce the inherent racism of the plan. Many black critics emphasized their long-standing argument that African Americans possessed an inherent right to remain in the United States, but others focused on attacking the more recent justifications for colonization. A black correspondent to the *Liberator* scathingly denounced the idea that African Americans might serve a dismal utilitarian role within U.S. imperial strategy. In doing so, he exposed how colonizationists drew false equivalencies between black and white homesteaders by wryly satirizing the president's claim to embody American free enterprise through his own biography as a self-made man who settled the Illinois frontier: "But, say you 'Coal land is the best thing I know of to begin an enterprise.' Astounding discovery! . . . Twenty-five Negroes digging coal in Central America! Mighty plan! Equal to about twenty-five Negroes splitting rails in Sangamon [Illinois]!"[97] Such a vociferous response to Lincoln's proposal shows that even if a viable colony had resulted, it would have faced significant resistance from well-organized northern free black communities that were essential for realizing the goals of any federal colonization effort.

Shortly after President Lincoln received this negative response from black leaders, he faced an even more formidable obstacle as it became increasingly apparent that several Central American nations were determined to actively resist any form of U.S. colony. While widespread racism against peoples of African descent helped mobilize opposition to the plans within several of these nations, there is even more evidence to suggest that their political leaders were far more preoccupied with the idea that such a colony would infringe on their political authority and invite further U.S. expansion into the region.[98] This reaction illustrates the fatal flaw of colonization plans for Central America, namely, that U.S. politicians had failed to consider questions about the sovereignty of existing governments while blithely promoting new black republics in them. In early 1862 Matías Romero backed away from the Yucatán proposal, citing his suspicion that it cloaked an agenda of U.S. expansionism, and soon after other nations began to follow. In the summer of 1862 colonization proposals received a wave of bad press in several Central American newspapers, particularly as they publicized U.S. colonizationists' imperialist agenda. Following extensive regional discussions about the nature of U.S. intentions for the colonies, Tomás Martínez, the president of Nicaragua, led an effort to convince other countries to reject all manifestations of U.S. settlement collectively.[99]

Even more than the United States' presumed economic designs, Central American citizens objected to the idea that the United States would maintain some form of ongoing political relationship with the proposed colonies. The negative coverage was capped off by the publication of Lincoln's August speech to the delegation of black leaders promising them continuing U.S. "protection." This struck many Central American observers as presumptuous, given that no governments had reached formal agreements with the United States that would have carved out the kind of quasi-sovereignty that Lincoln suggested for the colonies. While the previous years of public discussions in the United States reveal considerable ambiguity about precisely what relationship U.S. colonizationists envisioned, the notion that such a colony might threaten the sovereignty of any host state touched a nerve in a region where William Walker's exploits remained a fresh memory. A U.S. diplomat on the ground in Nicaragua attested to "much anxiety . . . by the people of this country" concerning colonization, asserting that "their opposition seems to be deep-rooted and strong." A Guatemalan minister noted that Mexico had suffered dire consequences when it had invited the Americans to colonize Texas several decades earlier. Although the colonization plans had a different rhetorical emphasis than the militarist filibusters, Latin Americans recognized that seemingly benign intentions could also have a disastrous effect by eroding regional sovereignty.[100]

Increasingly armed with a powerful set of anti-imperialist arguments, the governments of Central America quickly demonstrated remarkable unity in resisting any U.S. colonies. In September 1862 Luis Molina, a Costa Rican foreign minister stationed in Washington, D.C., was enlisted to represent the governments of Costa Rica, Nicaragua, and Honduras in their opposition to potential black colonies. In a letter to Seward, Molina forcefully condemned the idea that colonists would attempt to settle the Chiriquí province without the consent of people within the region. Invoking the United States' own policies against such an action, he characterized it as a violation of the Monroe Doctrine principle that the Americas should not be "colonized by any foreign power."[101]

After this trio of countries joined El Salvador and Mexico in the coalition of Central American republics opposing black colonies, only New Grenada, a country in the midst of civil war and riven by tenuous and competing political authorities, remained nominally receptive to the idea. However, Molina even questioned New Grenada's ability to dispose of the Chiriquí territory. He informed William Seward that this land was entangled in a territorial dispute and that "there is not an inch of ground on the isthmus of Chiriqui which does not belong either to Costa Rica or to New Granada."[102] As the diplomatic pressure from Central America began to threaten the viability of the Chiriquí plan, Lincoln's administration began to change course. By early October 1862 Secretary Seward had received months of negative diplomatic responses, and he advised President Lincoln to stop actively pursuing colonies in Central America. Lincoln agreed with this course of action.[103]

The growing diplomatic fallout was only one of the many factors that doomed the prospect of the Chiriquí colony. Renewed black opposition to colonizationism and mismanagement of the project by both Pomeroy and Thompson raised questions about the viability of the enterprise. Of course, this failure to plant a racial republic in Central America did not mean the end of Lincoln's colonization policy. His administration would continue to pursue other proposals throughout 1863 and 1864, the two most prominent being a small island settlement off Haiti's coast called Île-à-Vache and another in modern-day Belize, then the colony of British Honduras. Both efforts came to very little, as the Île-à-Vache expedition ended disastrously for the small group of settlers who attempted to found the colony, and the planned settlement in British Honduras never moved much beyond back-channel diplomatic discussions. Like the Central American governments, both Haitian leaders and British colonial officials were interested in using colonists as a new source of labor; however, the later colonies were notably different from the earlier colonization efforts. Although the Île-à-Vache scheme was similarly organized around an American businessman's economic plans for cotton production, Haiti was a proudly independent black republic that offered little prospect that a small and isolated American settlement off its coast would lead to U.S. domination of the nation's politics. Moreover, it offered far fewer of the economic and strategic advantages that many politicians presumed would come with quasi-independent settlements in Central America. In the case of British Honduras, the settlement would be located within a British crown colony that had been created, in large part, to establish a British imperial foothold in the Western Hemisphere. Thus, British leaders were very unlikely to accept a black colony that might threaten their control of that possession, let alone strengthen the United States' position in the region, the stated goal of most U.S. colonizationists during this period.[104]

Therefore, Lincoln's virtual abandonment of colonization projects in the independent Latin American states signified a shift toward scaling back ambitions for creating racial republics that would help shape the Western Hemisphere in the United States' image. This reflected a long-standing tension within the broader colonization movement in which domestic goals, such as removing African Americans from the United States or bringing an end to slavery, competed with foreign objectives, such as ending the slave trade, opening avenues for commerce, and spreading U.S. political institutions. The former set of objectives had tended to dominate discussion during the early years of the movement; since Liberian independence the latter had come to be increasingly important, but by the Civil War era the two goals had begun to assume nearly equal weight in colonizationist rhetoric. This tension was evident within the Lincoln administration's own fragmented colonization policy. The president initially favored some of the more explicitly imperialist arguments for colonization, as it had become an increasingly popular position within his party and one advocated by both of his secretaries of the interior. However, Lincoln sought a countervailing voice when he appointed James Mitchell to run the emigration office that was tasked with coordinating his administration's various colonization projects.

As a former organizer for the ACS, Mitchell was a veteran of the more domestically focused discussions about colonization in the Midwest. He had previously run the Indiana State Board of Negro Colonization in the 1850s, the body formed by that state's constitutional mandate to create a colonization program. These experiences led Mitchell to view colonization primarily as a means to end slavery and remove free black populations from the United States, rather than having any ancillary geopolitical goals. This view often put him at odds with the Department of the Interior and led to institutional disputes that characterized the general disarray of Lincoln's colonization program. While this bureaucratic conflict exemplifies the ongoing push and pull between the domestic and foreign aims of colonization policies, the two ideals were clearly interwoven and emphasized alternately depending on the context. This was evident when both Montgomery and Francis Blair, Sr., two men deeply responsible for reimagining colonizationism through an explicitly imperialist lens, shifted their support in favor of the Île-à-Vache colony when the Chiriquí plan began to look increasingly tenuous. While Chiriquí almost perfectly embodied the Blairs' template for a colonization program, in the end its broader imperial objectives could be jettisoned in favor of a program that seemed to have a better chance to actually remove African Americans from the United States, a goal they both felt was essential if white racial republicanism was to succeed in the absence of slavery.[105]

While Lincoln's administration would persist in pursuing smaller-scale colonization efforts until late in the war, the Central American governments' rebuke of the earlier proposals undermined the vision of hemispheric transformation embodied in Republicans' recent efforts to repurpose the colonizationist racial republic. That vision had relied on a fantasy that black settlers could be made into quasi-independent subjects within an expansive U.S. empire. While this had always been a minor theme within colonization proposals dating back to the Revolutionary era, it had grown to take on greater significance during the years leading up to the Civil War. However, the United States was rapidly confronted with the limits of that vision precisely because these motivations were clear to the people of Central America.

*   *   *

For more than a half century, white-led efforts to create black colonies were a recurring feature of U.S. political culture, yet the demise of the Lincoln administration's colonization plans represented both a high point and an endpoint for the colonization movement. After the Civil War, few white politicians would ever again publicly support colonization proposals in any serious way. Despite this denouement, the brief success of Central American colonizationism reveals fundamental transformations around race and U.S. expansion. Examined through the lens of these colonization proposals, the concept of manifest destiny functioned more as an open-ended set of ideas about U.S. expansion than a stable or coherent ideology. Historians have generally associated the filibustering campaigns of the 1850s closely with manifest destiny because they were largely an extension of the United States' efforts to build a continental empire during the first half of the nineteenth century, an impulse that had often been driven by those who wished to expand the reach of slavery. But the proponents of black colonies in Central America could lay equal claim to the legacy of manifest destiny. For them, this concept was not defined by the goals of annexation or expanding slavery but was a broader assertion of the United States' right to control territory, resources, and peoples far beyond its own borders. The House report accompanying the 1862 colonization bill made precisely this point when it argued that "'manifest destiny'" had been "perverted to the purposes" of filibusters and had become "so detestable" that it now required "a higher and nobler interpretation" provided by the spread of black republics into the tropics.[106]

Filibusters and colonizationists drew from a common reservoir of ideas, yet they often advanced different destinies for the future of U.S. imperialism. In the near term, both efforts to redefine manifest destiny would fail, but over the next century many colonizationist ideas would survive as part of the ethos of U.S. expansionism. Just as black colonists were tasked with shaping the peoples of Central America, the United States would increasingly encourage the spread of U.S. republicanism to other nonwhite peoples around the world. The racial republics such efforts sought to foster were often designed to become proxy states that would advance U.S. global interests. In this way, they would follow the Liberian model defined by one African colonizationist as "independent" yet "American in feeling, language, and interests" in order to serve as an "extension of American influence, trade and commerce."[107]

This reflects the United States' gradual move away from settler colonialism as the dominant strain of U.S. expansionism. While the United States would continue to colonize the North American continent by displacing indigenous populations, settler colonialism would play a less important role as the United States began to test new strategies aimed at managing an increasingly global empire. The beginning of this transformation was already evident in the Central American colonization plans. After nearly a half century of advocating for a black colony in Africa, colonizationists returned to the idea of planting colonies in the Western Hemisphere. At the turn of the nineteenth century, Americans had rejected similar colonies because they threatened the cohesion of the white settler state. By the 1850s a much larger and more powerful U.S. empire had violently asserted its sovereignty over a vast swath of the continent. And yet U.S. citizens remained ambivalent about settling parts of the world that contained large nonwhite populations, and therefore the plans for Central American colonies focused less on how to settle these regions and more on how they would be managed. In this way, the ideas of the African colonization movement had already contributed to developing a rhetoric of U.S. global power that would persist long after the end of colonizationism.

The Racial Geography of
America's Imperial Future

In the summer of 1862 President Abraham Lincoln signed a bill into law that established official diplomatic relations with the Republics of Haiti and Liberia. It was fitting that these two nations would be paired together at this moment. Against the Civil War backdrop of hundreds of thousands of enslaved people seizing their freedom in ways that would profoundly shape the United States' future, the nation's leaders formally reevaluated its relationship with two black republics: one forged through a slave insurrection and the other created to avoid it.[1] That the recognition of these nations had been deferred so long also spoke to a simple fact: since its founding, the United States had officially refused to concede that people of African descent could govern themselves. With slaveholding interests now largely absent from the federal government, Congress and the president were finally willing and able to recognize these long-denied nations.[2] The bill also passed during the United States' last significant effort to advance colonizationism. In a few short years, the end of the war and the efforts of enslaved people themselves to transform its emancipatory outcome would largely put to rest an idea around since the creation of the United States.[3] The circumstances of the bill's passage, during the last gasp of both slavery and colonizationism, speak to its profound implications for the evolving racial geography of the United States' empire.

The ensuing congressional debate on the subject demonstrated that an ongoing war over the future of domestic slavery contained within it a battle over how race would play into the United States' international agenda following the war. While Lincoln called on Congress to recognize these nations in the middle of his early push for a federal colonization program, it was actually a Radical Republican skeptic of colonization, the Massachusetts senator

Charles Sumner, who introduced the bill in Congress. Recognizing the tenuous coalition of abolitionist and colonizationist constituencies within his party, Sumner's decision to pair these two nations was likely premised on attracting the support of both groups.[4] The tense antislavery politics surrounding the bill are evident in the fact that most members of Congress who spoke in support of the legislation studiously avoided discussing either slavery or the racial composition of the two republics. When introducing the bill to the Senate, Sumner furnished extensive economic data purportedly showing that the United States was already engaged in substantial commercial relations with both nations, far exceeding that of many European states with which the United States had diplomatic relations. He accompanied this with anecdotal evidence from both countries suggesting that this economic activity could be expanded even further if the United States normalized relations with the countries. Sumner's subtext seemed to be that the United States' irrational policy toward both nations had damaged its prospects for leveraging these trade advantages to their fullest extent.[5]

Speaking on behalf of the House version of the bill, William D. Kelley, a representative from Pennsylvania, expanded on Sumner's pitch by linking Liberia's importance as a trading partner to its potential for improving on the United States' model of settler colonization in North America. Kelley noted that the nation was a republic "which has grown as the American colonies did not grow" because European colonists faced a "savage and hostile people," while Liberian settlers find a "loving but degraded people to absorb and elevate." In his estimation, this would lead to the nation's continued success as "year by year, the limits and influence of that republic have been extended, and they will continue to extend." Promising a tremendous advantage for the United States in West Africa, he predicted that in "a few generations . . . commercial relations with the republic of Liberia [will have] grown to a magnitude and importance of the leading nations of the world."[6]

Proponents of recognition expressed these exuberant forecasts within the context of anxious imperial competition. Kelley argued that while the bill was nominally about establishing "proper international relations" with two countries, it was more fundamentally about how the United States could help secure "adequate supplies of raw materials" for American "factories and workshops" in order to counteract the British, a "powerful commercial rival."[7] In a similar vein, Congressman Robert McKnight observed that trade with Liberia was already being "rapidly seized and appropriated by England," and the United States' nonrecognition of Haiti put its trade with the nation "far behind the monarchies of Europe."[8] For many in Congress, the United States' failure to establish normalized relations with Haiti and Liberia represented an abdication not only of its republican principles but also, and perhaps more importantly, its potential strategic advantages as a global empire.

Following the lead of the Central American colonizationists from the late 1850s, in recent years the ACS had increasingly begun to advance similar arguments in support of diplomatic recognition. John H. B. Latrobe, the ACS president in the early 1860s, frequently linked the importance of recognizing Liberian independence to the United States' potential to exploit its economic foothold in West Africa. In his 1862 annual address to the ACS, Latrobe encouraged Lincoln's efforts at "recognizing the Government of Liberia," which he believed should have no difficulty passing once U.S. leaders were able to acknowledge "the benefits that would be derived from it." Latrobe argued that as "a nation of manufacturers" the United States has "fought for markets in China, and spent hundreds of thousands of dollars in obtaining them in Japan" while "we voluntarily exclude ourselves from almost the only virgin market in the world." After noting the progress of the French and British empires in securing territory in Africa, he lamented that the United States was unable to draw on the "peculiar facilities, which its relationship to Liberia naturally afford" and feared that if the United States continued to neglect its "commercial destiny" in Africa this opportunity could be "lost to it forever."[9]

While supporters of recognition studiously avoided the question of slavery by fixating on recognition's commercial benefits, it was not long before skeptics of the legislation raised the racial subtext of the debate to the fore. Several members of Congress recognized the symbolic importance of accepting Haiti and Liberia as peers on the world stage. Samuel Cox, a representative from Ohio, claimed that supporters of the bill used inflated statistics to make disingenuous commercial arguments designed to mask the symbolic racial politics at the heart of the issue: "The object sought . . . in this bill is not so much to increase the commercial relations of the United States with the countries named as to give a sort of dignity and equality to these republics, because they are black republics. It is, therefore, literally a Black Republican measure." Cox claimed that the true purpose of such a law was emancipation and citizenship, by "giving national equality to the black republics."[10]

Other members of Congress staked out a more nuanced position by conceding that the United States should fully avail itself of commercial opportunities in these nations while stopping short of granting them full diplomatic equality. Sen. Garrett Davis endorsed both formally recognizing the nations and signing treaties with them, but he opposed sending ambassadors that would "establish terms of mutual and equal reciprocity between the two countries and us."[11] As if to drive home his point, Sen. Willard Saulsbury warned that if the bill passed, "some negro will walk upon the floor of the Senate of the United States."[12] These members of Congress were so invested in preventing the prospect of full diplomatic equality that they likely overestimated the degree to which this bill was an abolitionist ploy. Nevertheless, they did have a point. It is notable that Sumner, a strident opponent of slavery, spoke on behalf of these republics, according to one congressman, in a way that made it impossible to "tell whether the people of these republics were of the Caucasian, the Basque, the Indian, or African race."[13] While advocates were accused of using the question of U.S. imperialism to mask the domestic racial subtext of recognition, the debate revealed that it was actually about both at the same time, a feature of colonizationism since its inception.

Opponents of the bill did not acknowledge that, for many supporters of recognition, the United States' symbolic acceptance of diplomatic equality with black republics did not amount to an effort to dismantle white supremacy. Representative Gooch made it plain that the goal of recognition was not racial equality but a vision of racial internationalism, a prospect for which colonizationism had laid considerable groundwork over the last half century. He rejected the idea that diplomacy involved "the recognition of the equality of the races," instead positing that "it involves nothing but the recognition of the fact that Hayti and Liberia are independent, self-sustaining Governments, and are, in our opinion, entitled to a place among the independent Powers of the earth."[14] While Haiti had once represented a radical challenge to the racial foundations of white government in the United States, colonizationism and Liberia had slowly opened the door for black republics to be accepted not as threats but as potential sites of American global power. The bill's opponents again raised long-standing fears dating back to the Haitian revolution and the Congress of Panama; however, the Civil War had created a context in which these arguments increasingly held little sway. As a policy, colonizationism effectively died with the conclusion of the war, yet its ethos was deeply attuned to the prospect of the United States' global expansion in a postslavery world.

Since its founding, the United States' political and economic future had been predicated on establishing an empire that was rooted in both settler colonization and enslavement. As much as slavery had played a crucial role in advancing the United States' imperial agenda, the debate over recognition revealed how deeply it shaped, and even limited, expansion by prioritizing the reproduction of enslavement above all else.[15] Notably, both the recent discussion of Central American colonization and the recognition debate centered on how African Americans might help the United States expand its commercial and military presence overseas.¹⁶ At stake was no less than the future of racial capitalism: how the United States would manage its domestic and international economies when they were unbound from the institution of slavery.¹⁷

This shift illustrates how the United States' racial framework for expansion had transformed with the growing prospect of its global empire. Prior to the Civil War, the nation's dominant approach to expansion had focused on securing the territorial basis for a white settler republic within North America. As the nation expanded onto ever more distant lands, the question of whether it could continue to build its empire while maintaining white supremacy was both increasingly urgent and tenuous. The United States' recent war with Mexico had exposed the racial anxieties that accompanied the incorporation of large territories with nonwhite populations.¹⁸ This dynamic would resurface again when, shortly after the war, Congress contemplated and ultimately rejected the annexation of the Dominican Republic, largely based on concerns about the racial composition of its population. Such issues would only grow in importance as the United States further expanded its reach overseas during the second half of the nineteenth century.¹⁹

At the same time, colonizationism suggested a different path for the future of U.S. expansion. Colonizationists had long favored a conception of empire that was based around both maintaining racial distinctions and creating political states that would be amenable to the United States. By the Civil War era, this ethos was increasingly woven into the logic of U.S. expansion more broadly as a framework for imagining an international system of nominally sovereign yet unequal nation-states. In this vision, whites and nonwhites could have separate yet complementary racial destinies, and both would ultimately serve the domestic and international agendas of the United States. As the nation grew into an empire with truly global reach, it increasingly grappled with debates that centered on how the principle of self-government comported with the nonwhite polities around the world. Americans, whether they recognized it or not, lived in a world made by colonization.

NOTES

Introduction

1. A full version of the speech was published in *A Sketch of the Life of Com. Robert F. Stockton* (New York: Derby & Jackson, 1856), appendix, 67–69; for earlier press accounts of the speech, see "Colonization Society," *National Intelligencer*, February 28, 1825; "Colonization Society," *Raleigh Register*, March 1, 1825.

2. *Sketch of Robert F. Stockton*, appendix, 67–69. Stockton's reference to the "colonization of our aborigines" alludes to a recent speech by President James Monroe, which suggested that Native Americans might be colonized west of the Mississippi River. See James D. Richardson, "Message of Monroe, Jan. 27 1825," in *A Compilation of the Messages and Papers of the Presidents*, vol. 2 (New York: Bureau of National Literature, 1911), 280–83. For a fuller discussion of this proposal, see Chapter 3.

3. *Sketch of Robert F. Stockton*, 41–47; P. J. Staudenraus, *The African Colonization Movement, 1816–1865* (New York: Columbia University Press, 1961), 62–68.

4. Here and throughout the book I use the term colonizationism broadly to refer to the concept that African Americans, or other nonwhite peoples, should be resettled within colonies outside the United States. I use colonizationist, a term used consistently throughout much of this era, to refer to anyone who subscribed to this idea.

5. On colonization and the politics of slavery, see Staudenraus, *African Colonization Movement*; George M. Frederickson, *The Black Image in the White Mind: The Debate on Afro-American Character and Destiny, 1817–1914* (New York: Harper & Row, 1971); Paul Goodman, *Of One Blood: Abolitionism and the Origins of Racial Equality* (Berkeley: University of California Press, 2000), 23–64; Bruce Dorsey, "A Gendered History of African Colonization in the Antebellum United States," *Journal of Social History* 34, no. 1 (October 1, 2000): 77–103; Richard S. Newman, *The Transformation of American Abolitionism* (Chapel Hill: University of North Carolina Press, 2002), 86–130; Claude A. Clegg, *The Price of Liberty: African Americans and the Making of Liberia* (Chapel Hill: University of North Carolina Press, 2004); Eric Burin, *Slavery and the Peculiar Solution: A History of the American Colonization Society* (Gainesville: University Press of Florida, 2005); Marie Tyler-McGraw, *An African Republic: Black and White Virginians in the Making of Liberia* (Chapel Hill: University of North Carolina Press, 2007); Beverly Tomek, *Colonization and Its Discontents: Emancipation, Emigration, and Antislavery in Antebellum Pennsylvania* (New York: New York University Press, 2011). On the role of colonizationism within black politics, see Floyd John Miller, *The Search for a Black Nationality: Black Emigration and Colonization, 1787–1863* (Urbana: University of Illinois Press, 1975); Patrick Rael, *Black Identity and Black Protest in the Antebellum North* (Chapel Hill: University of North Carolina Press, 2002); James Sidbury, *Becoming African in America: Race and Nation in the Early Black*

Atlantic (New York: Oxford University Press, 2007); Ousmane K. Power-Greene, *Against Wind and Tide: The African American Struggle Against the Colonization Movement* (New York: New York University Press, 2014).

6. In recent years, historians have explored pieces of this story by showing how the colonization movement intersected with the United States' efforts to displace Native Americans and enact varieties of economic, military, and cultural imperialism around the globe. See Nicholas Guyatt, *Bind Us Apart: How Enlightened Americans Invented Racial Segregation* (New York: Basic Books, 2016); Nicholas Guyatt, "'The Outskirts of Our Happiness': Race and the Lure of Colonization in the Early Republic," *Journal of American History* 95, no. 4 (March 2009): 986–1011; Emily Conroy-Krutz, *Christian Imperialism: Converting the World in the Early American Republic* (Ithaca, NY: Cornell University Press, 2015); Bronwen Everill, *Abolition and Empire in Sierra Leone and Liberia* (London: Palgrave Macmillan, 2012); Eugene S. Van Sickle, "Reluctant Imperialists: The U.S. Navy and Liberia, 1819–1845," *Journal of the Early Republic* 31, no. 1 (Spring 2011): 107–34. These recent trends in scholarship are preceded by earlier work within American studies that situated the colonization movement within the cultural history of U.S. imperialism, such as David Kazanjian, *The Brink of Freedom: Improvising Life in the Nineteenth-Century Atlantic World* (Durham, NC: Duke University Press, 2016); David Kazanjian, *The Colonizing Trick: National Culture and Imperial Citizenship in Early America* (Minneapolis: University of Minnesota Press, 2003); Etsuko Taketani, *U.S. Women Writers and the Discourses of Colonialism, 1825–1861* (Knoxville: University of Tennessee Press, 2003); Amy Kaplan, "Manifest Domesticity," *American Literature* 70, no. 3 (September 1998): 581–606; Susan M. Ryan, "Errand into Africa: Colonization and Nation Building in Sarah J. Hale's Liberia," *New England Quarterly* 68, no. 4 (December 1995): 558–83.

7. On the problem of U.S. anti-imperial self-definition, see Walter Benn Michaels, "Anti-Imperial Americanism," in *Cultures of United States Imperialism*, ed. Donald E. Pease and Amy Kaplan (Durham, NC: Duke University Press, 1993); Walter LaFeber, "The American View of Decolonization, 1776–1920: An Ironic Legacy," in *The United States and Decolonization: Power and Freedom*, ed. David Ryan and Victor Pungong (Basingstoke, UK: Macmillan, 2000); Peter S. Onuf, *Jefferson's Empire: The Language of American Nationhood* (Charlottesville: University of Virginia Press, 2000); Mary Ann Heiss, "The Evolution of the Imperial Idea and U.S. National Identity," *Diplomatic History* 26, no. 4 (Fall 2002): 511–40.

8. My definition of "settler empire" is indebted to Aziz Rana's use of the concept in *The Two Faces of American Freedom* (Cambridge, MA: Harvard University Press, 2010). Recent scholarship has devoted growing attention to settler colonialism in the early United States, but none have addressed colonizationism in a sustained fashion. See Noenoe K. Silva, *Aloha Betrayed: Native Hawaiian Resistance to American Colonialism* (Durham, NC: Duke University Press, 2004); Frederick E. Hoxie, "Retrieving the Red Continent: Settler Colonialism and the History of American Indians in the US," *Ethnic and Racial Studies* 31, no. 6 (2008): 1153–67; Jean M. O'Brien, *Firsting and Lasting: Writing Indians out of Existence in New England* (Minneapolis: University of Minnesota Press, 2010); Lisa Ford, *Settler Sovereignty: Jurisdiction and Indigenous People in America and Australia, 1788–1836* (Cambridge, MA: Harvard University Press, 2010); Bethel Saler, *The Settlers' Empire: Colonialism and State Formation in America's Old Northwest* (Philadelphia: University of Pennsylvania Press, 2014). In recent decades, historians studying this transformation have typically focused on reframing the exceptionalist story of westward continental expansion as one of incipient empire building; however, efforts to integrate these narratives into a single frame of view have remained relatively provisional. See Michael Adas,

"From Settler Colony to Global Hegemon: Integrating the Exceptionalist Narrative of the American Experience into World History," *American Historical Review* 106, no. 5 (December 2001): 1692; Julian Go, *Patterns of Empire: The British and American Empires, 1688 to the Present* (New York: Cambridge University Press, 2011); A. G. Hopkins, *American Empire* (Princeton, NJ: Princeton University Press, 2018).

9. This approach is informed by several broader histories of this period that have, in various ways, pointed to the colonization movement's constitutive role in early U.S. racial ideology and nationalism. On colonizationism and racial ideology, see Frederickson, *Black Image in the White Mind*, 1–42; Lawrence Jacob Friedman, *Inventors of the Promised Land* (New York: Knopf, 1975), 180–258; Joanne Pope Melish, *Disowning Slavery: Gradual Emancipation and "Race" in New England, 1780–1860* (Ithaca, NY: Cornell University Press, 1998), 163–209; Peter S. Onuf, "'To Declare Them a Free and Independent People': Race, Slavery, and National Identity in Jefferson's Thought," *Journal of the Early Republic* 18, no. 1 (Spring 1998): 1–46; James Brewer Stewart, "The Emergence of Racial Modernity and the Rise of the White North, 1790–1840," *Journal of the Early Republic* 18, no. 2 (Summer 1998): 181–217; Bruce R. Dain, *A Hideous Monster of the Mind: American Race Theory in the Early Republic* (Cambridge, MA: Harvard University Press, 2002); Guyatt, *Bind Us Apart*.

10. In his examination of colonization, David Kazanjian has made similar observations, arguing that colonizationist rhetoric used the language of liberal citizenship "by representing itself as a merely technical, governmental realization of the necessary relationships among freedom, race, and nation." David Kazanjian, "Racial Governmentality: The African Colonization Movement," in *Colonizing Trick*, 97.

11. Rosemarie Zagarri, "The Significance of the 'Global Turn' for the Early American Republic: Globalization in the Age of Nation-Building," *Journal of the Early Republic* 31, no. 1 (2011): 1–37. Some examples of recent work that highlight the dynamic relationship between U.S. settlement and global empire include Aims McGuinness, *Path of Empire: Panama and the California Gold Rush* (Ithaca, NY: Cornell University Press, 2008); Brian Rouleau, *With Sails Whitening Every Sea: Mariners and the Making of an American Maritime Empire* (Ithaca, NY: Cornell University Press, 2014); Eliga H. Gould, *Among the Powers of the Earth: The American Revolution and the Making of a New World Empire*, reprint ed. (Cambridge, MA: Harvard University Press, 2014); Conroy-Krutz, *Christian Imperialism*; Matthew Karp, *This Vast Southern Empire: Slaveholders at the Helm of American Foreign Policy* (Cambridge, MA: Harvard University Press, 2016).

Chapter 1

1. James Monroe to Thomas Jefferson, June 15, 1801, in *The Writings of James Monroe*, ed. Stanislaus Murray Hamilton, vol. 3 (New York: G. P. Putnam's Sons, 1903), 293.

2. Thomas Jefferson to James Monroe, November 24, 1801, in *The Works of Thomas Jefferson*, ed. Paul Leicester Ford, vol. 9 (New York: G. P. Putnam's Sons, 1905), 315–19.

3. When formed in December 1816, the ACS initially called itself the American Society for Colonizing Free People of Color, but by the late 1810s it was more commonly known by the shortened version. For simplicity, I refer to the organization as the American Colonization Society or ACS throughout the book.

4. While some of these proposals have been widely discussed, historians have devoted less attention to the early colonization proposals aimed at North America than the later movement focused on Africa. When discussed they have been largely presented as incoherent and

unsuccessful precursors to the formidable organization that would coalesce behind African colonization, rather than an incipient movement in their own right. For prominent examples of scholarship on African colonization that offer only a partial discussion of these proposals, see Henry Noble Sherwood, "Early Negro Deportation Projects," *Mississippi Valley Historical Review* 2, no. 4 (March 1916): 484–508; P. J. Staudenraus, *The African Colonization Movement, 1816–1865* (New York: Columbia University Press, 1961), 1–3; George M. Frederickson, *The Black Image in the White Mind: The Debate on Afro-American Character and Destiny, 1817–1914* (New York: Harper & Row, 1971); Amos Jones Beyan, *The American Colonization Society and the Creation of the Liberian State: A Historical Perspective, 1822–1900* (Lanham, MD: University Press of America, 1991), 2–3. For colonization scholarship that offers little or no mention of western proposals, see Claude A. Clegg, *The Price of Liberty: African Americans and the Making of Liberia* (Chapel Hill: University of North Carolina Press, 2004), 21–22. For work that provides some background on these early efforts as a precursor to African colonization, see Eric Burin, *Slavery and the Peculiar Solution: A History of the American Colonization Society* (Gainesville: University Press of Florida, 2005), 7–13; Marie Tyler-McGraw, *An African Republic: Black and White Virginians in the Making of Liberia* (Chapel Hill: University of North Carolina Press, 2007), 9–12. Nicholas Guyatt's recent work is an exception to this tendency and offers a far more detailed look at these early efforts. See Nicholas Guyatt, *Bind Us Apart: How Enlightened Americans Invented Racial Segregation* (New York: Basic Books, 2016); Nicholas Guyatt, "'The Outskirts of Our Happiness': Race and the Lure of Colonization in the Early Republic," *Journal of American History* 95, no. 4 (March 2009): 1–3.

5. Ira Berlin, *Many Thousands Gone: The First Two Centuries of Slavery in North America* (Cambridge, MA: Belknap Press of Harvard University Press, 1998), 277–85; Peter Kolchin, *American Slavery, 1619–1877* (New York: Hill & Wang, 1993), 78–81.

6. Thomas Jefferson, *Notes on the State of Virginia* (Richmond, VA: J. W. Randolph, 1853), 149.

7. Winthrop D. Jordan, *White over Black: American Attitudes Toward the Negro, 1550–1812* (Chapel Hill: University of North Carolina Press, 1968), 546–47; John Chester Miller, *The Wolf by the Ears: Thomas Jefferson and Slavery* (New York: Free Press, 1977), 21–22.

8. Peter S. Onuf, "'To Declare Them a Free and Independent People': Race, Slavery, and National Identity in Jefferson's Thought," *Journal of the Early Republic* 18, no. 1 (Spring 1998): 3–6, 8–10; Jefferson, *Notes on the State of Virginia*, 175.

9. On the significance of slave revolution in the French Caribbean to the questions of race and republicanism, see Robin Blackburn, "Haiti, Slavery, and the Age of the Democratic Revolution," *William and Mary Quarterly* 63, no. 4 (October 2006): 643–74; Laurent Dubois, *A Colony of Citizens: Revolution and Slave Emancipation in the French Caribbean, 1787–1804* (Chapel Hill: University of North Carolina Press, 2004); Carolyn E. Fick, *The Making of Haiti: The Saint Domingue Revolution from Below* (Knoxville: University of Tennessee Press, 1990). On the symbolic dimensions of European and American disavowal of the Haitian revolution, see Sibylle Fischer, *Modernity Disavowed: Haiti and the Cultures of Slavery in the Age of Revolution* (Durham, NC: Duke University Press, 2004).

10. On American reactions to the Haitian revolution, see Ashli White, *Encountering Revolution: Haiti and the Making of the Early Republic* (Baltimore, MD: Johns Hopkins University Press, 2010); Bruce R. Dain, *A Hideous Monster of the Mind: American Race Theory in the Early Republic* (Cambridge, MA: Harvard University Press, 2002); Michael Zuckerman, "The Power of Blackness: Thomas Jefferson and the Revolution in St. Domingue," in *Almost Chosen People:*

Oblique Biographies in the American Grain (Berkeley: University of California Press, 1993); Alfred N. Hunt, *Haiti's Influence on Antebellum America: Slumbering Volcano in the Caribbean* (Baton Rouge: Louisiana State University Press, 1988).

11. On African Americans' engagement with the Haitian revolution, see Chris Dixon, *African America and Haiti: Emigration and Black Nationalism in the Nineteenth Century* (Westport, CT: Greenwood Press, 2000); Julius Sherrard Scott, "The Common Wind: Currents of Afro-American Communication in the Era of the Haitian Revolution" (Ph.D. diss., Duke University Press, 1986).

12. William Thornton, "To the Honorable Henry Clay, Chairman of the Assembly for Promoting the Establishment of a Free and Independent Nation of Blacks in Africa," in *William Thornton and Negro Colonization*, ed. Gaillard Hunt (Worcester, MA: American Antiquarian Society, 1921), 29–30. Thornton would eventually come to support the ACS during its early years, even drawing up a street grid for the eventual capital of Monrovia. See Figure 2 in Chapter 2.

13. Floyd John Miller, *The Search for a Black Nationality: Black Emigration and Colonization, 1787–1863* (Urbana: University of Illinois Press, 1975), 11–21; Lamont D. Thomas, *Paul Cuffe: Black Entrepreneur and Pan-Africanist* (Urbana: University of Illinois Press, 1986); Dickson D. Bruce, Jr., "National Identity and African-American Colonization, 1773–1817," *Historian* 58, no. 1 (1995), 17–19.

14. Although Craighead published nothing on the subject at the time, his plans were recounted fifty years later in Archibald Alexander's history of the African colonization movement, *A History of Colonization on the Western Coast of Africa* (Philadelphia: W. S. Martien, 1846), 61–62. See also Virginia Historical Society, *Collections of the Virginia Historical Society*, vol. 6 (Richmond: Virginia Historical Society, 1887), 24; James Geddes Craighead, *The Craighead Family: A Genealogical Memoir of the Descendants of Rev. Thomas and Margaret Craighead, 1658–1876* (Philadelphia: Sherman, 1876), 56–57.

15. Othello, "Essay on Negro Slavery," *American Museum*, November 1788.

16. St. George Tucker, *Blackstone's Commentaries: With Notes of Reference, to the Constitution and Laws, of the Federal Government of the United States; and of the Commonwealth of Virginia*, vol. 4 (Philadelphia, 1803).

17. St. George Tucker, *Dissertation on Slavery: With a Proposal for the Gradual Abolition of It, in the State of Virginia* (Philadelphia: Mathew Carey, 1796), 94–95.

18. Ibid.

19. Quoted in Douglas R. Egerton, *Gabriel's Rebellion: The Virginia Slave Conspiracies of 1800 and 1802* (Chapel Hill: University of North Carolina Press, 1993), 14–15; see also Jordan, *White over Black*, 558–60.

20. Thomas Jefferson to St. George Tucker, August 28, 1797, in Ford, *Works of Thomas Jefferson*, 8:231.

21. Anthony Benezet published several of his letters on slavery during his lifetime, and they were later compiled in Roberts Vaux, *Memoirs of the Life of Anthony Benezet* (Philadelphia: W. Alexander, 1817), 39; "Letters of Anthony Benezet," *Journal of Negro History* 2, no. 1 (January 1917): 83, 85–86.

22. On the postrevolutionary transformation in northern slavery, see Joanne Pope Melish, *Disowning Slavery: Gradual Emancipation and "Race" in New England, 1780–1860* (Ithaca, NY: Cornell University Press, 1998), 50–83; John Wood Sweet, *Bodies Politic: Negotiating Race in the American North, 1730–1830* (Baltimore: Johns Hopkins University Press, 2003), 225–67; James Oliver Horton, *In Hope of Liberty: Culture, Community, and Protest Among Northern Free*

Blacks, 1700–1860 (New York: Oxford University Press, 1997), 71–75; David Brion Davis, *The Problem of Slavery in the Age of Revolution, 1770–1823* (Ithaca, NY: Cornell University Press, 1975), 120–30.

23. For a brief biographical sketch of Fisk, see "Moses Fisk, M.A.," in B. B. Edwards and W. Cogswell, *The American Quarterly Register*, vol. 12 (Boston: Perkins & Marvin, 1840), 382.

24. Moses Fisk, *Tyrannical Libertymen a Discourse upon Negro-Slavery in the United States: Composed at -- in New Hampshire, on the Late Federal Thanksgiving-Day* (Hanover, NH: Eagle Office, 1795), 5, 9–11.

25. Ibid., 9–11.

26. Lacy Ford has argued that early colonization plans emerged from a political context in which Federalists increasingly argued that states such as Virginia should be weaned off of dependence on slavery because it was incompatible with both political liberty and economic prosperity. Lacy K. Ford, *Deliver Us from Evil: The Slavery Question in the Old South* (New York: Oxford University Press, 2011), 57–58.

27. Egerton, *Gabriel's Rebellion*, 45–48, 69–79.

28. *Journal of the House of Delegates of the Commonwealth of Virginia* (Richmond, VA: Thomas Nicolson, 1801), 47–48.

29. George Tucker, *Letter to a Member of the General Assembly of Virginia on the Subject of the Late Conspiracy of the Slaves; with a Proposal for Their Colonization* (Baltimore, MD: Bonsal & Niles, 1801).

30. Ibid., 6–7, 18, 21.

31. Egerton, *Gabriel's Rebellion*, 152.

32. James Monroe to Thomas Jefferson, June 15, 1801, in Hamilton, *Writings of James Monroe*, 3:293.

33. Thomas Jefferson to James Monroe, November 24, 1801, in Ford, *Works of Thomas Jefferson*, 9:315–19.

34. Ibid.

35. Jefferson, *Notes on the State of Virginia*, 149–55; Richard Holland Johnston, "Thomas Jefferson to Captain Hendrick, the Delawares, Mohicans, and Munries, December 21, 1808," in *The Writings of Thomas Jefferson*, vol. 16 (Washington, DC: Thomas Jefferson Memorial Association of the United States, 1903).

36. Jordan, *White over Black*, 393–94.

37. *Journal of the House of Delegates*, 47–48; General Assembly, House of Delegates, Virginia, January 22, 1805, General Assembly, House of Delegates, Office of the Speaker, Executive Communications, January 12, 1805, Library of Virginia; General Assembly, House of Delegates, Virginia, January 16, 1805, General Assembly, House of Delegates, Office of the Speaker, Executive Communications, January 12, 1805, Library of Virginia. For a detailed history of Virginia's pursuit of various western colonization proposals following Gabriel's Rebellion, see Egerton, *Gabriel's Rebellion*, 147–62. On how these proposals contributed to the origins of the national African colonization movement, see Douglas R. Egerton, "'Its Origin Is Not a Little Curious': A New Look at the American Colonization Society," *Journal of the Early Republic* 5, no. 4 (Winter 1985): 463–80.

38. David Roediger has observed that the Louisiana Purchase reflected a shift in thinking about how slavery would end: from a problem that would be solved in time to one that would be solved through space. David R. Roediger, *How Race Survived U.S. History: From Settlement and Slavery to the Obama Phenomenon* (London: Verso, 2008), 61–63.

39. Peter J. Kastor, "'What Are the Advantages of the Acquisition?': Inventing Expansion in the Early American Republic," *American Quarterly* 60, no. 4 (December 2008): 1005; James P.

Ronda, "'We Have a Country': Race, Geography, and the Invention of Indian Territory," *Journal of the Early Republic* 19, no. 4 (Winter 1999): 739–55. See also Reginald Horsman, *Race and Manifest Destiny: The Origins of American Racial Anglo-Saxonism* (Cambridge, MA: Harvard University Press, 1981).

40. St. George Tucker published his pamphlet in support of the Louisiana Purchase under the pen name "Sylvestris." Sylvestris, *Reflections, on the Cession of Louisiana to the United States* (Washington, DC: Samuel Harrison Smith, 1803), 25–26. On the prevalence of climate-based racial theories, see Dain, *Hideous Monster of the Mind*.

41. Beverly Tomek, "'From Motives of Generosity, as Well as Self-Preservation': Thomas Branagan, Colonization, and the Gradual Emancipation Movement," *American Nineteenth Century History* 6, no. 2 (June 2005), 121–47.

42. Thomas Branagan, *Serious Remonstrances, Addressed to the Citizens of the Northern States, and Their Representatives; Being an Appeal to Their Natural Feelings & Common Sense* (Philadelphia: Thomas T. Stiles, 1805), 22, 24, 34, 41, 43, 48–53.

43. John Parrish, *Remarks on the Slavery of Black People; Addressed to the Citizens of the United States Particularly to Those Who Are in Legislative or Executive Stations in the General or State Governments; and Also to Such Individuals as Hold Them in Bondage* (Philadelphia: Kimber, Conrad, 1806), 8–9, 41, 43; Staudenraus, *African Colonization Movement*, 4.

44. For Thornton's earlier skepticism about black settler colonies in North America, see Thornton, "To the Honorable Henry Clay," 29–30. Thornton was the son of a British planter in the West Indies, and shortly after coming to the United States he gained access to powerful politicians. As a result of these connections, he would ultimately help design the U.S. Capitol and become the first superintendent of patents. Thornton's interest in colonization plans went back decades: in the mid-1780s he unsuccessfully attempted to send a group of free African Americans to populate the new British colony in Sierra Leone, and in 1802 he proposed purchasing Puerto Rico from Spain for the purposes of colonizing it with emancipated slaves. See Hunt, *William Thornton and Negro Colonization*, 4–11, 24.

45. William Thornton, *Political Economy Founded in Justice and Humanity in a Letter to a Friend* (Washington, DC: Samuel Harrison Smith, 1804), 16–17.

46. Ibid., 9, 16–17, 21–22.

47. Ibid., 22–23. On "domestic dependent nationhood" as it pertained to Indian nations following the John Marshall's critical trilogy of Supreme Court decisions in the 1820s and 1830s, see Priscilla Wald, "Terms of Assimilation: Legislating Subjectivity in the Emerging Nation," in *Cultures of United States Imperialism*, ed. Donald E. Pease and Amy Kaplan (Durham, NC: Duke University Press, 1993), 672; Robert A. Williams, *Like a Loaded Weapon: The Rehnquist Court, Indian Rights, and the Legal History of Racism in America* (Minneapolis: University of Minnesota Press, 2005), 47–70.

48. Fisk, *Tyrannical Libertymen*, 9–11.

49. Branagan, *Serious Remonstrances*, 22–24.

50. Tucker, *Letter to a Member of the General Assembly of Virginia*, 18, 20–21.

51. Lewis Dupré, *Rational & Benevolent Plan for Averting Some of the Calamitous Consequences of Slavery, Being a Practable, Seasonable, and Profitable Institution for the Progressive Emancipation of Virginia and Carolina Slaves* (Charleston, SC, 1810), 4.

52. Unlike other pre-ACS pamphleteers, Dupré attempted to use his proposal to create a colonizationist organization. In this pamphlet he also includes the "Articles of the Virginia and Carolina Emancipation Society," which featured explicit plans for emancipation of slaves and the purchase of territory on which to colonize them. While Dupré's organization gained

no following in the South at the time, it could be considered one of the earliest attempts to give colonizationism an institutional form outside of government-based efforts. For more on Dupré, see Alice Dana Adams, *The Neglected Period of Anti-Slavery in America (1808–1831)* (Boston: Ginn, 1908), 30–31.

53. For a good overview of the scholarly debate around colonizationism's status as an antislavery effort, see Burin, *Slavery and the Peculiar Solution*, 1–2.

54. Parrish, *Remarks on the Slavery of Black People*, 41, 43. On the ways that Americans continually reinvented "the West" as a geopolitical space in the early republic, see Kastor, "'What Are the Advantages of the Acquisition?'"; Ronda, "'We Have a Country.'"

55. On early civilization policy, see Francis Paul Prucha, *The Great Father: The United States Government and the American Indians*, abridged ed. (Lincoln: University of Nebraska Press, 1984), 48–54; Reginald Horsman, *The Indian Policy of an "Empire for Liberty,"* ed. Frederick E. Hoxie, Ronald Hoffman, and Peter J. Albert (Charlottesville: University of Virginia Press, 1999), 51–52.

56. R. David Edmunds, *The Shawnee Prophet* (Lincoln: University of Nebraska Press, 1983), 92–93; John Sugden, *Tecumseh: A Life* (New York: Henry Holt, 1998), 187–90.

57. Gregory Evans Dowd, *A Spirited Resistance: The North American Indian Struggle for Unity, 1745–1815* (Baltimore: Johns Hopkins University Press, 1992), xiv, 129; R. Douglas Hurt, *The Indian Frontier, 1763–1846* (Albuquerque: University of New Mexico Press, 2002), 123–33.

58. On Tecumseh's wide-reaching efforts at establishing pan-Indian diplomacy, see Claudio Saunt, *A New Order of Things: Property, Power, and the Transformation of the Creek Indians, 1733–1816* (Cambridge: Cambridge University Press, 1999), 249–72; John Sugden, "Early Pan-Indianism: Tecumseh's Tour of the Indian Country, 1811–1812," *American Indian Quarterly* 10, no. 4 (Autumn 1986): 273–304.

59. Robert S. Finley, *Thoughts on the Colonization of Free Blacks* (Washington, DC, 1816), 6.

60. George Washington Edwards Phillips, "Diary of George Washington Edwards Phillips," 1817, 110–11, George Washington Edwards Phillips Papers, Duke University, Special Collections.

61. American Colonization Society, *A View of Exertions Lately Made for the Purpose of Colonizing the Free People of Colour, in the United States, in Africa, or Elsewhere* (Washington, DC, 1817), 7.

62. Scott, "Common Wind," 273–74; Daniel Rasmussen, *American Uprising: The Untold Story of America's Largest Slave Revolt* (New York: Harper, 2011), 88–90.

63. Kevin Mulroy, *Freedom on the Border: The Seminole Maroons in Florida: The Indian Territory-Coahuila and Texas* (Lubbock: Texas Tech University Press, 1993), 13–15; Kenneth Wiggins Porter, *The Black Seminoles: History of a Freedom-Seeking People* (Gainesville: University Press of Florida, 1996), 13–24.

64. Saunt, *New Order of Things*, 235–40, 269–70.

65. Frederick T. Davis, ed., "United States Troops in Spanish East Florida, 1812–13 (letters of Lieut. Col. T. A. Smith)," *Florida Historical Quarterly* 9 (April 1931): 269.

66. Quoted in "Report on Colonizing the Free People of Color of the United States," *Daily National Intelligencer*, March 28, 1817.

67. "Colonization of Free People of Color," *National Register*, April 5, 1817.

68. General Assembly of Virginia, December 23, 1816, House of Delegates, Resolutions, Library of Virginia. While this resolution suggested Africa as a possible destination, it did not meaningfully distinguish between this and other locations. As such, it indicates that members of the assembly recognized that western colonization proposals were on the decline. Herman

Vandenburg Ames, *State Documents on Federal Relations: The States and the United States* (New York: Longman, Green, 1904), 3–4.

69. *Minutes of the Proceedings of a Special Meeting of the Fifteenth American Convention for Promoting the Abolition of Slavery, and Improving the Condition of the African Race* (Philadelphia: Hall & Atkinson, 1818), 49. On the relationship between the ACPAS and the emergence of the colonization movement, see Robert Duane Sayre, "The Evolution of Early American Abolitionism: The American Convention for Promoting the Abolition of Slavery and Improving the Condition of the African Race, 1794–1837" (Ph.D. diss., Ohio State University, 1987); *Minutes of the Sixteenth American Convention for Promoting the Abolition of Slavery, and Improving the Condition of the African Race* (Philadelphia: William Fry, 1819), 51. There is some evidence that black communities might have preferred western colonies to resettlement in Africa. A witness to a meeting of the free people of color in Richmond, Virginia, reported: "They will prefer colonization in any quarter of their native land, to being exiled into a foreign country, and hope that a situation may be allowed them on the Missouri, or elsewhere in North America." See Jesse Torrey, *A Portraiture of Domestic Slavery, in the United States: With Reflections on the Practicability of Restoring the Moral Rights of the Slave, without Impairing the Legal Privileges of the Possessor: And a Project of a Colonial Asylum for Free Persons of Colour* (Philadelphia: John Bioren, 1817), 93–94.

70. *Minutes of the Sixteenth American Convention*, 51–52.

71. *Minutes of the Seventeenth Session of the American Convention for Promoting the Abolition of Slavery, and Improving the Condition of the African Race* (Philadelphia: Atkinson & Alexander, 1821), 647–77; Stephen Aron, *American Confluence: The Missouri Frontier from Borderland to Border State* (Bloomington: Indiana University Press, 2006); Adam Rothman, *Slave Country: American Expansion and the Origins of the Deep South* (Cambridge, MA: Harvard University Press, 2007); François Furstenberg, "The Significance of the Trans-Appalachian Frontier in Atlantic History," *American Historical Review* 113, no. 3 (June 2008): 647–77.

72. Aron, *American Confluence*; Rothman, *Slave Country*; Furstenberg, "Significance of the Trans-Appalachian Frontier."

73. "Communication," *National Intelligencer*, March 22, 1825.

74. On the rejection of Tucker's bill in the House of Representatives, see *Register of Debates*, 18th Cong., 2nd sess. (1825): 735–36, 740. For his earlier colonization proposal, see Tucker, *Letter to a Member*.

75. "Communication."

76. Ibid.

77. "The Reports of the American Society for Colonizing the Free People of Colour in the United States.—1818, 19, 20, 21, 22, 23," *Christian Spectator* 5 (October 1823); Bacon's speech was later republished in the *National Intelligencer*, a consistent early advocate for the African colonization movement. See "The African Colonization Plan Review of the Reports of the American Society for Colonizing the Free People of Color in the United States," *Daily National Intelligencer*, November 1, 1823. While Bacon was part of the northern antislavery community, southern slaveholders were just as likely to link the threat of Native American and African American revolution after having witnessed examples of their collaboration in recent decades. Two years later a southern slaveholder and opponent of African colonization, Whitemarsh Seabrook, published a pamphlet that paraphrased Bacon, making the claim that a "Toussaint, or a Spartacus, or an African Tecumseh" will "demand by what authority we hold them in subjection." Whitemarsh B. Seabrook, *A Concise View of the Critical Situation and Future Prospects of the Slave-Holding*

States, in Relation to Their Coloured Population (Charleston, SC: Agricultural Society of St. John's Colleton, 1825), 4. Bacon was an influential evangelical activist in the northern colonization movement who was increasingly obsessed with the possibility of race war following the Missouri crisis of 1819–20. See Hugh Davis, "Northern Colonizationists and Free Blacks, 1823–1837: A Case Study of Leonard Bacon," *Journal of the Early Republic* 17, no. 4 (Winter 1997): 655.

Chapter 2

1. Warburton, "To the Editors," *Daily National Intelligencer*, December 20, 1819.

2. I am influenced here by Jay Sexton's suggestion that William Appleman Williams's concept of "imperial anticolonialism" is key to understanding the contradictions of the heart of the Monroe Doctrine. Jay Sexton, *The Monroe Doctrine: Empire and Nation in Nineteenth-Century America* (New York: Hill & Wang, 2012), 5. See also William Appleman Williams, *The Tragedy of American Diplomacy* (New York: W. W. Norton, 1972), 1858.

3. Warburton, "To the Editors." On the United States' pursuit of Spanish territory during this period, see William Earl Weeks, *John Quincy Adams and American Global Empire* (Lexington: University Press of Kentucky, 2002); Frank Lawrence Owsley and Gene A. Smith, *Filibusters and Expansionists: Jeffersonian Manifest Destiny, 1800–1821* (Tuscaloosa: University of Alabama Press, 1997). On the state of the Spanish empire during this period, see David Weber, *The Spanish Frontier in North America* (New Haven, CT: Yale University Press, 1994).

4. James Monroe, Seventh Annual Address, December 2, 1823, in *A Compilation of the Messages and Papers of the Presidents*, 11 vols., ed. James D. Richardson (New York: Bureau of National Literature and Art, 1911), 2:787.

5. Warburton, "To the Editors." While the proposal was modeled on the ideas of the ascendant ACS, Warburton lamented that his plan would likely fall on deaf ears because the nation's leading colonizationists seem to have "decided on Africa as the most proper place."

6. On how the context of British abolitionism and imperialism shaped the project in Sierra Leone, see Christopher Leslie Brown, *Moral Capital: Foundations of British Abolitionism* (Chapel Hill: University of North Carolina Press, 2006), 259–330; Bronwen Everill, *Abolition and Empire in Sierra Leone and Liberia* (London: Palgrave Macmillan, 2012). On how Americans sought to distance themselves from Britishness in an effort to assert the particular foundations of their own nationhood, see Kariann Akemi Yokota, *Unbecoming British: How Revolutionary America Became a Postcolonial Nation* (New York: Oxford University Press, 2011).

7. On how the American Revolution set into motion the prospect of emancipation and British imperial reorganization, see Sylvia R. Frey, *Water from the Rock: Black Resistance in a Revolutionary Age* (Princeton, NJ: Princeton University Press, 1993), 172–205; Mary Louise Clifford, *From Slavery to Freetown: Black Loyalists After the American Revolution* (Jefferson, NC: McFarland, 1999); Cassandra Pybus, *Epic Journeys of Freedom: Runaway Slaves of the American Revolution and Their Global Quest for Liberty* (New York: Beacon Press, 2007). On the broader Atlantic world context for these migrations, see Alexander X. Byrd, *Captives and Voyagers: Black Migrants Across the Eighteenth-Century British Atlantic World* (Baton Rouge: Louisiana State University Press, 2008).

8. On Granville Sharp's idealistic vision for the colony, see Christopher Fyfe, *A History of Sierra Leone* (Oxford: Oxford University Press, 1962), 16–30; John Peterson, *Province of Freedom: A History of Sierra Leone, 1787–1870* (London: Faber, 1969), 17–27. For a broader exploration of how Granville Sharp's humanitarian outlook was shaped by his perception of British imperial crisis, see Brown, *Moral Capital*, 155–206.

9. See, for instance, Henry Smeathman's influential plan for creating the colony in Sierra Leone and its emphasis on economic issues. Henry Smeathman, *Plan of a Settlement to Be Made near Sierra Leone on the Grain Coast of Africa Intended More Particularly for the Service and Happy Establishment of Blacks and People of Colour, to Be Shipped as Freemen Under the Direction of the Committee for Relieving the Black Poor, and Under the Protection of the British Government* (London: G. Kearsley, 1786).

10. On the larger context for the convergence of economic and humanitarian rhetoric in the founding of Sierra Leone, see Brown, *Moral Capital*, 259–82.

11. James Madison, "Memorandum on an African Colony for Freed Slaves," in *The Papers of James Madison*, ed. William T. Hutchinson and William M. E. Rachal, vol. 12 (Chicago: University of Chicago Press, 1991), 437–38.

12. Around the same time, the prominent Virginian slaveholder Ferdinando Fairfax similarly advocated on behalf of an African colony because it would be located "at such a distance as to prevent" danger to "the peace of society . . . between two neighboring states" in North America that would be separated by racial distinction. Ferdinando Fairfax, "Plan for Liberating the Negroes within the United States," *American Museum* 8, no. 6 (December 1790): 285–87.

13. Thomas Jefferson to James Monroe, November 24, 1801, in *The Works of Thomas Jefferson*, ed. Paul Leicester Ford, vol. 9 (New York: G. P. Putnam's Sons, 1905), 315–19; Lacy K. Ford, *Deliver Us from Evil: The Slavery Question in the Old South* (New York: Oxford University Press, 2011), 62–63.

14. Thomas Jefferson to Rufus King, July 13, 1802, Thomas Jefferson Papers, Library of Congress (hereafter Jefferson Papers), Ser. 1, Reel 26.

15. Rufus King to Thomas Jefferson, December 18, 1802, Jefferson Papers, Ser. 1, Reel 27.

16. Rufus King to Thomas Jefferson, May 12, 1803, Jefferson Papers.

17. For a summary of Jefferson's view on the dissolution of this plan after the fact, see Thomas Jefferson to John Lynch, January 21, 1811, Jefferson Papers.

18. George Arnold Salvador, *Paul Cuffe, the Black Yankee, 1759–1817* (New Bedford, MA: Reynolds-DeWalt, 1969), 12–15, 30; Sally Loomis, "The Evolution of Paul Cuffe's Black Nationalism," in *Black Apostles at Home and Abroad: Afro-Americans and the Christian Mission from the Revolution to Reconstruction*, ed. David Wills and Richard S. Newman (Boston: G. K. Hall, 1982), 298–99; Floyd John Miller, *The Search for a Black Nationality: Black Emigration and Colonization, 1787–1863* (Urbana: University of Illinois Press, 1975), 30–31.

19. P. J. Staudenraus, *The African Colonization Movement, 1816–1865* (New York: Columbia University Press, 1961), 29–30.

20. "African Colonization," *National Advocate*, November 5, 1817.

21. Lamont D. Thomas, *Paul Cuffe: Black Entrepreneur and Pan-Africanist* (Urbana: University of Illinois Press, 1986), 117.

22. For reprintings of Jefferson's letter, see "Colonization of Free Blacks," *Daily National Intelligencer*, April 14, 1817; *National Advocate*, April 16, 1817; "African Colonization," *Niles' Weekly Register*, April 19, 1817; "Colonization of Free Blacks," *Boston Recorder*, April 29, 1817; "American Colonization Society," *Christian Herald*, January 31, 1818; "Mr. Jefferson's Letter," *Christian Messenger*, February 28, 1818. For Jefferson's original letter, see Jefferson to Lynch, January 21, 1811, *Jefferson Papers*, Ser. 1, Reel 45.

23. For Clay's speech praising Sierra Leone at the first ACS meeting, see "Meeting at Washington City, on the Colonization of Free Blacks," *American Watchman*, December 28, 1816.

24. "Colonization of Free Blacks," *National Advocate*, December 30, 1816.

25. American Colonization Society, *A View of Exertions Lately Made for the Purpose of Colonizing the Free People of Colour, in the United States, in Africa, or Elsewhere* (Washington, DC, 1817), 17; reprinted in "Report on Colonizing the Free People of Color of the United States," *Daily National Intelligencer*, March 28, 1817; Staudenraus, *African Colonization Movement*, 33–35.

26. "Free People of Color," *Daily National Intelligencer*, May 5, 1817.

27. "Colonization," *National Advocate*, July 23, 1817.

28. "The Colonization Scheme," *Niles' Weekly Register*, October 4, 1817.

29. "To H. Niles," *Niles' Weekly Register*, November 8, 1817.

30. "Auxiliary Colonization Society," *Christian Herald*, October 18, 1817.

31. "African Colonization," *National Advocate*, November 17, 1817.

32. "The Colonization of the Free Blacks," *National Register*, November 8, 1817; "The Colonization of the Free Blacks—No. II," *National Register*, November 20, 1817; "The Colonization of the Free Blacks—No. III," *National Register*, November 22, 1817.

33. *Georgetown Register* article cited in *Raleigh Register, and North-Carolina Gazette*, August 8, 1817; "Colonization of Free Blacks," *Christian Messenger*, July 12, 1817.

34. Eric Burin, "The Slave Trade Act of 1819: A New Look at Colonization and the Politics of Slavery," *American Nineteenth Century History* 13, no. 1 (2012): 1–14.

35. James Sidbury, *Becoming African in America: Race and Nation in the Early Black Atlantic* (New York: Oxford University Press, 2007); Staudenraus, *African Colonization Movement*, 37–47, 50–56.

36. Ford, *Deliver Us from Evil*, 63–64.

37. *Annals of Congress*, 15th Cong., 1st sess. (1818): 1771–74. On Mercer's role in initiating the early colonization movement, see Douglas R. Egerton, " 'Its Origin Is Not a Little Curious': A New Look at the American Colonization Society," *Journal of the Early Republic* 5, no. 4 (Winter 1985): 463–80.

38. "Proceedings, Board of Managers," March 4, 1819, American Colonization Society Papers, Library of Congress, Washington, DC, Ser. 5, Reel 289.

39. Charles Francis Adams, ed., *Memoirs of John Quincy Adams, Comprising Portions of His Diary from 1795 to 1848*, vol. 4 (Philadelphia: J. B. Lippincott, 1875), 292–94.

40. Ibid., 4:437–38.

41. On Monroe's initial reluctance to exert federal authority, see "Proceedings, Board of Managers." This meeting notes that Monroe suggested that the ACS should purchase the territory but that the United States could play a support role without overstepping its legal mandate.

42. On William Wirt's decision, see Benjamin Hall, ed., *Official Opinions of the Attorneys General of the United States*, vol. 1 (Washington, DC: R. Farnham, 1852), 314–20; Staudenraus, *African Colonization Movement*, 53–57.

43. On the emergence of a specifically American vision of settler expansion that was used to protest the strictures of British imperialism, see Peter Silver, *Our Savage Neighbors: How Indian War Transformed Early America* (New York: W. W. Norton, 2009).

44. David C. Hendrickson, *Union, Nation, or Empire: The American Debate over International Relations, 1789–1941* (Lawrence: University Press of Kansas, 2009), 78–93; Sexton, *Monroe Doctrine*, 47–84; Paul Constantine Pappas, *The United States and the Greek War for Independence, 1821–1828* (New York: Columbia University Press, 1985); John J. Johnson, *A Hemisphere Apart: The Foundations of United States Policy Toward Latin America* (Baltimore: Johns Hopkins University Press, 1990), 80–87. On John Quincy Adams's role in fostering the ideas behind the Monroe Doctrine, see Weeks, *John Quincy Adams*.

45. Dexter Perkins, *Monroe Doctrine, 1823–1826* (Gloucester, MA: Peter Smith, 1965), 103. The literary scholar Gretchen Murphy has elaborated on Perkins's assertion by convincingly showing how the flexible ideas of the Monroe Doctrine were evident "in the air" through a variety of cultural narratives in the early United States. Gretchen Murphy, *Hemispheric Imaginings: The Monroe Doctrine and Narratives of U.S. Empire* (Durham, NC: Duke University Press, 2005).

46. American Society for Colonizing the Free People of Colour of the United States, *Memorial of the President and Board of Managers of the American Society for Colonizing the Free People of Colour of the United States: January 14, 1817: Read and Ordered to Lie upon the Table* (Washington, DC: William A. Davis, 1817), 3.

47. *Daily National Intelligencer*, November 27, 1818.

48. Angelo Repousis, "'The Cause of the Greeks': Philadelphia and the Greek War for Independence, 1821–1828," *Pennsylvania Magazine of History and Biography* 123, no. 4 (October 1999): 345. On the broader movement to support Greek independence in the United States, see Pappas, *United States and the Greek War for Independence.*

49. Harmodius, "Greece," *National Gazette*, December 25, 1823. Such rhetoric would be revived with even greater force following Liberian independence in the late 1840s. For instance, Edward Everett would continue to champion such arguments about a Christian settler republic modeled after the United States in the 1850s that echoed the fervent advocacy of himself and other pro-Greek colleagues in the 1820s. See Edward Everett, *Address of the Hon. Edward Everett, Secretary of State, at the Anniversary of the Am. Col. Society, 18th Jan., 1853* (Boston: T. R. Marvin, 1853).

50. Matthew Carey, *Letters on the Colonization Society; with a View of Its Probable Results* (Philadelphia, 1838), 5–6. On Carey's central role in advocating for colonization within the nationalist political economy of the "American System," see Beverly Tomek, *Colonization and Its Discontents: Emancipation, Emigration, and Antislavery in Antebellum Pennsylvania* (New York: New York University Press, 2011), 63–92.

51. Pelham, "To the Editors," *Daily National Intelligencer*, November 13, 1824.

52. *American Traveller*, December 9, 1825.

53. Reuben Smith, *Africa Given to Christ* (Chauncy Goodrich, 1830), 12–14.

54. Ibid.

55. Sexton, *Monroe Doctrine*, 73–81; Hendrickson, *Union, Nation, or Empire*, 97–103; Jeffrey J. Malanson, "The Congressional Debate over U.S. Participation in the Congress of Panama, 1825–1826: Washington's Farewell Address, Monroe's Doctrine, and the Fundamental Principles of U.S. Foreign Policy," *Diplomatic History* 30, no. 5 (November 2006): 813–38.

56. *Register of Debates*, 19th Cong., 1st sess. (1826): 112–14.

57. On the racial character of the Congress of Panama debate, see N. Andrew N. Cleven, "The First Panama Mission and the Congress of the United States," *Journal of Negro History* 13, no. 3 (July 1, 1928): 225–54. On Randolph's colonization politics, see Nicholas Wood, "John Randolph of Roanoke and the Politics of Slavery in the Early Republic," *Virginia Magazine of History and Biography* 120, no. 2 (March 2012): 106–43.

58. On the context for the political divisions within revolutionary and postrevolutionary Haiti, see David Nicholls, *From Dessalines to Duvalier: Race, Colour, and National Independence in Haiti*, rev. ed. (New Brunswick, NJ: Rutgers University Press, 1996), 33–66; Carolyn E. Fick, *The Making of Haiti: The Saint Domingue Revolution from Below* (Knoxville: University of Tennessee Press, 1990), 183–236.

59. For examples of Niles's vocal support for Haitian recognition and emigration, see *Niles' Weekly Register*, September 27, 1823, June 26, 1824.

60. On African American support for Haitian emigration, see Chris Dixon, *African America and Haiti: Emigration and Black Nationalism in the Nineteenth Century* (Westport, CT: Greenwood Press, 2000), 32–37; Ousmane K. Power-Greene, *Against Wind and Tide: The African American Struggle Against the Colonization Movement* (New York: New York University Press, 2014), 17–45; Bruce R. Dain, *A Hideous Monster of the Mind: American Race Theory in the Early Republic* (Cambridge, MA: Harvard University Press, 2002), 97–104; Maurice Jackson and Jacqueline Bacon, "'The Black Republic': The Influence of the Haitian Revolution on Northern Black Political Consciousness," in *African Americans and the Haitian Revolution: Selected Essays and Historical Documents*, ed. Maurice Jackson and Jacqueline Bacon (London: Routledge, 2010); Miller, *Search for a Black Nationality*, 76–82.

61. Loring D. Dewey, *Correspondence Relative to the Emigration to Hayti, of the Free People of Colour, in the United States Together with Instructions to the Agent Sent Out by President Boyer* (New York: Mahlon Day Press, 1824).

62. *United States Literary Gazette* 1, no. 10 (September 1, 1824).

63. "Minutes, Board of Managers," June 11, 1824, American Colonization Society Papers, Business Papers.

64. *Daily National Intelligencer*, July 5, 1824. A few weeks later, the paper published another article arguing that Liberia was much better suited than Haiti to deliver "the blessings of free and enlightened government." "African Colonization," *Daily National Intelligencer*, July 24, 1824.

65. "The Colonization Plan," *Daily National Intelligencer*, September 20, 1824.

66. See Nicholas Guyatt, *Bind Us Apart: How Enlightened Americans Invented Racial Segregation* (New York: Basic Books, 2016); Joanne Pope Melish, *Disowning Slavery: Gradual Emancipation and "Race" in New England, 1780–1860* (Ithaca, NY: Cornell University Press, 1998). On how early colonizationism was linked to concerns about maintaining social order, see Egerton, "'Its Origin Is Not a Little Curious'"; on environmentalism and the early racial theory behind colonization, see George M. Frederickson, *The Black Image in the White Mind: The Debate on Afro-American Character and Destiny, 1817–1914* (New York: Harper & Row, 1971), 6–27.

67. L. L. Hamline, *An Address Delivered in Zanesville, Ohio at the Request of a Committee of the Zanesville and Putnam Colonization Society* (Zanesville, OH: Peters & Pelham, 1830).

68. "Emigration to Africa and Hayti," *North American Review* 20, no. 46 (January 1825): 203.

69. For a typical example of this religious variant where the Liberian colony is given a role in the "final renovation of Africa," see Smith, *Africa Given to Christ*.

70. "Annual Meeting of the American Colonization Society," *African Repository and Colonial Journal* 3, no. 11 (January 1828). On how the African colonization movement posited "abstract equality" between citizenship in the United States and Liberia, see David Kazanjian, "Racial Governmentality: The African Colonization Movement," in *The Colonizing Trick: National Culture and Imperial Citizenship in Early America* (Minneapolis: University of Minnesota Press, 2003).

71. Gardiner Spring, *Memoirs of the Rev. Samuel J. Mills: Late Missionary to the South Western Section of the United States and Agent of the American Colonization Society Deputed to Explore the Coast of Africa / by Gardiner Spring* (New York: New York Evangelical Missionary Society, 1820), 139.

Chapter 3

1. James D. Richardson, "Message of Monroe, Jan. 27 1825," in *A Compilation of the Messages and Papers of the Presidents*, vol. 2 (New York: Bureau of National Literature, 1911), 280–83.

2. Robert Stockton connected Monroe's Indian colonization plan to the African colonization movement in his speech before the ACS annual meeting in 1825. See "Colonization Society," *National Intelligencer*, February 28, 1825. For a fuller discussion of this speech, see Introduction.

3. Nicholas Guyatt has published the most sustained inquiries into the relationship between colonizationism and removal policy. See Nicholas Guyatt, *Bind Us Apart: How Enlightened Americans Invented Racial Segregation* (New York: Basic Books, 2016); Nicholas Guyatt, " 'The Outskirts of Our Happiness': Race and the Lure of Colonization in the Early Republic," *Journal of American History* 95, no. 4 (March 2009): 988. For more limited prior examinations of this topic, see Mary Young, "Racism in Red and Black: Indians and Other Free People of Color in Georgia, Law, Politics, and Removal Policy," *Georgia Historical Quarterly* 73, no. 3 (1989): 492–518; Lawrence Jacob Friedman, *Inventors of the Promised Land* (New York: Knopf, 1975), 199–215; Susan M. Ryan, *The Grammar of Good Intentions: Race and the Antebellum Culture of Benevolence* (Ithaca, NY: Cornell University Press, 2003), 25–45.

4. "Notice of Publications in Behalf of the American Colonization Society," *African Repository and Colonial Journal* 6, no. 10 (December 1830): 290.

5. Reginald Horsman, "The Indian Policy of an 'Empire for Liberty,' " ed. Frederick E. Hoxie, Ronald Hoffman, and Peter J. Albert (Charlottesville: University of Virginia Press, 1999), 370; Anthony F. C. Wallace, *Jefferson and the Indians: The Tragic Fate of the First Americans* (Cambridge, MA: Belknap Press of Harvard University Press, 1999), 207–40.

6. Richard Holland Johnston, "Thomas Jefferson to Captain Hendrick, the Delawares, Mohicans, and Munries, December 21, 1808," in *The Writings of Thomas Jefferson*, vol. 16 (Washington, DC: Thomas Jefferson Memorial Association of the United States, 1903), 452.

7. Thomas Jefferson to William Henry Harrison, February 27, 1803, Thomas Jefferson Papers, Library of Congress, Ser. 1, Reel 27.

8. Reginald Horsman, *Race and Manifest Destiny: The Origins of American Racial Anglo-Saxonism* (Cambridge, MA: Harvard University Press, 1981), 191–95.

9. Honor Sachs, *Home Rule: Households, Manhood, and National Expansion on the Eighteenth-Century Kentucky Frontier* (New Haven, CT: Yale University Press, 2015).

10. George A. Schultz, *An Indian Canaan: Isaac McCoy and the Vision of an Indian State* (Norman: University of Oklahoma Press, 1972), 67–68.

11. On African colonization's place within the development of antebellum religious reform, see Emily Conroy-Krutz, *Christian Imperialism: Converting the World in the Early American Republic* (Ithaca, NY: Cornell University Press, 2015); Beverly Tomek, *Colonization and Its Discontents: Emancipation, Emigration, and Antislavery in Antebellum Pennsylvania* (New York: New York University Press, 2011); Ronald G. Walters, *American Reformers, 1815–1860* (New York: Hill & Wang, 1978); Indiana Colonization Society, "Constitution of the Indiana Auxiliary American Colonization Society," *Abolition Intelligencer and Missionary Magazine* 1, no. 2 (June 1822): 22.

12. Schultz, *Indian Canaan*, 33.

13. Isaac McCoy, *Remarks on the Practicability of Indian Reform, Embracing Their Colonization* (New York, 1827), 10.

14. Brian W. Dippie, *The Vanishing American: White Attitudes and U.S. Indian Policy* (Middletown, CT: Wesleyan University Press, 1982), 48–61.

15. George M. Frederickson, *The Black Image in the White Mind: The Debate on Afro-American Character and Destiny, 1817–1914* (New York: Harper & Row, 1971), 154–64. For an example of this thinking from the most prominent national spokesperson for African colonization, see Henry Clay, "An Address; Delivered to the Colonization Society of Kentucky, at Frankfort, December 17, 1829, by the Hon. Henry Clay, at the Request of the Board of Managers," *Daily National Intelligencer*, January 12, 1830. For an earlier iteration of this ideology within colonizationist discourse, see William Thornton's pamphlet that connected Indians and African Americans as populations that needed "protection." William Thornton, *Political Economy Founded in Justice and Humanity in a Letter to a Friend* (Washington, DC: Samuel Harrison Smith, 1804).

16. "Indian Colonization," *Columbian Star and Christian Index* 1, no. 11 (September 12, 1829): 171.

17. McCoy, *Remarks on the Practicability of Indian Reform*, 30, 40.

18. Isaac McCoy, "Address to Philanthropists in the United States Generally, and to Christians in Particular, on the Condition and Prospects of the American Indians," in *History of Baptist Indian Missions* (Washington, DC: William M. Morrison, 1831), 432.

19. William Gerald McLoughlin, *Cherokee Renascence in the New Republic* (Princeton, NJ: Princeton University Press, 1986), 248–52, 430–35. On how this struggle was located within the wider politics of the global missionary efforts, see Emily Conroy-Krutz, *Christian Imperialism: Converting the World in the Early American Republic* (Ithaca, NY: Cornell University Press, 2015), 138–41.

20. John A. Andrew, *From Revivals to Removal: Jeremiah Evarts, the Cherokee Nation, and the Search for the Soul of America* (Athens: University of Georgia Press, 2007), 151–61.

21. Schultz, *Indian Canaan*, 67–69; Francis Paul Prucha, *The Great Father: The United States Government and the American Indians* (Lincoln: University of Nebraska Press, 1984), 183–91.

22. Thomas Loraine McKenney, *Memoirs, Official and Personal: With Sketches of Travels Among the Northern and Southern Indians: Embracing a War Excursion, and Descriptions of Scenes Along the Western Borders* (New York: Paine & Burgess, 1846), 34.

23. Ibid., 229.

24. On McKenney's critical role in establishing federal Indian policy during this era, see Herman J. Viola, *Thomas L. McKenney: Architect of America's Early Indian Policy, 1816–1830* (Chicago: Sage Books, 1974); Richard Drinnon, *Facing West: The Metaphysics of Indian-Hating and Empire-Building* (Minneapolis: University of Minnesota Press, 1980), 165–90.

25. "A Bill for the Preservation and Civilization of the Indian Tribes within the United States," *Senate Bills and Resolutions*, 18th Cong., 2d sess. (1825): S. 45.

26. *Register of Debates*, 18th Cong., 2d sess. (1825): 639–49.

27. On James Barbour's continuation of Monroe's Indian colonization policy, see Prucha, *Great Father*, 66–67. Alexander Saxton offers astute analysis of Barbour's policy as an aspect of Whig approaches to a regulated policy for western expansion. However, I believe this plan should also be viewed as bearing the direct imprint of the colonization discourses of the era. Alexander Saxton, *The Rise and Fall of the White Republic: Class Politics and Mass Culture in Nineteenth-Century America* (London: Verso, 1990), 54–59.

28. Ronald N. Satz, *American Indian Policy in the Jacksonian Era* (Lincoln: University of Nebraska Press, 1974), 11–12.

29. Schultz, *Indian Canaan*, 120–25, 131–33.

30. Andrew Jackson, "First Annual Message to Congress, December 8, 1829," in *A Compilation of Messages and Papers of the Presidents*, ed. United States Congress Joint Committee on Printing, vol. 3 (Bureau of National Literature, 1897), 1005–25.

31. Horsman, *Race and Manifest Destiny*, 191–92. Alexander Saxton has argued that "soft" and "hard" rhetorics of racism appealed to different audiences but worked to sustain white supremacy. Saxton, *Rise and Fall of the White Republic*, 53–72.

32. For McCoy's exceptions for "civilized" tribes, see McCoy, *Remarks on the Practicability of Indian Reform*, 16–17, 26, 40, 46.

33. On the relationship between the rhetoric of "civilization" and racial identity among many southern tribes, see Gregory Evans Dowd, *A Spirited Resistance: The North American Indian Struggle for Unity, 1745–1815* (Baltimore: Johns Hopkins University Press, 1992), 152–54; McLoughlin, *Cherokee Renascence in the New Republic*, xvi.

34. Mary Young, "The Cherokee Nation: Mirror of the Republic," *American Quarterly* 33, no. 5 (Winter 1981): 502–24.

35. Theda Perdue, "Cherokee Planters, Black Slaves, and African Colonization," *Chronicles of Oklahoma* 60, no. 3 (1982): 322–31.

36. Walter Lowrie, Walter S. Franklin, and Matthew St. Clair Clark, eds., "McKenney to James Barbour, Sept. 2, 1825," in *American State Papers*, 2 vols. (Washington, DC, 1832), 2: 651–52; Perdue, "Cherokee Planters."

37. "Extracts from a Letter of Mr. Chamberlin, Dated 8th of January 1829," *Missionary Herald*, April 1829, 119–20. A record of the donations made by the African Benevolent Society is published in *African Repository and Colonial Journal* 6, no. 2 (April 1830): 63.

38. For examples of articles illustrating Cherokee advocacy for African colonization, see "A Scene in Africa," *Cherokee Phoenix*, March 6, 1828; "The African Colony," *Cherokee Phoenix*, June 23, 1828; "The African Colony," *Cherokee Phoenix*, October 8, 1828; "Colonization," *Cherokee Phoenix*, July 15, 1829; "The Coast of Africa," *Cherokee Phoenix*, December 3, 1829; "American Spectator and Washington City Chronicle," *Cherokee Phoenix*, July 2, 1831.

39. "Rights of Blacks in Michigan," *Cherokee Phoenix*, May 22, 1830.

40. A similar article in the paper decried the unjust treatment of a black man by a Florida court: "Land of Liberty," *Cherokee Phoenix*, July 21, 1828.

41. Tiya Miles, *Ties That Bind: The Story of an Afro-Cherokee Family in Slavery and Freedom* (Berkeley: University of California Press, 2005), 100–128; Michael D. Green, *The Politics of Indian Removal: Creek Government and Society in Crisis* (Lincoln: University of Nebraska Press, 1982), 69–72. On the broader context of evolving Cherokee nationalism, see McLoughlin, *Cherokee Renascence in the New Republic*.

42. Young, "Racism in Red and Black."

43. "Indians," *Cherokee Phoenix*, March 3, 1830.

44. E. S. Abdy, *Journal of A Residence and Tour in the United States of North America, from April, 1833, to October, 1834*, vol. 3 (London: John Murray, 1835), 86.

45. Peter Williams, *A Discourse Delivered in St. Philip's Church for the Benefit of the Coloured Community of Wilberforce, in Upper Canada, on the Fourth of July, 1830* (New York: G. F. Bunce, 1830).

46. Maria W. Stewart, *Maria W. Stewart, America's First Black Woman Political Writer: Essays and Speeches* (Bloomington: Indiana University Press, 1987), 63–64.

47. "A Voice from Providence" in William Lloyd Garrison, *Thoughts on African Colonization: Or an Impartial Exhibition of the Doctrines, Principles and Purposes of the American*

Colonization Society. Together with the Resolutions, Addresses and Remonstrances of the Free Peo-ple of Color (New York: Garrison & Knapp, 1832), 44.

48. "An Address to the Citizens of New York," *Liberator*, February 12, 1831.

49. "From the Annual Meeting of the New-England Anti-Slavery Society," *Liberator*, January 26, 1833.

50. "A Voice from Baltimore," *Liberator*, April 2, 1831.

51. "Extreme Courtesy," *Liberator*, April 9, 1831.

52. Mary Hershberger, "Mobilizing Women, Anticipating Abolition: The Struggle Against Indian Removal in the 1830s," *Journal of American History* 86, no. 1 (June 1999): 39; Alisse Portnoy, *Their Right to Speak: Women's Activism in the Indian and Slave Debates* (Cambridge, MA: Harvard University Press, 2005).

53. Garrison, *Thoughts on African Colonization*, 16.

54. "Georgia and the Colonization Society," *Liberator*, August 17, 1833.

55. "Congressional Debate House of Representatives—Feb. 20, 1828," *Daily National Intelligencer*, March 12, 1828.

56. Ibid.

57. Charles Francis Adams, ed., *Memoirs of John Quincy Adams, Comprising Portions of His Diary from 1795 to 1848*, vol. 4 (Philadelphia: J. B. Lippincott, 1875), 292–94.

58. P. J. Staudenraus, *The African Colonization Movement, 1816–1865* (New York: Columbia University Press, 1961), 53–57.

59. Ibid., 170–71.

60. R. R. Gurley, "Colonization Society," *African Repository and Colonial Journal* 1, no. 9 (November 1825): 261–62.

61. Staudenraus, *African Colonization Movement*, 173–74.

62. *Controversy Between Caius Gracchus and Opimius: In Reference to the American Society for Colonizing the Free People of Colour of the United States: First Published in the Richmond Enquirer* (Washington, DC: Georgetown, 1827), 11.

63. Ibid., 38.

64. Ibid., 65.

65. Sen. Robert Hayne, "The Colonization Society," *Register of Debates*, 19th Cong., 2d sess. (1827): 289–90.

66. Robert James Turnbull, *The Crisis: Or, Essays on the Usurpations of the Federal Government* (Charleston, SC: A. E. Miller, 1827), 7.

67. On the relationship between anticolonization and antifederalism among Jacksonians, see Staudenraus, *African Colonization Movement*, 175.

68. *Report of the Senate Committee on Foreign Relations, April 28, 1828*, 20th Cong., 1st sess., Senate Document no. 178, serial 167 (Washington, DC, 1828), 3, 5–6.

69. Ibid.

70. The legal scholar Robert Williams has outlined the logic behind this distinction between continental and global empire by showing the role of "discovery" in legitimating native dispossession. Robert A. Williams, *Like a Loaded Weapon: The Rehnquist Court, Indian Rights, and the Legal History of Racism in America* (Minneapolis: University of Minnesota Press, 2005).

71. Ryan, *Grammar of Good Intentions*, 25–45.

72. *Register of Debates*, 21st Cong., 1st sess. (1830): 1111–12.

73. "Judge Test's Address," *African Repository and Colonial Journal* 9, no. 9 (May 1833): 68.

74. *Register of Debates*, 18th Cong., 2d sess. (1825): 623.

75. Kentucky Colonization Society, "Memorial of the Kentucky Colonization Society," *African Repository and Colonial Journal* 5, no. 11 (January 1830): 347–48.

76. "Petitions of Congress," *Daily National Intelligencer*, February 12, 1831.

77. On the place of colonization policy within the Whigs' "American System," see Daniel Walker Howe, *The Political Culture of the American Whigs* (Chicago: University of Chicago Press, 1979), 134–37.

78. *Register of Debates*, 22d Cong., 1st sess. (1832): 1098, 1100–1101.

79. Ibid., 1116–17.

80. *Register of Debates*, 22d Cong., 1st sess. (1832): 1116–17; *Register of Debates*, 22d Cong., 2d sess. (1833): 75, 790.

81. *Report of the Senate Committee on Public Lands, May 18, 1832*, 22d Cong., 1st sess., Senate Document no. 145, serial 214 (Washington, DC, 1832), 16.

82. *Register of Debates*, 22d Cong., 2d sess. (1833): 75, 233.

83. Staudenraus, *African Colonization Movement*, 184–87; Claude A. Clegg, *The Price of Liberty: African Americans and the Making of Liberia* (Chapel Hill: University of North Carolina Press, 2004), 149.

Chapter 4

1. William Lloyd Garrison, "A Voice from New-Bedford," in *Thoughts on African Colonization: Or an Impartial Exhibition of the Doctrines, Principles and Purposes of the American Colonization Society. Together with the Resolutions, Addresses and Remonstrances of the Free People of Color* (New York: Garrison & Knapp, 1832), 50–51.

2. Richard C. Wade, "The Negro in Cincinnati, 1800–1830," *Journal of Negro History* 39, no. 1 (January 1954): 50–55; Nikki Taylor, "Reconsidering the 'Forced' Exodus of 1829: Free Black Emigration from Cincinnati, Ohio to Wilberforce, Canada," *Journal of African American History* 87 (Summer 2002): 283–302.

3. The term "settler citizen" is used to highlight the fact that within antebellum U.S. political discourse, citizenship was linked to the presumed right to settle on indigenous lands.

4. "For the National Intelligencer a Counter Memorial Proposed to Be Submitted to Congress in Behalf of the Free People of Colour of the District of Columbia," *Daily National Intelligencer*, December 30, 1816.

5. Ousmane Power-Greene, *Against Wind and Tide: The African American Struggle Against the Colonization Movement* (New York: New York University Press, 2014); Paul Goodman, *Of One Blood: Abolitionism and the Origins of Racial Equality* (Berkeley: University of California Press, 2000), 23–35; Leonard P. Curry, *The Free Black in Urban America, 1800–1850: The Shadow of the Dream* (Chicago: University of Chicago Press, 1981), 231–38; Albert G. Oliver, "The Protest and Attitudes of Blacks Towards the American Colonization Society and the Concepts of Emigration and Colonization in Africa, 1817–1865" (Ph.D. diss., St. John's University, 1978), 45–122; P. J. Staudenraus, *The African Colonization Movement, 1816–1865* (New York: Columbia University Press, 1961), 29–31; Louis R. Mehlinger, "The Attitude of the Free Negro Toward African Colonization," *Journal of Negro History* 1, no. 3 (June 1916): 276–301.

6. David Walker, *Walker's Appeal, in Four Articles: Together with a Preamble to the Colored Citizens of the World, but in Particular and Very Expressly to Those of the United States of America* (Boston, 1829), 68. On the implications of Walker's anticolonizationism within the context of U.S. empire, see David Kazanjian, *The Colonizing Trick: National Culture and Imperial Citizenship in Early America* (Minneapolis: University of Minnesota Press, 2003), 89–138.

7. "From the Annual Meeting of the New-England Anti-Slavery Society," *Liberator*, January 26, 1833.

8. "Address of C. C. Harper: Extract from a Late Address of Charles Carroll Harper to the Voters of Baltimore," *African Repository and Colonial Journal* 2, no. 6 (August 1826): 188–90.

9. On how white leaders viewed colonization as an effort to reconcile republicanism with racial hierarchy, see Douglas R. Egerton, "'Its Origin Is Not a Little Curious': A New Look at the American Colonization Society," *Journal of the Early Republic* 5, no. 4 (Winter 1985): 463–80; David M. Streifford, "The American Colonization Society: An Application of Republican Ideology to Early Antebellum Reform," *Journal of Southern History* 45, no. 2 (May 1979): 201–20.

10. "Address of C. C. Harper," 188–90.

11. Dorothy Burnett Porter, ed., "Resolutions of the People of Color, at a Meeting Held on 25th of January, 1831. With an Address to the Citizens of New York, 1831. In Answer to Those of the New York Colonization Society," in *Early Negro Writing, 1760–1837* (Boston: Beacon Press, 1971), 283.

12. "Address of C. C. Harper," 188–90.

13. On the relationship between settler identity and white male citizenship in both the Revolutionary and early republic eras, see Bethel Saler, *The Settlers' Empire: Colonialism and State Formation in America's Old Northwest* (Philadelphia: University of Pennsylvania Press, 2014); Aziz Rana, *The Two Faces of American Freedom* (Cambridge, MA: Harvard University Press, 2010); Peter Silver, *Our Savage Neighbors: How Indian War Transformed Early America* (New York: W. W. Norton, 2009).

14. *Essex Register (Salem, MA)*, December 17, 1817.

15. "Thirty-First Annual Report of the American Colonization Society; 18 January, 1848," *African Repository and Colonial Journal* 24, no. 3 (March 1848): 65.

16. "Colonization Hints," *Liberator*, February 12, 1831.

17. Saler, *Settlers' Empire*. On the process of asserting a "native" settler identity in the context of New England, see Jean M. O'Brien, *Firsting and Lasting: Writing Indians out of Existence in New England* (Minneapolis: University of Minnesota Press, 2010).

18. James Brown Ray, "Speech to the Indiana General Assembly," in *Papers of James Brown Ray*, ed. Dorothy Riker and Gayle Thornbough (Indianapolis: Indiana Historical Bureau, 1954), 472–73.

19. Thomas D. Matijasic, "The Foundations of Colonization: The Peculiar Nature of Race Relations in Ohio During the Early Ante-Bellum Period," *Queen City Heritage* 49, no. 4 (1991): 23–25; Eugene H. Berwanger, *The Frontier Against Slavery: Western Anti-Negro Prejudice and the Slavery Extension Controversy* (Urbana: University of Illinois Press, 2002), 31.

20. *The Cincinnati Directory for the Year 1829* (Cincinnati: Robinson & Fairbank, 1829).

21. Wade, "Negro in Cincinnati," 43–44.

22. *Cincinnati Daily Gazette*, July 24, 1829.

23. Leonard L. Richards, *Gentlemen of Property and Standing: Anti-Abolition Mobs in Jacksonian America* (New York: Oxford University Press, 1970), 34; Staudenraus, *African Colonization Movement*, 139; Wade, "Negro in Cincinnati," 54.

24. David Smith, *The First Annual Report of the Ohio State Society for Colonizing the Free People of Colour of the United States* (Columbus, OH, 1828).

25. Richard C. Wade, *The Urban Frontier: Pioneer Life in Early Pittsburgh, Cincinnati, Lexington, Louisville, and St. Louis* (Chicago: University of Chicago Press, 1967), 226; J. Reuben Sheeler, "The Struggle of the Negro in Ohio for Freedom," *Journal of Negro History* 31, no. 2 (April 1946): 210–12; Curry, *Free Black in Urban America*, 104–5.

26. Quoted from the *Cincinnati Emporium* in the "Colored People in Ohio," *Scioto Gazette*, July 22, 1829; this letter was republished to a wider audience of ACS members as "Coloured People in Ohio," *African Repository and Colonial Journal* 5, no. 6 (August 1829): 185.

27. John Malvin, *The Autobiography of John Malvin* (Cleveland, OH: Leader Printing Company, 1879), 12–13.

28. Wade, "Negro in Cincinnati," 50–55; John M. Werner, *Reaping the Bloody Harvest: Race Riots in the United States During the Age of Jackson, 1824–1849* (New York: Garland, 1986), 56–57. On the role of self-determination in black migration plans, see Taylor, "Reconsidering the 'Forced' Exodus of 1829," 283–302.

29. Henry Noble Sherwood, "The Movement in Ohio to Deport the Negro," *Quarterly Publication of the Historical and Philosophical Society of Ohio* 7 (June 1912): 53–87; Richards, *Gentlemen of Property and Standing*, 34–35. For firsthand reporting on the events, see *Western Times*, August 22, 1829; *Western Star*, August 29, 1829.

30. *Western Times*, August 22, 1829.

31. Robert S. Finley to R. R. Gurley, November 9, 1826, American Colonization Society Papers, Library of Congress, Ser. 1, Reel 1.

32. Walker, *Walker's Appeal*, 64.

33. Staudenraus, *African Colonization Movement*, 207–23; Richards, *Gentlemen of Property and Standing*, 26–27; John Jentz, "Artisans, Evangelicals, and the City: A Social History of Abolition and Labor Reform in Jacksonian New York" (Ph.D. diss., City University of New York, 1977), 245–46; Werner, *Reaping the Bloody Harvest*, 138–40.

34. *New York Courier and Enquirer*, July 9, 1834.

35. Milo Osborn to C. W. Lawrence, July 12, 1834, Miscellaneous Riots, 1834, New-York Historical Society. On the preceding anti-abolitionist violence fostered by colonizationists in late 1833 and early 1834, see John Neal to R. R. Gurley, October 2, 1833, ACS Papers, Incoming Correspondence; E. S. Abdy, *Journal of a Residence and Tour in the United States of North America, from April, 1833, to October, 1834*, 3 vols. (London: John Murray, 1835), 1:389; Joel Tyler Headley, *The Great Riots of New York, 1712 to 1873* (New York: E. B. Treat, 1873), 82–83; Bertram Wyatt-Brown, *Lewis Tappan and the Evangelical War Against Slavery* (Cleveland, OH: Case Western Reserve University Press, 1969), 115–16.

36. Abdy, *Journal*, 3:317.

37. As in Ohio, the antiblack climate in Pennsylvania had been aided by the state government, which had systematically marginalized free African Americans while supporting African colonization as a solution. In 1829 the state's legislative assembly publicly endorsed the efforts of the ACS and two years later passed legislation that outlawed black settlement in the state. See Leon F. Litwack, *North of Slavery: The Negro in the Free States, 1790–1860* (Chicago: University of Chicago Press, 1961), 69. John Runcie has argued that African colonization only played a partial role in the riot. I agree that it was not a primary factor, but I am more interested in how its logic was embedded within the context in which rioters acted, rather than a search for direct inspiration. John Runcie, " 'Hunting the Nigs' in Philadelphia: The Race Riot of August 1834," *Pennsylvania History* 39 (1972): 190; Acting Committee, Pennsylvania Abolition Society, "Report on the Aug. 12–14, 1834 Riot Against Blacks by a Philadelphia Mob," 1834, Pennsylvania Abolition Society Papers, Historical Society of Pennsylvania, cited in Werner, *Reaping the Bloody Harvest*, 170; Edwin Atlee, "The Mobs in Philadelphia—Their Causes—Their Character," *New York Emancipator*, August 26, 1834. Edward Abdy also noted that several colonization-friendly newspapers played a role in stirring potential rioters. Abdy, *Journal*, 3:318; *Commercial Herald*, August 11, 1834; *Poulson's American Daily Advertiser*, August 20, 1834.

38. Job R. Tyson, *Discourse Before the Young Men's Colonization Society of Pennsylvania: Delivered October 24, 1834, in St. Paul's Church, Philadelphia* (Philadelphia, 1834), 14–16.

39. On official repudiation of the riots by ACS members, see "Abolition Riots," *New-York Spectator*, July 14, 1834; "Address of Rev. Peter Williams," *New-York Spectator*, July 17, 1834.

40. Elizur Wright to Amos Phelps, August 8, 1834, Elizur Wright Papers, Library of Congress.

41. Abdy, *Journal*, 3:115; Werner, *Reaping the Bloody Harvest*, 142.

42. Richards, *Gentlemen of Property and Standing*, 150–55. See also Paul A. Gilje, *The Road to Mobocracy: Popular Disorder in New York City, 1763–1834* (Chapel Hill: University of North Carolina Press, 1987), 165–66.

43. "Further Colonization Riots," *Workingman's Advocate*, July 12, 1834; "Five Points," *New York Evening Post*, July 12, 1834.

44. Abdy, *Journal*, 3:324.

45. Linda Kerber has posited that racialized labor competition was the central concern of rioters. Linda Kerber, "Abolitionists and Amalgamators: The New York City Race Riots of 1834," *New York History* 48, no. 1 (January 1967): 165–66. On the race and class politics for the workers involved in the riot, see David R. Roediger, *The Wages of Whiteness: Race and the Making of the American Working Class* (London: Verso, 1999), 107–11. On how New York rioters had addressed a similar issue by targeting higher-status black residents and referencing minstrel show burlesques of black respectability, see Eric Lott, *Love and Theft: Blackface Minstrelsy and the American Working Class* (New York: Oxford University Press, 1995), 131–35; Runcie, "'Hunting the Nigs' in Philadelphia," 200–201. For descriptions of the Philadelphia riots, see "Town Meeting.—Riots," *Hazard's Register of Pennsylvania, Devoted to the Preservation of Facts and Documents, and Every Kind of Useful Information Respecting the State of Pennsylvania* 14, no. 13 (September 27, 1834); *Niles' Weekly Register*, August 30, 1834.

46. Samuel Joseph May, *Some Recollections of Our Antislavery Conflict* (Boston: Fields, Osgood, 1869).

47. Gary B. Nash, *Forging Freedom: The Formation of Philadelphia's Black Community, 1720–1840* (Cambridge, MA: Harvard University Press, 1988), 272–75.

48. William Lloyd Garrison, *An Address Delivered Before the Free People of Color in Philadelphia, New-York, and Other Cities, During the month of June 1831* (Boston: Stephen Foster, 1831), 18–19.

49. *Columbia Spy (Pennsylvania)*, August 23, 1834; William Frederic Worner, "The Columbia Race Riots," *Lancaster County Historical Society Papers* 26 (1922): 177–78.

50. "Philadelphia Riots," *Columbia Spy (Pennsylvania)*, August 23, 1834.

51. William Frederic Worner, "The Lancaster County Colonization Society," *Lancaster County Historical Society Papers* 26 (1922): 109.

52. B., "Remarks on the Rise, Condition, and Prospect of the Colony at Liberia, No. 4," *Columbia Spy (Pennsylvania)*, June 14, 1832.

53. Leroy T. Hopkins, "The Emergence of Black Columbia, 1726–1861," *Journal of the Lancaster County Historical Society* 89 (1985): 110–32.

54. "A Voice from Columbia, PA!," *Liberator*, August 20, 1831.

55. *Columbia Spy (Pennsylvania)*, May 24, 1834.

56. *Columbia Spy (Pennsylvania)*, August 23, 1834.

57. Ibid.

58. Ibid.

59. *Columbia Spy (Pennsylvania)*, September 6, 1834; "Notice," *Columbia Spy (Pennsylvania)*, September 13, 1834. Nearly a month after the initial violence, another mob attacked several houses inhabited by African Americans, allegedly in reaction to the recent marriage of a black man and a white woman. See "Occurrences of a Night," *Columbia Spy (Pennsylvania)*, October 4, 1834.

60. Terry Bouton, *Taming Democracy: "The People," the Founders, and the Troubled Ending of the American Revolution* (New York: Oxford University Press, 2009), 53–54.

61. On the broader political context for black disenfranchisement in Pennsylvania, see Nicholas Wood, "'A Sacrifice on the Altar of Slavery': Doughface Politics and Black Disenfranchisement in Pennsylvania, 1837–1838," *Journal of the Early Republic* 31, no. 1 (Spring 2011): 75–106.

62. *Proceedings and Debates of the Convention of the Commonwealth of Pennsylvania, to Propose Amendments to the Constitution, Commenced . . . at Harrisburg, on the Second Day of May, 1837*, 14 vols. (Harrisburg, PA: Packer, Barrett, and Parke, 1837), 9:389.

63. Ibid.

64. Ibid., 10:8.

65. Ibid., 10:23.

66. Ibid., 2:200–201.

67. Ibid., 5:456.

68. Ibid., 2:200.

69. "Proceedings and Debates of the Constitutional Convention," *Indiana State Journal*, November 9, 1850.

70. *The Constitutional Debates of 1847* (Springfield: Trustees of the Illinois State Historical Library, 1919), 203.

71. "Illinois Constitutional Convention—June 24, 1847," *Sangamon Journal*, July 1, 1847.

72. George A. Gordon, "Negroes," *Indiana State Journal*, February 7, 1851.

73. "Proceedings and Debates of the Constitutional Convention," *Indiana State Journal*, February 6, 1851.

74. "Remarks of Mr. Gregg, of Jefferson." *Indiana State Journal*, November 23, 1850.

75. *Constitutional Debates of 1847*, 211–12.

76. Milo M. Quaife, *The Convention of 1846*, vol. 27 (Madison: Wisconsin Historical Society, 1919), 214–15.

77. *Report of the Proceedings and Debates in the Convention to Revise the Constitution of the State of Michigan, 1850* (Lansing, MI: R. W. Ingals, 1850), 290–91.

78. "Negro Suffrage," *Indiana State Journal*, November 9, 1850.

79. William Blair Lord, Charles B. Collar, and Henry M. Parkhurst, *The Debates of the Constitutional Convention* (Davenport, IA: Luse, Lane, 1857), 700.

80. *Constitutional Debates of 1847*, 207.

81. *Report of the Debates and Proceedings of the Convention for the Revision of the Constitution of the State of Ohio, 1850–51* (Columbus, OH: S. Medary, 1851), 56.

82. See article 13, section 1 of the 1851 Indiana constitution in *Constitution of the State of Indiana: And the Address of the Constitutional Convention* (New Albany, IA: Kent & Norman, 1851).

83. "Meeting of the Citizens of Indiana in Behalf of Colonization," *Lafayette Daily Courier*, February 9, 1852.

84. "Benevolence to the African Race," *African Repository* 27, no. 7 (July 1851): 208.

85. Samuel W. Parker, *Speech of Hon. S. W. Parker of Indiana, in the House of Representatives, April 28, 1852* (Washington, DC, 1852).

86. "Letter from Liberia," *Lafayette Daily Courier*, March 30, 1853.

87. Ohio Committee of Correspondence, of the American Colonization Society, *Ohio in Africa* (Cincinnati, 1851).

88. Edward Wesley Shunk, "Ohio in Africa," *Ohio State Archaeological and Historical Quarterly* 51 (1942); Sherwood, "Movement in Ohio"; Thomas D. Matijasic, "Conservative Reform in the West: The African Colonization Movement in Ohio, 1826–1839" (Ph.D. diss., Miami University, 1982), 195–99; Stephen Middleton, *The Black Laws: Race and the Legal Process in Early Ohio* (Athens: Ohio University Press, 2005), 144–56.

89. *Report of the . . . Constitution of the State of Ohio*, 56–59; "Negro Exclusion," *African Repository* 29, no. 4 (April 1853): 110; "Blacks and Mulattoes," *Liberator*, January 7, 1853; "Revival of the Negro Laws in Ohio," *New York Daily Times*, December 17, 1852.

90. "Remarks of Robert Christy," *Ohio Statesman*, April 10, 1859.

91. "Anti-Colonization Meeting," *Liberator*, April 15, 1853.

92. "A New Party Question," *Frederick Douglass' Paper*, March 18, 1853.

Chapter 5

1. *Liberia Herald*, April 15, 1847.

2. "Liberia—Colonization," *Daily National Intelligencer*, May 22, 1847.

3. On the United States' "anti-imperial" stance during the early national era, see Mary Ann Heiss, "The Evolution of the Imperial Idea and U.S. National Identity," *Diplomatic History* 26 (Fall 2002): 511–40; Walter LaFeber, "The American View of Decolonization, 1776–1920: An Ironic Legacy," in *The United States and Decolonization: Power and Freedom*, ed. David Ryan and Victor Pungong (Basingstoke, UK: Palgrave Macmillan, 2000), 24–40; William Earl Weeks, "American Nationalism, American Imperialism: An Interpretation of United States Political Economy, 1789–1861," *Journal of the Early Republic* 14 (Winter 1994): 485–95.

4. Nicholas Guyatt, " 'The Outskirts of Our Happiness': Race and the Lure of Colonization in the Early Republic," *Journal of American History* 95 (March 2009): 987.

5. Bronwen Everill and Gale Kenny have recently examined how expansionist arguments informed black emigrationism during this period. Bronwen Everill, " 'Destiny Seems to Point Me to That Country': Early Nineteenth-century African American Migration, Emigration, and Expansion," *Journal of Global History* 7 (March 2012): 53–77; Gale L. Kenny, "Manliness and Manifest Racial Destiny: Jamaica and African American Emigration in the 1850s," *Journal of the Civil War Era* 2, no. 2 (2012): 151–78; Gale L. Kenny, *Contentious Liberties: American Abolitionists in Post-Emancipation Jamaica, 1834–1866* (Athens: University of Georgia Press, 2010). While the ideology of manifest destiny bolstered such arguments, the ethos of expansion reflected in support for Liberia was more in line with what Amy Greenberg has identified as the "restrained manhood" behind Hawaiian colonization than the "martial manhood" of filibustering expeditions following the Mexican-American War. Amy S. Greenberg, *Manifest Manhood and the Antebellum American Empire* (Cambridge: Cambridge University Press, 2005).

6. On African colonization and U.S. empire, see Eugene S. Van Sickle, "Reluctant Imperialists: The U.S. Navy and Liberia, 1819–1845," *Journal of the Early Republic* 31 (Spring 2011): 107–34; Bronwen Everill, "British West Africa or 'The United States of Africa'? Imperial Pressures on the Transatlantic Anti-slavery Movement, 1839–1842," *Journal of Transatlantic Studies* 9 (June 2011): 136–50; David Kazanjian, *The Colonizing Trick: National Culture and Imperial Citizenship*

in Early America (Minneapolis: University of Minnesota Press, 2003); Etsuko Taketani, "Postcolonial Liberia: Sarah Josepha Hale's Africa," *American Literary History* 14 (Autumn 2002): 479–504; Amy Kaplan, "Manifest Domesticity," *American Literature* 70 (September 1998): 581–606; Susan M. Ryan, "Errand into Africa: Colonization and Nation Building in Sarah J. Hale's Liberia," *New England Quarterly* 68 (December 1995): 558–83.

7. Historians of colonizationism and early Liberian history have generally minimized the significance of independence aside from its role in altering the colony's relationship to the ACS or its impact on the governing structures within Liberia. See Eric Burin, *Slavery and the Peculiar Solution: A History of the American Colonization Society* (Gainesville: University Press of Florida, 2005); Amos Jones Beyan, *The American Colonization Society and the Creation of the Liberian State: A Historical Perspective, 1822–1900* (Lanham, MD: University Press of America, 1991); James Wesley Smith, *Sojourners in Search of Freedom: The Settlement of Liberia by Black Americans* (Lanham, MD: University Press of America, 1987); P. J. Staudenraus, *The African Colonization Movement, 1816–1865* (New York: Columbia University Press, 1961). Exceptions to this trend are found in the work of Claude Clegg and Ousmane Greene, who have detailed the complicated reception of Liberian independence by black audiences. Claude A. Clegg, *The Price of Liberty: African Americans and the Making of Liberia* (Chapel Hill: University of North Carolina Press, 2004), 179–200; Ousmane Greene, "Against Wind and Tide: African Americans' Response to the Colonization Movement and Emigration, 1770–1865" (Ph.D. diss., University of Massachusetts Amherst, 2007), 358–72. David Kazanjian has also thoughtfully addressed Liberian independence by calling into question the "historicist" framework that assumes black settlers progressed on an inevitable path toward liberal citizenship and state formation before 1847. David Kazanjian, "The Speculative Freedom of Colonial Liberia," *American Quarterly* 63 (December 2011): 863–93. On how the Liberian republic was viewed within the context of British imperialism, see Zoë Laidlaw, "Slavery, Settlers and Indigenous Dispossession: Britain's Empire Through the Lens of Liberia," *Journal of Colonialism and Colonial History* 13, no. 1 (2012).

8. On how expanded political participation was defined by the exclusion of black citizens, see Alexander Keyssar, *The Right to Vote: The Contested History of Democracy in the United States*, rev. ed. (New York: Basic Books, 2009), 23–60; Christopher Malone, *Between Freedom and Bondage: Race, Party, and Voting Rights in the Antebellum North* (New York: Routledge, 2007), 23–100; Sean Wilentz, *The Rise of American Democracy: Jefferson to Lincoln* (New York: W. W. Norton, 2006), 330–58, 547–76; David Waldstreicher, *In the Midst of Perpetual Fetes: The Making of American Nationalism, 1776–1820* (Chapel Hill: University of North Carolina Press, 1997), 294–348; James H. Kettner, *The Development of American Citizenship, 1608–1870* (Chapel Hill: University of North Carolina Press, 1978), 287–333; Leon F. Litwack, *North of Slavery: The Negro in the Free States, 1790–1860* (Chicago: University of Chicago Press, 1961), 64–112.

9. On the specific role colonizationism played in excluding African Americans from northern conceptions of the national polity, see John Wood Sweet, *Bodies Politic: Negotiating Race in the American North, 1730–1830* (Baltimore: Johns Hopkins University Press, 2003), 349–67; Joanne Pope Melish, *Disowning Slavery: Gradual Emancipation and "Race" in New England, 1780–1860* (Ithaca, NY: Cornell University Press, 1998), 163–209; James Brewer Stewart, "The Emergence of Racial Modernity and the Rise of the White North, 1790–1840," *Journal of the Early Republic* 18 (Summer 1998): 181–217.

10. On the decline of colonizationism following the organizational crises of the ACS, see Clegg, *Price of Liberty*, 129–62; Burin, *Slavery and the Peculiar Solution*, 79–99; Kurt Lee Kocher, "A Duty to America and Africa: A History of the Independent African Colonization Movement

in Pennsylvania," *Pennsylvania History* 51, no. 2 (1984): 118–53; George M. Frederickson, *The Black Image in the White Mind: The Debate on Afro-American Character and Destiny, 1817–1914* (New York: Harper & Row, 1971), 27–32.

11. On how black critiques of African colonization transformed into new assertions of black nationalism, see Patrick Rael, *Black Identity and Black Protest in the Antebellum North* (Chapel Hill: University of North Carolina Press, 2002), 209–78; James Sidbury, *Becoming African in America: Race and Nation in the Early Black Atlantic* (New York: Oxford University Press, 2007), 157–79, 201–10. From 1848 to 1857 the ACS sent 5,125 colonists to Liberia, while from 1838 to 1847 it sent only 1,108. Staudenraus, *African Colonization Movement*, 251.

12. The view that Liberia was distinct from U.S. territorial empire in North America was rooted in discussions during the Monroe administration, when Secretary of State John Quincy Adams worried that the establishment of the settlement would burden the United States with an unconstitutional "colonial system." Charles Francis Adams, ed., *Memoirs of John Quincy Adams, Comprising Portions of His Diary from 1795 to 1848*, 12 vols. (Philadelphia: J. B. Lippincott & Co., 1875), 4:292–94. For the contours of this debate, see Chapter 1.

13. Young Men's Colonization Society of New York, *Address and Constitution of the Young Men's Colonization Society* (Philadelphia, 1834).

14. "Extract of a Letter from New Orleans," *African Repository and Colonial Journal* 16, no. 8 (April 15, 1840): 116.

15. Tom W. Shick, *Behold the Promised Land: A History of Afro-American Settler Society in Nineteenth-Century Liberia* (Baltimore: Johns Hopkins University Press, 1980), 37–38; Staudenraus, *African Colonization Movement*, 82–93.

16. George William Brown, *The Economic History of Liberia* (Washington, DC: Associated Publishers, 1941), 127–30; Svend E. Holsoe, "A Study of Relations Between Settlers and Indigenous Peoples in Western Liberia, 1821–1847," *African Historical Studies* 4, no. 2 (1971): 331–62.

17. On the tension between the indigenous populations of West Africa and American civilizing missions, see Joseph Yannielli, "George Thompson Among the Africans: Empathy, Authority, and Insanity in the Age of Abolition," *Journal of American History* 96 (March 2010): 979–1000; Tunde Adeleke, *UnAfrican Americans: Nineteenth-Century Black Nationalists and the Civilizing Mission* (Lexington: University Press of Kentucky, 1998).

18. "Edward Everett to Earl of Aberdeen, December 30, 1843," in *Colony of Liberia, in Africa: message from the President of the United States, accompanied with a report of the Secretary of State, relative to the colony of Liberia* (Washington, DC: Blair & Rives Printers, 1844), 5.

19. "R. R. Gurley to John Tyler, February 2, 1844," in ibid, 11.

20. Comm. W. Jones, September 9, 1844, Records of the Massachusetts Colonization Society, Massachusetts Historical Society, Boston.

21. Charles Henry Huberich, *The Political and Legislative History of Liberia*, 2 vols. (New York: Central Book, 1947), 1:774. In 1842 Secretary of State Daniel Webster responded to British inquiries about the colony's status and ruled that Liberia was effectively independent and not a possession of the United States. For a detailed examination of this question, see Van Sickle, "Reluctant Imperialists," 129–32.

22. An excerpt from the *Commercial Advertiser* article was reprinted in "Trouble in Liberia," *Emancipator and Weekly Chronicle*, July 2, 1845.

23. "Mr. John P. Kennedy's Report on Our African Colonies and Commerce," *Daily National Intelligencer*, November 8, 1843.

24. "Reviews," *African Repository and Colonial Journal* 20, no. 3 (March 1844): 65.

25. Joseph Tracy, "Sovereignty of Liberia," *African Repository and Colonial Journal* 21, no. 4 (April 1845): 97–102.

26. Joseph Tracy to Simon Greenleaf, April 26, 1845, Simon Greenleaf Papers, Harvard Law School Library, Cambridge, MA.

27. "Oration," *Liberia Herald*, February 5, 1847.

28. *Liberia Herald*, January 15, 1847.

29. William McLain to Joseph Roberts, May 1846, American Colonization Society Papers, Library of Congress, Washington, DC (hereafter ACS Papers), Ser. 2, Reel 187.

30. William McLain to Joseph Roberts, August 28, 1846, ACS Papers, Ser. 2, Reel 187.

31. "Board of Directors, Executive Committee Journal," January 20, 1847, ACS Papers, Ser. 5, Reel 292.

32. William McLain to Joseph Roberts, April 12, 1847, ACS Papers, Ser. 2, Reel 188.

33. On the alienation of indigenous groups from the early Liberian state, see Jeremy I. Levitt, *The Evolution of Deadly Conflict in Liberia: From "Paternaltarianism" to State Collapse* (Durham, NC: Duke University Press, 2005), 89–94.

34. On the domination of the Liberian political bureaucracy by the colony's merchant settler elite, see Amos Jones Beyan, "The Antitheses of Liberia's Independence in Historical Perspective, 1822–1990," *Liberian Studies Journal* 22, no. 1 (1997): 4–5; Magdalene S. David, "The Love of Liberty Brought Us Here (An Analysis of the Development of the Settler State in 19th Century Liberia)," *Review of African Political Economy* 31 (December 1984): 63–64; Robert T. Brown, "Simon Greenleaf and the Liberian Constitution of 1847," *Liberian Studies Journal* 9, no. 2 (1980): 52–53.

35. "Declaration of Independence in Convention," in *Liberian Statutes, 1847–1857* (Monrovia: Herald Office, J. C. Minor, 1857), 4. See Article 5, Sections 12 and 13 of the Constitution of the Republic of Liberia, in *Liberian Statutes*, 18.

36. See Constitution of the Republic of Liberia, Article 5, Sections 12 and 13, 18. The creation of different rights for black and white residents already had some precedent in the laws of the separate colony operated by the Maryland State Colonization Society in Cape Palmas. *Constitution and Laws of Maryland in Liberia with an Appendix of Precedents* (Baltimore: John D. Toy, 1847), 103–9.

37. Elliot Cresson to Simon Greenleaf, February 15, 1848, Simon Greenleaf Papers, Harvard Law School Library. While at least two other accounts of the convention were kept at the time, including the convention's official minutes, both were either lost or destroyed, making the sections of Lugenbeel's journal sent in a letter to the ACS the only extant record of its proceedings. J. W. Lugenbeel to William McLain, October 9, 1847, ACS Papers, Ser. 1, Reel 53.

38. Samuel Benedict to Simon Greenleaf, April 4, 1848, Simon Greenleaf Papers, Harvard Law School Library.

39. "Thirtieth Annual Report of the American Colonization Society," *African Repository and Colonial Journal* 23, no. 3 (March 1847): 65.

40. "New York State Colonization Society," *New York Herald*, May 10, 1848; "The Republic of Liberia," *Daily National Intelligencer*, May 5, 1848.

41. Timothy Mason Roberts, *Distant Revolutions: 1848 and the Challenge to American Exceptionalism* (Charlottesville: University of Virginia Press, 2009); Andre M. Fleche, *The Revolution of 1861: The American Civil War in the Age of Nationalist Conflict* (Chapel Hill: University of North Carolina Press, 2012). In the case of the Italian nationalist struggle, Paola Gemme has argued that the United States has legitimized its designs of imperial expansion through the

"myth of the United States as a catalyst and model of global liberal movements." Paola Gemme, *Domesticating Foreign Struggles: The Italian Risorgimento and Antebellum American Identity* (Athens: University of Georgia Press, 2005), 5. For an older literature on the United States' long relationship with political revolutions and nation building, see William Appleman Williams, *America Confronts a Revolutionary World, 1776–1976* (New York: Morrow, 1976), 15–119; David Brion Davis, *Revolutions: Reflections on American Equality and Foreign Liberations* (Cambridge, MA: Harvard University Press, 1990); Paul Constantine Pappas, *The United States and the Greek War for Independence, 1821–1828* (New York: Columbia University Press, 1985); Arthur Preston Whitaker, *The United States and the Independence of Latin America, 1800–1830* (New York: Russell & Russell, 1962). For the creation of colonizationist doctrine within the context of republican revolution, see Chapter 2.

42. "Liberia," *Niles' National Register* 22, no. 7 (April 17, 1847); "Liberia," *Niles' National Register* 22, no. 9 (May 1, 1847); "National Convention of Colored People," *Niles' National Register* 23, no. 11 (November 13, 1847); "Republic of Liberia," *Niles' National Register* 23, no. 14 (December 4, 1847); "The Republic of Liberia," *Niles' National Register* 23, no. 16 (December 25, 1847).

43. *Journal of Commerce* article cited in "The Republic of Liberia," *Pittsfield (MA) Sun*, March 23, 1848.

44. "A Republic in Africa," *New York Sun*, January 5, 1847.

45. On the relationship between U.S. imperialism and antebellum missionary endeavors, see Emily Conroy-Krutz, *Christian Imperialism: Converting the World in the Early American Republic* (Ithaca, NY: Cornell University Press, 2015).

46. "Liberia," *New Hampshire Sentinel*, December 23, 1847.

47. "The Republic of Liberia," *Barre (MA) Patriot*, November 19, 1847.

48. "Independence of Liberia," *Hartford Daily Courant*, November 30, 1847.

49. For articles listing government officials, see "Meeting of the Legislature," *New London (CT) Morning News*, March 8, 1848; "Appointment by the President of Liberia, with the Consent of the Senate," *Hudson River Chronicle*, July 11, 1848. For articles highlighting Liberia's U.S.-inspired flag, see "Liberia," *Vermont Chronicle*, December 29, 1847; "Flag and Seal of the Republic of Liberia," *Wachusett Star*, January 18, 1848; "Liberia," *Ohio Observer*, January 19, 1848.

50. "Republic of Liberia," *Farmer's Cabinet* 46, no. 14 (November 18, 1847): 2.

51. Article from the *Christian Statesman* reprinted in "Frederick Douglass and Augustus Washington," *Frederick Douglass' Paper*, September 4, 1851.

52. "Turn About Is Fair Play," *New London (CT) Morning News*, December 24, 1847. A few months later, the paper reiterated this point in a three-sentence bulletin on Liberia, which explained that "no white man can vote in Liberia." "Events of 1847," *New London (CT) Morning News*, February 2, 1848.

53. From the *Liberia Advocate*, May 1846, printed in "Liberia an Independent Republic," *Christian Advocate and Journal*, May 20, 1846.

54. "Thirtieth Annual Report of the American Colonization Society," *African Repository and Colonial Journal* 23, no. 3 (March 1847): 65.

55. "But Will They Go?" *African Repository* 26, no. 10 (October 1850): 292.

56. Geo. S. L. Starks, "Analogy Between the Anglo-American and the Liberian," *African Repository* 27, no. 11 (November 1851): 345.

57. John A. M'Clung, *Proceedings of the Annual Meeting of the Kentucky Colonization Society* (Frankfort, KY: A. G. Hodges, 1848), 17–20.

58. "Noble Enterprise—Ohio in Africa," *Cincinnati Daily Gazette*, August 26, 1848; "Annual Report of the American Colonization Society," *African Repository* 27, no. 3 (March 1851): 65.

59. "Blacks and Mulattoes," *Liberator*, January 7, 1853.

60. Susan M. Ryan, "Errand into Africa: Colonization and Nation Building in Sarah J. Hale's Liberia," *New England Quarterly* 68, no. 4 (December 1995): 558–83; Amy Kaplan, "Manifest Domesticity," *American Literature* 70, no. 3 (September 1998): 581–606; Etsuko Taketani, "Postcolonial Liberia: Sarah Josepha Hale's Africa," *American Literary History* 14, no. 3 (Autumn 2002): 479–504; Etsuko Taketani, *U.S. Women Writers and the Discourses of Colonialism, 1825–1861* (Knoxville: University of Tennessee Press, 2003).

61. "The New Republic—A Thrilling Sketch," *Farmer's Cabinet* 48, no. 37 (April 25, 1850): 1. On the print culture of sensationalist stories about the Mexican-American War, see Shelley Streeby, *American Sensations: Class, Empire, and the Production of Popular Culture* (Berkeley: University of California Press, 2002).

62. Helen C. Knight, *The New Republic* (Boston: Massachusetts Sabbath School Society, 1851), 64–70. The book was also republished under the title *Africa Redeemed: Or, The Means of Her Relief Illustrated by the Growth and Prospects of Liberia* (London: James Nisbet, 1851).

63. Knight, *New Republic*, 228–35, 241, 247. While it is unclear how much impact Knight's book made, a colonizationist newspaper claimed that it had "extensive circulation" and was successful in making "many new friends" to support an independent Liberia. "Review of The New Republic, by Helen C. Knight," *Colonization Herald*, July 1850.

64. Harriet Beecher Stowe, *Uncle Tom's Cabin* (New York: W. W. Norton, 1993), 374–75.

65. Ryan, "Errand into Africa," 563. While Hale focused on responding to Stowe, she also acknowledged a debt to Knight in the book's preface. Sarah J. Hale, *Liberia Or, Mr. Peyton's Experiments* (New York: Harper & Brothers, 1853).

66. Hale, *Liberia*, 194, 202–29.

67. While Liberia was marginal to Stowe's story, the literary critic, Michelle Burnham has argued that "the colonizing gesture" was "central to *Uncle Tom's Cabin*" because it implicitly negated "the 'alarming' possibilities of a black colony not in the service of the Christian and maternal empire of white America." Michelle Burnham, *Captivity and Sentiment: Cultural Exchange in American Literature, 1682–1861* (Hanover, NH: Dartmouth College Press, 1997), 121, 146.

68. On the Fugitive Slave Act of 1850 and African American interest in both Liberia and black-led emigration efforts, see Kenny, "Manliness and Manifest Racial Destiny"; Beverly Tomek, *Colonization and Its Discontents: Emancipation, Emigration, and Antislavery in Antebellum Pennsylvania* (New York: New York University Press, 2011), 199–201; Sidbury, *Becoming African in America*, 203–10. For classic studies that explore this topic, see Benjamin Quarles, *Black Abolitionists* (New York: Oxford University Press, 1969), 213–22; Litwack, *North of Slavery*, 252–66.

69. On emigrationism and the growth of black nationalism, see Rael, *Black Identity and Black Protest*, 209–36; Kwando Mbiassi Kinshasa, *Emigration vs. Assimilation: The Debate in the Antebellum African-American Press, 1827–1861* (Jefferson, NC: McFarland Publishing, 1988), 63–193; Sterling Stuckey, *Slave Culture: Nationalist Theory and the Foundations of Black America* (New York: Oxford University Press, 1987), 166–85; Floyd John Miller, *The Search for a Black Nationality: Black Emigration and Colonization, 1787–1863* (Urbana: University of Illinois Press, 1975), 94–231; Howard H. Bell, "The Negro Emigration Movement, 1849–1854: A Phase of Negro Nationalism," *Phylon* 20 (Summer 1959): 132–42.

70. On the ACS and African Americans' conflicted identification with Africa in the early republic, see Sidbury, *Becoming African in America*; Rael, *Black Identity and Black Protest*, 82–117; Stuckey, *Slave Culture*, 193–244. Ben Schiller has argued that these studies of African diasporic discourse are limited by their focus on a small minority of free black intellectuals. Ben Schiller, "US Slavery's Diaspora: Black Atlantic History at the Crossroads of 'Race,' Enslavement, and Colonisation," *Slavery and Abolition* 32, no. 2 (2011): 199–212.

71. On the Haitian revolution's crucial symbolic role in shaping racial politics in the United States, see Ashli White, *Encountering Revolution: Haiti and the Making of the Early Republic* (Baltimore: Johns Hopkins University Press, 2010); Matthew J. Clavin, *Toussaint Louverture and the American Civil War: The Promise and Peril of a Second Haitian Revolution* (Philadelphia: University of Pennsylvania Press, 2010); Bruce R. Dain, *A Hideous Monster of the Mind: American Race Theory in the Early Republic* (Cambridge, MA: Harvard University Press, 2002), 81–111; Chris Dixon, *African America and Haiti: Emigration and Black Nationalism in the Nineteenth Century* (Westport, CT: Greenwood Press, 2000); Alfred N. Hunt, *Haiti's Influence on Antebellum America: Slumbering Volcano in the Caribbean* (Baton Rouge: Louisiana State University Press, 1988). On the impact of British emancipation on these discussions of race and nationhood, see Kenny, *Contentious Liberties*; Edward Bartlett Rugemer, *The Problem of Emancipation: The Caribbean Roots of the American Civil War* (Baton Rouge: Louisiana State University Press, 2008).

72. "National Convention of Colored People" and "Duties of Colored Men," *New York Colonization Journal*, December 1850.

73. "The Free Colored People's Convention," *Frederick Douglass' Paper*, August 13, 1852.

74. Ibid. On black nationalists' dialogue with U.S. nationalism, see Rael, *Black Identity and Black Protest*, 209–36. On the persistence of American identity among Liberian settlers, see Schiller, "US Slavery's Diaspora," 199–212.

75. Carter G. Woodson compiled a significant number of the letters written to the ACS from 1817 to 1860. Of these letters, more than half came from the six years following the independence of Liberia in 1847. Carter G. Woodson, *The Mind of the Negro as Reflected in Letters Written During the Crisis, 1800–1860* (Washington, DC: Association for the Study of Negro Life and History, 1926). In quoting from these letters I have corrected some grammar and spelling errors to allow for the best readability. A word in brackets indicates that it has been changed to reflect the likely intention of the writer.

76. Peter Butler to the American Colonization Society, November 17, 1848, ACS Papers, Ser. 1, Reel 57.

77. N. D. Artist to the American Colonization Society, July 18, 1849, ACS Papers, Ser. 1, Reel 59.

78. Nathaniel Bowen to the American Colonization Society, April 26, 1853, ACS Papers, Ser. 1, Reel 70.

79. Lewis Holbert to the American Colonization Society, October 2, 1847, ACS Papers, Ser. 1, Reel 53; Lewis Holbert to American Colonization Society, September 7, 1847, ACS Papers, Ser. 1, Reel 53.

80. Bruce Dorsey, "A Gendered History of African Colonization in the Antebellum United States," *Journal of Social History* 34, no. 1 (2000): 94. See also Bruce Dorsey, *Reforming Men and Women: Gender in the Antebellum City* (Ithaca, NY: Cornell University Press, 2002), 136–94.

81. "African Colonization," *African Repository and Colonial Journal* 23, no. 6 (June 1847): 186.

82. "Remarks on the Constitution by the Editor of the Liberia Herald," *African Repository and Colonial Journal* 24, no. 1 (January 1848): 13.

83. Benjamen S. Bebee to the American Colonization Society, August 1850, ACS Papers, Ser. 1, Reel 63.

84. S. Wesley Jones, "Extract from a letter of a Free Colored Man in Alabama," *African Repository* 28, no. 5 (May 1852): 149.

85. H. B. Stewart to the American Colonization Society, July 17, 1848, ACS Papers, Ser. 1, Reel 56; N. D. Artist to the American Colonization Society, October 5, 1851, ACS Papers, Ser. 1, Reel 66A.

86. Augustus Washington, "African Colonization by a Man of Color," *New York Daily Tribune*, July 3, 1851.

87. "African Colonization," *Frederick Douglass' Paper*, July 31, 1851.

88. "Frederick Douglass and Augustus Washington," *Christian Statesman*, August 9, 1851.

89. See also Wilson Jeremiah Moses, *Liberian Dreams: Back-to-Africa Narratives from the 1850s* (University Park: Pennsylvania State University Press, 1998), 181–83. On how the abolitionist movement upheld middle-class notions of masculinity, see Kristin L. Hoganson, "Garrisonian Abolitionists and the Rhetoric of Gender, 1850–1860," *American Quarterly* 45, no. 4 (December 1993): 558–95.

90. William W. Findlay, "Appeal of Wm. W. Findlay, to the Colored People of Indiana," *African Repository and Colonial Journal* 25, no. 6 (June 1849): 177.

91. "No Colonization," *North Star*, August 17, 1849.

92. "Minutes and Address of the State Convention of the Colored Citizens of Ohio, Convened at Columbus, January 10th, 11th, 12, & 13th, 1849," in *Proceedings of the Black State Conventions, 1840–1865*, ed. Philip Foner and George E. Walker, vol. 1 (Philadelphia: Temple University Press, 1980), 223.

93. *Report of the Proceedings of the Colored National Convention Held at Cleveland, Ohio, on Wednesday, September 6, 1848* (Rochester, NY: John Dick, 1848), 16.

94. "Proceedings of the State Convention of Colored People Held at Albany, New-York, on the 22nd, 23rd and 24th of July, 1851," in *Proceedings of the Black State Conventions*, 1:67.

95. "Letter from Mr. E. W. Blyden," *African Repository* 30, no. 8 (August 1854): 238–39.

96. American and Foreign Anti-Slavery Society, *The Thirteenth Annual Report of the American and Foreign Anti-Slavery Society* (New York: American and Foreign Anti-Slavery Society, 1853), 192–93.

97. "Mrs. Stowe's Position," *Frederick Douglass' Paper*, May 6, 1853. For another harsh critique of Stowe's fate for Harris, see "George Harris," *Toronto Provincial Freeman*, July 22, 1854.

98. Miller, *Search for a Black Nationality*, 94–231; Stuckey, *Slave Culture*, 138–92; Sterling Stuckey, *The Ideological Origins of Black Nationalism* (Boston: Beacon Press, 1972); Kinshasa, *Emigration vs. Assimilation*; Bell, "Negro Emigration Movement."

99. "Liberia," *North Star*, March 2, 1849.

100. Martin Robison Delany, *The Condition, Elevation, Emigration, and Destiny of the Colored People of the United States* (Philadelphia, 1852), 169. Paul Gilroy has argued that Delany rejected Liberia as an "autonomous, black nation state" because it "was not an adequate or sufficiently serious vehicle for the hopes and dreams of black citizen soldiers." Paul Gilroy, *The Black Atlantic: Modernity and Double Consciousness* (Cambridge, MA: Harvard University Press, 1993), 23.

101. William Nesbit, *Four Months in Liberia or, African Colonization Exposed* (Pittsburgh: J. T. Shryock, 1855), 29, 33–34, 50, 56.

102. "Proceedings of the State Convention of Colored People Held at Albany, New-York," 69.

103. *Proceedings of the Colored National Convention, Held in Rochester, July 6th, 7th and 8th, 1853* (Rochester, NY: Office of Frederick Douglass' Paper, 1853).

104. "Colonization. This Scheme of Our Yankee Enemies Is Gathering," *Toronto Provincial Freeman*, March 24, 1854.

Chapter 6

1. Robert J. (Robert John) Walker, *Letter of Mr. Walker, of Mississippi, Relative to the Annexation of Texas: In Reply to the Call of the People of Carroll County, Kentucky, to Communicate His Views on That Subject* (Washington, DC, 1844), 14.

2. Sam W. Haynes, "Anglophobia and the Annexation of Texas," in *Manifest Destiny and Empire: American Antebellum Expansionism* (College Station: Texas A&M University Press, 1997), 128–29.

3. Robert J. Walker, "The Union," *Continental Monthly: Devoted to Literature and National Policy* 2, no. 5 (November 1862): 576–77. Walker's claims about the success of black civilizing efforts in Liberia were a more extreme example of contradictory colonizationist sentiments around the capability of African Americans for self-government. One of the central arguments in his Texas annexation letter misleadingly twisted census data to claim that African Americans were overrepresented among the physically and mentally disabled population and thus unfit for citizenship in northern states.

4. The colonization proposals of the late 1850s and early 1860s are generally disconnected from the African colonization movement within scholarly accounts. Most scholars of the subject have focused on Liberia and ACS efforts, often only referencing these plans as a footnote. Scholarship that dealt with these plans generally did so within the volatile sectional politics over slavery in the 1850s and made only passing references to their relationship to the longer trajectory of African colonization, usually by noting Abraham Lincoln's history of interest in the idea. Therefore, the ironic outcome is that the greatest federal intervention on behalf of colonizationism is generally relegated to the margins of the African colonization story. This chapter makes the case that the Central American plans were perhaps the fullest expression of the racial republic idea advanced by the colonization movement, even as they differed from the ACS project in some significant ways. For examples of scholarship that only include the Civil War colonization efforts as a footnote, see Eric Burin, *Slavery and the Peculiar Solution: A History of the American Colonization Society* (Gainesville: University Press of Florida, 2005); P. J. Staudenraus, *The African Colonization Movement, 1816–1865* (New York: Columbia University Press, 1961); Beverly Tomek, *Colonization and Its Discontents: Emancipation, Emigration, and Antislavery in Antebellum Pennsylvania* (New York: New York University Press, 2011).

5. Some of the best examples of this work include Walter Johnson, *River of Dark Dreams: Slavery and Empire in the Cotton Kingdom* (Cambridge, MA: Belknap Press of Harvard University Press, 2013); Amy S. Greenberg, *Manifest Manhood and the Antebellum American Empire* (Cambridge: Cambridge University Press, 2005); Shelley Streeby, *American Sensations: Class, Empire, and the Production of Popular Culture* (Berkeley: University of California Press, 2002); Robert E. May, *Manifest Destiny's Underworld: Filibustering in Antebellum America* (Chapel Hill: University of North Carolina Press, 2002). For a small sampling of the extensive literature that has primarily approached this topic in relation to the politics of slavery and sectional conflict, see Phillip W. Magness and Sebastian N. Page, *Colonization After Emancipation: Lincoln and the Movement for Black Resettlement* (Columbia: University of Missouri Press, 2011); Michael Vorenberg, "Abraham Lincoln and the Politics of Black Colonization," *Journal of the Abraham*

Lincoln Association 14, no. 2 (Summer 1993): 23–46; James D. Bilotta, *Race and the Rise of the Republican Party, 1848–1865* (New York: Peter Lang, 1992); G. S. Boritt, "The Voyage to the Colony of Linconia: The Sixteenth President, Black Colonization, and the Defense Mechanism of Avoidance," *Historian* 37, no. 4 (August 1975): 619–32; Eric Foner, *Free Soil, Free Labor, Free Men: The Ideology of the Republican Party Before the Civil War* (New York: Oxford University Press, 1970). For the handful of scholars who have analyzed these plans in terms of expansionist sentiment, see Sharon Hartman Strom, "Labor, Race, and Colonization: Imagining a Post-Slavery World in the Americas," in *The Problem of Evil: Slavery, Freedom, and the Ambiguities of American Reform*, ed. Steven Mintz and John Stauffer (Amherst: University of Massachusetts Press, 2007); Thomas Schoonover, "Misconstrued Mission: Expansionism and Black Colonization in Mexico and Central America During the Civil War," *Pacific Historical Review* 49, no. 4 (November 1, 1980): 607–20; Tinsley Lee Spraggins, "Economic Aspects of Negro Colonization During the Civil War" (Ph.D. diss., American University, 1957).

6. "Republic of Liberia," *Richmond Republican*, October 1847.

7. "Notes on New Books," *Daily National Intelligencer*, January 2, 1847.

8. On the proliferation of filibuster schemes during this era, see Johnson, *River of Dark Dreams*; Greenberg, *Manifest Manhood*; Streeby, *American Sensations*; May, *Manifest Destiny's Underworld*; Robert E. May, *The Southern Dream of a Caribbean Empire, 1854–1861: With a New Preface*, 1st ed. (Gainesville: University Press of Florida, 2002); Thomas R. Hietala, *Manifest Design: American Exceptionalism and Empire* (Ithaca, NY: Cornell University Press, 2002); Charles H. (Henry) Brown, *Agents of Manifest Destiny: The Lives and Times of the Filibusters* (Chapel Hill: University of North Carolina Press, 1980).

9. Hietala, *Manifest Design: American Exceptionalism and Empire*, 170–71.

10. On the "All Mexico" movement, see Thomas R. Hietala, *Manifest Design: Anxious Aggrandizement in Late Jacksonian America* (Ithaca, NY: Cornell University Press, 1985), 159–65; Paul W. Foos, *A Short, Offhand, Killing Affair: Soldiers and Social Conflict During the Mexican-American War* (Chapel Hill: University of North Carolina Press, 2002), 149–54.

11. A number of scholars have examined the Republican campaigns that led to the pursuit of Central American colonies during the Civil War. Much of the early work on this subject has examined the racial, political, and economic dimensions of these plans within Republican Party policy. See Frederic Bancroft, "The Colonization of American Negroes from 1801 to 1865," in *Frederic Bancroft—Historian*, ed. Jacob E. Cooke (Norman: University of Oklahoma Press, 1957); Spraggins, "Economic Aspects of Negro Colonization"; Foner, *Free Soil, Free Labor, Free Men*; Bilotta, *Race and the Rise of the Republican Party*. More recently, a short book chapter by Sharon Hartman Strom considered these colonization efforts within the context of southern filibustering campaigns. I build on her insights by placing the pursuit of Central American colonies within a larger narrative about the relationship between colonizationism and U.S. expansionism. See Strom, "Labor, Race, and Colonization."

12. The growing support for black-led emigration efforts was most evident in the fact that it increasingly became the subject of northern black political conventions of this era, the most prominent of which was the National Emigration Convention held in Cleveland during the summer of 1854. Martin Delany, the fierce critic of Liberian colonization, attended the convention and become one of the most prominent advocates of this position, particularly after his *Condition, Elevation, Emigration, and Destiny of the Colored People of the United States* advanced the idea of emigration to Central and South America. White advocates of such colonies would mostly ignore the efforts of black leaders and referenced them only as a way to illustrate that

these colonies might have more support within black communities than Liberia. See *Proceedings of the National Emigration Convention of Colored People* (Pittsburgh, PA, 1854); Bronwen Everill, " 'Destiny Seems to Point Me to That Country': Early Nineteenth-Century African American Migration, Emigration, and Expansion," *Journal of Global History* 7, no. 1 (2012): 53–77; Ousmane K. Power-Greene, *Against Wind and Tide: The African American Struggle Against the Colonization Movement* (New York: New York University Press, 2014), 129–57; Floyd John Miller, *The Search for a Black Nationality: Black Emigration and Colonization, 1787–1863* (Urbana: University of Illinois Press, 1975), 134–69. An example of the instrumental use of black voices to support the Central American colonization idea appeared in the report issued by the House of Representatives, which cited at length the proceedings of the National Emigration Convention of Colored People. "H.R. Doc. No. 148," in *Reports of Committees of the House of Representatives, Made During the Second Session of the Thirty-Seventh Congress, 1861–'62*, vol. 4 (Washington, DC: Government Printing Office, 1862), 37–59.

13. On the role of the Blair family in antebellum U.S. politics, see William Ernest Smith, *The Francis Preston Blair Family in Politics*, 2 vols. (New York: Macmillan, 1933). On the Blair family's growing interest in Central American colonization, see William Earl Parrish, *Frank Blair: Lincoln's Conservative* (Columbia: University of Missouri Press, 1998). It is unclear when the Blairs first considered promoting Central American colonization plans, but through early 1857 they exchanged some letters that discussed the prospect. See Francis P. Blair to William Henry Beecher, January 15, 1857, Blair-Lee Papers, Box 6, Folder 1, Princeton University, Special Collections; Frank P. Blair, Jr., to Francis P. Blair, March 23, 1857, Blair-Lee Papers, Box 6, Folder 5.

14. For examples of the most prominent writings of Squier and Wells, see E. G. (Ephraim George) Squier, *Nicaragua, Its People, Scenery, Monuments, and the Proposed Interoceanic Canal* (New York: D. Appleton, 1852); E. G. Squier, *The States of Central America* (New York: Harper & Brothers, 1858); Wells William Vincent, *Explorations and Adventures in Honduras, Comprising Sketches of Travel in the Gold Regions of Olancho, and a Review of the History and General Resources of Central America* (New York: Harper & Brothers, 1857). On the culture of Central American boosterism among travel writers, see Greenberg, *Manifest Manhood*, 55–58.

15. For examples of references to the Central American travel writers, see Frank P. Blair, Jr., to Francis P. Blair, August 5, 1858, Blair-Lee Papers, Box 6, Folder 5; Frank P. Blair, Jr., *Speech of Hon. Francis P. Blair, Jr., of Missouri, on the Acquisition of Central America; Delivered in the House of Representatives, January 14, 1858* (Washington, DC: Congressional Globe Office, 1858), 8–9.

16. Sharon Hartman Strom, " 'If Success Depends upon Enterprise': Central America, U.S. Foreign Policy, and Race in the Travel Narratives of E. G. Squier," *Diplomatic History* 35, no. 3 (2011): 403–43; Charles L. Stansifer, "E. George Squier and the Honduras Interoceanic Railroad Project," *Hispanic American Historical Review* 46, no. 1 (February 1, 1966): 1–27. While Squier's writing helped inspire all sorts of interest in Central America, he never directly promoted either type of scheme and, in fact, publicly opposed filibusters. Charles Stansifer, "The Central American Career of E. George Squier" (Ph.D. diss., Tulane University, 1959).

17. E. G. Squier, "The Nicaragua Question," *U.S. Magazine and Democratic Review* 41 (February 1858): 115.

18. For references to Squier's influence on Blair's thinking, see Frank P. Blair, Jr., to Francis P. Blair, undated (1858), Blair-Lee Papers, Box 6, Folder 5.

19. *Remarks on the Colonization of the Western Coast of Africa by the Free Negroes of the United States, and the Consequent Civilization of Africa and Suppression of the Slave Trade* (New York: W. L. Burroughs' Steam Power Press, 1850), 24.

20. *New York Daily Tribune*, May 9, 1857.

21. Parrish, *Frank Blair*, 69–71.

22. *Congressional Globe*, 35th Cong., 1st sess. (1858): 298. Blair's speech was also reprinted in pamphlet form for wider distribution. Blair, Jr., *Speech of Hon. Francis P. Blair, Jr.*

23. *Congressional Globe*, 35th Cong., 1st sess. (1858): 227–31.

24. The response to Thayer's speech revealed support for such "Americanization" efforts by northern Democrats, such as Rep. Garnett Adrain from New Jersey. *New York Herald*, March 11, 1860.

25. *Congressional Globe*, 35th Cong., 2d sess. (1859): 907, 967; *Congressional Globe*, 36th Cong., Senate Special sess. (1859): 1685.

26. Frank P. Blair, Jr., to Francis P. Blair, November 2, 1859, Blair-Lee Papers, Box 6, Folder 5. This letter from Frank Blair to his father in late 1859 demonstrates the cascading effect of support that followed Senator Doolittle's advocacy of the cause, which influenced both Samuel Kirkwood and James Harlan to support it. The letter also gives a sense of the elder Blair's maneuvering behind the scenes as it references his efforts to convince William Dennison. For a letter detailing Doolittle's successful lobbying efforts with Kirkwood, see "Frank P. Blair Jr. to James Doolittle, November 2, 1859," *Southern Historical Association* 10, no. 5 (September 1906): 285–86; William Dennison, "Inaugural Address," in *Messages and Reports to the General Assembly and Governor of the State of Ohio: For the Year 1859*, vol. 2 (Columbus, OH: Richard Nevins, 1860). On Dennison's decision to include this in his inaugural address, see William Dennison to Benjamin Wade, November 30, 1859, Benjamin Wade Papers, Library of Congress, Washington, DC, General Correspondence, Reel 2; Francis P. Blair to Martin Van Buren, February 13, 1860, Martin Van Buren Papers, Library of Congress, Washington, DC, Ser. 2, Reel 34.

27. One of Blair's pamphlets published to support the effort included letters and testimonials from many of these prominent individuals. Frank P. Blair, Jr., *The Destiny of the Races of the Continent, an Address, Delivered Before the Mercantile Library Association of Boston, Massachusetts on the 26th of January, 1859* (Washington, DC: Buell & Blanchard, 1859); "Montgomery Blair to James Doolittle, November 11, 1859," *Southern Historical Association* 10, no. 5 (September 1906): 287.

28. *Congressional Globe*, 35th Cong., 1st sess. (1858): 294.

29. *National Era*, February 24, 1859.

30. *Congressional Globe*, 36th Cong., 1st sess., Appendix (1860): 57.

31. "Hayti and Liberia," *New York Evening Post*, February 17, 1859.

32. *Congressional Globe*, 35th Cong., 1st sess. (1858): 293–95. Blair's speech was also reprinted in pamphlet form for wider distribution. See Blair, Jr., *Speech of Hon. Francis P. Blair, Jr.* On the common trope of redemptive masculinity in the African colonization movement, see Bruce Dorsey, "A Gendered History of African Colonization in the Antebellum United States," *Journal of Social History* 34, no. 1 (October 1, 2000): 77–103.

33. "Lecture of Senator Doolittle of Wisconsin," *Missouri Democrat*, March 21, 1859; Greenberg, *Manifest Manhood*, 135–69.

34. James Doolittle to Hannibal Hamlin, August 20, 1859, and September 18, 1859, Hannibal Hamlin Papers, University of Maine, Portland, ME, General Correspondence, Reel 5.

35. Dennison, "Inaugural Address."

36. Haynes, "Anglophobia and the Annexation of Texas."

37. *Congressional Globe*, 35th Cong., 1st sess. (1858): 297–98.

38. *National Era*, February 24, 1859.

39. *Congressional Globe*, 35th Cong., 2d sess. (1859): 907; *Congressional Globe*, 35th Cong., 1st sess. (1858): 293.

40. Francis P. Blair, Sr., to Simon Cameron, March 22, 1859, Simon Cameron Papers, Library of Congress, Washington, DC, General Correspondence, Reel 5.

41. Doolittle to Hamlin, August 20, 1859.

42. "Lecture of Senator Doolittle of Wisconsin," *Missouri Democrat*, March 21, 1859.

43. Frank P. Blair, Jr., to Francis P. Blair, September 10, 1858, Blair-Lee Papers, Box 6, Folder 5.

44. *Congressional Globe*, 35th Cong., 1st sess. (1858): 298, 2207.

45. "Mr. Preston King's New Lights upon the Nigger Question," *New York Herald*, May 20, 1858.

46. "Lecture of Senator Doolittle of Wisconsin." Doolittle made very similar comments about a "homestead policy for free blacks" in James Doolittle to Lyman Trumbull, November 10, 1860, Lyman Trumbull Papers (hereafter Trumbull Papers), Library of Congress, Washington, DC, General Correspondence, Reel 6.

47. *Congressional Globe*, 36th Cong., 1st sess., Appendix (1860): 57.

48. James Bilotta has demonstrated how thoroughly the Republican colonizationists made appeals to build colonies based on ideals of racial superiority in order to realize a homogenous white republic. See Bilotta, *Race and the Rise of the Republican Party*.

49. Frank P. Blair, Jr., to Montgomery D. Blair, October 16, 1858, Blair-Lee Papers, Box 42, Folder 2.

50. *New York Tribune*, May 9, 1857.

51. Blair elaborated his obsession with racial "destiny" privately in a number of letters to his father and publicly in a speech called "The Destiny of the Races of the Continent," which was eventually published as a pamphlet. Blair, Jr., to Blair, undated (1858); Frank P. Blair, Jr., to Francis P. Blair, October 22, 1858, Blair-Lee Papers, Box 6, Folder 5; Blair, Jr., *Destiny of the Races of the Continent*.

52. Doolittle to Hamlin, September 18, 1859.

53. *Congressional Globe*, 35th Cong., 1st sess. (1858): 296.

54. *New York Daily Tribune*, May 9, 1857.

55. *National Era*, February 24, 1859.

56. *Congressional Globe*, 35th Cong., 2d sess. (1859): 907.

57. *New York Daily Tribune*, May 9, 1857. For examples, see editorials in the *New York Daily Tribune*, February 25, 1858; Blair, Jr., *Destiny of the Races of the Continent*.

58. Blair, Jr., to Blair, August 5, 1858, Blair-Lee Papers, Box 6, Folder 5.

59. For a few typical examples of the extensive coverage of colonization by the *Missouri Democrat*, see "Lecture of Senator Doolittle of Wisconsin," August 15, 1859, as well as issues from February 7, December 1, and December 21, 1859; July 16 and August 3, 1860.

60. Frank P. Blair, Jr., to Francis P. Blair, April 16, 1859, Blair-Lee Papers, Box 6, Folder 5; *New York Tribune*, February 25, 1858. For other examples of positive national coverage of the plan, see "Senator Doolittle's Views of the Negro Question," *New York Times*, July 9, 1859.

61. Frank P. Blair, Jr., to Francis P. Blair, November 29, 1860, Blair-Lee Papers, Box 6, Folder 5.

62. Blair, Jr., *Destiny of the Races of the Continent*; Frank P. Blair, Jr., *Colonization and Commerce: An Address Before the Young Men's Mercantile Library Association of Cincinnati, Ohio, November 29, 1859* (Cincinnati, OH, 1859).

63. Blair, Jr., to Blair, October 16, 1858, Blair-Lee Papers, Box 42, Folder 2.

64. J. McKibben to Lyman Trumbull, December 26, 1859, Trumbull Papers, General Correspondence, Reel 5.

65. H. C. Trinne to Lyman Trumbull, December 18, 1859, Trumbull Papers, General Correspondence, Reel 4.

66. "Montgomery Blair to James Doolittle, November 11, 1859."

67. Frank P. Blair, Jr., to Francis P. Blair, October 6, 1859, Blair-Lee Papers, Box 6, Folder 5.

68. *New York Herald*, March 11, 1860. For Wade's endorsement, see *Congressional Globe*, 36th Cong., 1st sess., Appendix (1860): 154–55.

69. National Republican Convention, *National Republican Platform Adopted by National Republican Convention, Held in Chicago, May 17, 1860* (Chicago: Chicago Press & Tribune Office, 1860).

70. James Doolittle to Christopher C. Sholes, May 21, 1860, James R. Doolittle Papers, Reel 1, Wisconsin State Historical Society.

71. Blair, Jr., to Blair, November 29, 1860.

72. While the body of work on Lincoln and colonization is extensive, see these examples for the general scope of debate on the subject: Magness and Page, *Colonization After Emancipation*; Sebastian N. Page, "Lincoln and Chiriquí Colonization Revisited," *American Nineteenth Century History* 12, no. 3 (2011): 289–325; Mark E. Neely, Jr., "Colonization and the Myth That Lincoln Prepared the People for Emancipation," in *Lincoln's Proclamation: Emancipation Reconsidered*, ed. William A. Blair and Karen Fisher Younger (Chapel Hill: University of North Carolina Press, 2009); Phillip Shaw Paludan, "Lincoln and Colonization: Policy or Propaganda?" *Journal of the Abraham Lincoln Association* 25, no. 1 (January 1, 2004): 23–37; Vorenberg, "Abraham Lincoln"; Richard K. Fleischman, "The Devil's Advocate: A Defense of Lincoln's Attitude Toward the Negro, 1837–1863," *Lincoln Herald* 81 (Fall 1979): 172–86; Boritt, "Voyage to the Colony of Linconia"; Robert Zoellner, "Negro Colonization: The Climate of Opinion Surrounding Lincoln," *Mid-America* 42, no. 3 (1960): 131–50.

73. Abraham Lincoln, "First Annual Message," in *A Compilation of the Messages and Papers of the Presidents*, ed. James D. Richardson, vol. 6 (Washington, DC: Bureau of National Literature and Art, 1903), 54.

74. *Congressional Globe*, 37th Cong., 2d sess., Appendix (1862): 83–84, 87.

75. Ibid., 98–99.

76. "H.R. Doc. No. 148," 19–31.

77. "A Bill to Confiscate the Property of Rebels for the Payment of the Expenses of the Present Rebellion, and for Other Purposes," *Senate Bills and Resolutions*, 37th Cong., 2d sess. (1862): 25–26.

78. Salmon Portland Chase, "Diary and Correspondence of Salmon P. Chase," in *Annual Report of the American Historical Association for the Year 1902: Sixth Report of Historical Manuscripts Commission: With Diary and Correspondence of Salmon P. Chase*, vol. 2 (Washington, DC: Government Printing Office, 1903), 92–93.

79. The House report published before the colonization bill was passed spent a considerable portion of its appendix explaining the potential benefits of a black colony in Chiriquí, in addition to the Yucatán Peninsula and northern Venezuela. "H.R. Doc. No. 148," 74–83.

80. Caleb Smith to Abraham Lincoln, November 4, 1861, Ambrose W. Thompson Papers (hereafter Thompson Papers), Library of Congress, Washington, DC, Chiriqui Improvement Company File, Box 43; Ambrose Thompson to Caleb Smith, April 26, 1862, Thompson Papers,

Chiriqui Improvement Company File, Box 43. See also U.S. Department of the Interior, "Message from the President of the United States, Communicating, in Compliance with a Resolution of the Senate of the 25th Ultimo, Information Touching the Transaction of the Executive Branch of the Government Respecting the Transportation, Settlement, and Colonization of Persons of the African Race," in *Senate Executive Documents for the First Session of the Thirty-Ninth Congress of the United States of America, 1865–66*, 39th Cong., 1st sess., Senate Executive Document 55, vol. 2 (Washington, DC: Government Printing Office, 1866), 6.

81. Aims McGuinness, *Path of Empire: Panama and the California Gold Rush* (Ithaca, NY: Cornell University Press, 2008).

82. On the disputed political and territorial claims in Colombia during this period, see Page, "Lincoln and Chiriquí Colonization Revisited."

83. On Thompson's business plans for the region, see J. Hubley Ashton, ed., *Official Opinions of the Attorneys General of the United States*, vol. 9 (Washington, DC: W. H. & O. H. Morrison, 1869), 286–91; Ninan Edwards to Abraham Lincoln, August 9, 1861, Abraham Lincoln Papers (hereafter Lincoln Papers), Ser. 1, Reel 24; "H.R. Doc. No. 568," in *Reports of Committees of the House of Representatives, Made During the First Session of the Thirty-Sixth Congress, 1859–60*, vol. 4 (Washington, DC, 1860).

84. For criticism of Thompson's business plans in Congress, see *Congressional Globe*, 36th Cong., 2d sess. (1861): 730–35. For a summary of Smith's pursuit of private partnerships, see Caleb Smith to Abraham Lincoln, May 9, 1862, Thompson Papers, Chiriqui Improvement Company File, Box 43; U.S. Department of the Interior, "Message from the President of the United States," 7–8.

85. On the range of business-oriented colonization proposals during this period, see Spraggins, "Economic Aspects of Negro Colonization," 100–103.

86. Francis P. Blair to Abraham Lincoln, "Important Considerations for Congress," November 16, 1861, Lincoln Papers, Ser. 1, Reel 29.

87. "Matías Romero to Ministro de Relaciones Exteriores, June 6, 1861," in *Correspondencia de la legación mexicana en Washington durante la intervención extranjera, 1860–1868: Coleccion de documentos para formar la historia de la intervencion*, 10 vols., ed. Matías Romero (Mexico City: Imprenta del Gobierno en Palacio, 1870), 1:412.

88. Elisha Oscar Crosby and James Doolittle, November 20, 1861, James R. Doolittle Papers, Reel 1; Schoonover, "Misconstrued Mission," 613–14.

89. Bilotta, *Race and the Rise of the Republican Party*, 358–60.

90. For the House committee's suggestion that Central American colonization would be more desirable to black audiences, see "H.R. Doc. No. 148," 37–59.

91. Abraham Lincoln, *The Collected Works of Abraham Lincoln*, ed. Roy P. Basler, vol. 5 (New Brunswick, NJ: Rutgers University Press, 1955), 370–75.

92. Eric Foner, *The Fiery Trial: Abraham Lincoln and American Slavery* (New York: W. W. Norton, 2011), 223–25; James Oakes, *The Radical and the Republican: Frederick Douglass, Abraham Lincoln, and the Triumph of Antislavery Politics* (New York: W. W. Norton, 2008), 191–93.

93. Kate Masur, "The African American Delegation to Abraham Lincoln: A Reappraisal," *Civil War History* 56, no. 2 (June 2010): 138–39. For the place of these events within the wider context of black politics within Washington, DC, see also Kate Masur, *An Example for All the Land: Emancipation and the Struggle over Equality in Washington, D.C.* (Chapel Hill: University of North Carolina Press, 2012).

94. "Colonization of the Blacks," *Liberator*, September 19, 1862.

95. *Baltimore Sun*, August 23, 1862.

96. Frederick Douglass, "The President and His Speeches," *Douglass' Monthly*, September 1862.

97. "A Colored Man's Reply to President Lincoln on Colonization," *Liberator*, September 5, 1862.

98. Thomas Schoonover has demonstrated that Latin American officials were more preoccupied with questions of national sovereignty and U.S. expansionism. See Schoonover, "Misconstrued Mission." There are several examples of diplomats reporting that Latin Americans were unwilling to admit African populations, which they considered racially inferior. See United States, Department of State, "A. B. Dickinson to William Seward, September 12, 1862," in *Papers Relating to the Foreign Relations of the United States, 1862* (Washington, DC, 1863); Friedrich Hassaurek to William Seward, January 16, 1863, Diplomatic Dispatches, Ecuador, T50, Reel 6, General Records of the Department of State, National Archives and Record Administration, Record Group 59. For an exploration of the role of racism in undermining colonization plans in Ecuador, see Robert L. Gold, "Negro Colonization Schemes in Ecuador, 1861–1864," *Phylon* 30, no. 3 (1969): 306–16.

99. "Matías Romero to Ministro de Relaciones Exteriores, February 1, 1862," in Romero, *Correspondencia*, 2:32–34. An example of this press coverage was when the official newspaper of Honduras republished an article from the *Boston Daily Advertiser* implying that the United States was creating colonies to commercially dominate Central America. *Gaceta Oficial de Honduras*, July 20, 1862.

100. United States, Department of State, "A. B. Dickinson to William Seward, September 12, 1862," 893–94; United States, Department of State, "Pedro Zeledon to A. B. Dickinson, September 12, 1862," in *Papers Relating to the Foreign Relations of the United States, 1862* (Washington, DC, 1863), 897–98; Schoonover, "Misconstrued Mission," 22.

101. United States, Department of State, "Luis Molina to William Seward, September 19, 1862," in *Papers Relating to the Foreign Relations of the United States, 1862*, 900–902.

102. United States, Department of State, "Luis Molina to William Seward, September 29, 1862," in *Papers Relating to the Foreign Relations of the United States, 1862*, 905.

103. United States, Department of State, "Luis Molina to William Seward, September 19, 1862," 900–902; United States, Department of State, "Luis Molina to William Seward, September 29, 1862," 905.

104. Magness and Page, *Colonization After Emancipation*; Chris Dixon, *African America and Haiti: Emigration and Black Nationalism in the Nineteenth Century* (Westport, CT: Greenwood Press, 2000); Miller, *Search for a Black Nationality*, 232–49.

105. For Mitchell's understanding of the issue of colonization, see James Mitchell, *Letters on the Relation of White and African Races in the United States: Showing the Necessity of the Colonization of the Latter* (Springfield, IL, 1860); Spraggins, "Economic Aspects of Negro Colonization," 100, 127–28; Page, "Lincoln and Chiriquí Colonization Revisited," 314.

106. "H.R. Doc. No. 148," 27.

107. *African Repository and Colonial Journal* 16, no. 8 (April 15, 1840): 113.

Epilogue

1. President Lincoln helped initiate this process of recognition by including a call for it in his first message to Congress in 1861. See James D. Richardson, "Message of Lincoln, Dec. 3, 1861," in *A Compilation of the Messages and Papers of the Presidents*, vol. 4 (New York: Bureau of National Literature, 1911), 47.

2. Tim Matthewson, *A Proslavery Foreign Policy: Haitian-American Relations During the Early Republic* (Westport, CT: Praeger, 2003); Ashli White, *Encountering Revolution: Haiti and the Making of the Early Republic* (Baltimore: Johns Hopkins University Press, 2010); Matthew Clavin, *Toussaint Louverture and the American Civil War: The Promise and Peril of a Second Haitian Revolution* (Philadelphia: University of Pennsylvania Press, 2010); Caitlin A. Fitz, *Our Sister Republics: The United States in an Age of American Revolutions* (New York: Liveright, 2017).

3. While the end of the war did represent the end of serious consideration of colonizationism among white leaders in the United States, it is worth noting that the ACS persisted in supporting Liberia through the early twentieth century, formally ceasing to exist in 1963. See P. J. Staudenraus, *The African Colonization Movement, 1816–1865* (New York: Columbia University Press, 1961). Aspects of colonizationism would have a second life within black-led emigration efforts. These began following the collapse of Reconstruction and continued, in various guises, well into the twentieth century, ultimately playing a crucial role in the development of black nationalism. See Edwin S. Redkey, *Black Exodus: Black Nationalist and Back-to-Africa Movements, 1890–1910* (New Haven, CT: Yale University Press, 1970); James T. Campbell, *Middle Passages: African American Journeys to Africa, 1787–2005* (New York: Penguin Press, 2006); Steven Hahn, *A Nation Under Our Feet: Black Political Struggles in the Rural South from Slavery to the Great Migration* (Cambridge, MA: Belknap Press, 2005).

4. *Congressional Globe*, 37th Cong., 2d sess. (1862): 1755.

5. Ibid., 1773–74, 1815. The bill's champions in the House, William Gooch and William D. Kelley, took a similar approach by providing an overwhelming array of trade data on the two nations. See *Congressional Globe*, 37th Cong., 2d sess., 2498–2502, 2528.

6. *Congressional Globe*, 37th Cong., 2d sess. (1862): 2528.

7. Ibid., 2527.

8. Ibid., 2530–31.

9. John H. B. Latrobe, "Annual Meeting of the American Colonization Society," *African Repository* 38, no. 2 (February 1862): 33. European states were far ahead in establishing diplomatic relations with both Liberia and Haiti. Although many Americans looked on Liberian independence in 1847 as a realization of the United States' exceptional republican ideals, Europe took the lead in recognizing Liberia, largely in an effort to establish economic ties with the nation. England and France recognized the nation's independence in 1848 and 1852, respectively, followed by treaties of commerce with several other smaller European states in the 1850s. Department of State, Republic of Liberia, *Treaties and Conventions Concluded Between the Republic of Liberia Foreign Powers, 1848–1892* (Monrovia, 1907), pp. 9–30. On the connection between Liberia and U.S. imperialism in the Pacific, see Eugene S. Van Sickle, "Reluctant Imperialists: The U.S. Navy and Liberia, 1819–1845," *Journal of the Early Republic* 31 (Spring 2011): 107–34.

10. *Congressional Globe*, 37th Cong., 2d sess. (1862): 2501.

11. Ibid., 1806.

12. Ibid., 1815.

13. Ibid., 2527.

14. Ibid., 2536.

15. On the dimensions of slaveholder imperialism, see Matthew Karp, *This Vast Southern Empire: Slaveholders at the Helm of American Foreign Policy* (Cambridge, MA: Harvard University Press, 2016); Walter Johnson, *River of Dark Dreams: Slavery and Empire in the Cotton Kingdom* (Cambridge, MA: Belknap Press of Harvard University Press, 2013).

16. On the conflict between pro- and antislavery visions of expansion, see Robert E. May, *Slavery, Race, and Conquest in the Tropics: Lincoln, Douglas, and the Future of Latin America* (New York: Cambridge University Press, 2013); Sharon Hartman Strom, "Labor, Race, and Colonization: Imagining a Post-Slavery World in the Americas," in *The Problem of Evil: Slavery, Freedom, and the Ambiguities of American Reform*, ed. Steven Mintz and John Stauffer (Amherst: University of Massachusetts Press, 2007).

17. On racial capitalism, see Cedric J. Robinson, *Black Marxism: The Making of the Black Radical Tradition* (Chapel Hill: University of North Carolina Press, 1983), 1–24. On how Britain had already reoriented its empire around its version of postslavery racial capitalism, see Christopher Leslie Brown, *Moral Capital: Foundations of British Abolitionism* (Chapel Hill: University of North Carolina Press, 2006); Thomas C. Holt, *The Problem of Freedom: Race, Labor, and Politics in Jamaica and Britain, 1832–1938* (Baltimore: Johns Hopkins University Press, 1992).

18. On the debate over the racial politics of annexation during the Mexican-American War, see Reginald Horsman, *Race and Manifest Destiny: The Origins of American Racial Anglo-Saxonism* (Cambridge, MA: Harvard University Press, 1981), 229–48; Thomas R. Hietala, *Manifest Design: American Exceptionalism and Empire* (Ithaca, NY: Cornell University Press, 2002), 159–71; Paul W. Foos, *A Short, Offhand, Killing Affair: Soldiers and Social Conflict During the Mexican-American War* (Chapel Hill: University of North Carolina Press, 2002), 139–54.

19. On the continuing role that racial ideology played in both justifying and limiting U.S. foreign interventions in the late nineteenth and early twentieth centuries, see Michael H. Hunt, *Ideology and U.S. Foreign Policy* (New Haven, CT: Yale University Press, 1987); Eric T. L. Love, *Race over Empire: Racism and U.S. Imperialism, 1865–1900* (Chapel Hill: University of North Carolina Press, 2004); Mary A. Renda, *Taking Haiti: Military Occupation and the Culture of U.S. Imperialism, 1915–1940* (Chapel Hill: University of North Carolina Press, 2001); Paul A. Kramer, *The Blood of Government: Race, Empire, the United States, and the Philippines* (Chapel Hill: University of North Carolina Press, 2006).

INDEX

Figures and tables are indicated by page numbers followed by *fig.* and *tab.*, respectively.

ACKNOWLEDGMENTS

This book is a collective endeavor that was supported by countless individuals and institutions. They have shaped the evolution of this project, in ways large and small, and I would like to acknowledge the many contributions that it possible.

My years at Michigan State University and the University of Illinois at Urbana-Champaign made me into the historian I am today. At MSU, I found an extremely caring, thoughtful, and attentive group of scholars, which included Kirsten Fermaglich, Frank Manista, Thomas Summerhill, and Greg Thomas. I particularly want to thank Pero Dagbovie and David Bailey, who sparked and encouraged my passion for historical research. At UIUC, I am indebted to the many people who created such a nurturing intellectual environment there. This list includes Jeff Ahlman, Jean Allman, Jim Barrett, Andy Bruno, Vernon Burton, Betsy Esch, Sarah Frohardt-Lane, Ian Hartman, Natalie Havlin, Karlos Hill, Abdulai Iddrisu, Jason Kozlowski, Anna Kurhajic, Clarence Lang, Ed Onaci, Liz Pleck, Mike Rosenow, and Ellen Swain. Julilly Kohler-Hausmann, Kwame Holmes, Anthony Sigismondi, and Brian Yates were crucial to shaping this work during its formative stages. I must especially acknowledge Kristin Hoganson, Dave Roediger, Antoinette Burton, and Fred Hoxie, who offered vital commentary on this project and helped me envision its scope and stakes.

Over the last several years I have had the privilege of working within amazing communities of scholars at McGill University and University of Colorado Denver. At McGill, I received both critical feedback and support from my colleagues Elizabeth Elbourne, Lorenz Lüthi, Len Moore, Jason Opal, Layla Parsons, Jon Soske, and John Zucchi. At UCD, I would particularly like to recognize Marjorie Levine-Clark, Pam Laird, Kariann Yokota, and Chris Agee, who have served as wise and encouraging department chairs during my time here. I have also had so many lively conversations about my work with UCD colleagues over the years. For that valuable feedback and support, I would like to thank Ryan Crewe, Jay Fell, Sarah Fields, Gabriel

Finkelstein, Mia Fischer, Susan Gustin, Sarah Hagelin, Rebecca Hunt, Jo Luloff, Katy Mohrman, Tom Noel, Kelly Palmer, Gillian Silverman, Richard Smith, Dale Stahl, Chris Sundberg, John Tinnell, Sarah Tyson, Bill Wagner, and Greg Whitesides. I would also like to thank Tabitha Fitzpatrick, who has facilitated the research for this project in countless ways.

Numerous organizations have provided me with financial and institutional support that made this book possible. A fellowship from the Gilder Lehrman Institute helped fund travel for my early research, and the Virginia Winship Memorial Fund provided many years of fellowship support. A William Appleman Williams Junior Faculty Research Grant from the Society for Historians of American Foreign Relations supported me while I conducted additional research in the latter stages of the project. I would also like to thank the McNeil Center for Early American Studies for travel support to present part of this research at its "Making a Republic Imperial" Conference. I would like to thank the staff at the Boston Public Library, Cincinnati Historical Society, Connecticut Historical Society, Countway Library of Harvard Medical School, Duke University Library, Filson Historical Society, Harvard Law School Library, Indiana Historical Society, Library of Congress, Library of Virginia, Massachusetts Historical Society, New-York Historical Society, New York Public Library, Ohio Historical Society, Ohio State Archives, Pennsylvania Historical Society, Princeton University Library, Schomberg Center for Research in Black Culture, University of North Carolina Library, University of Virginia, and the Virginia Historical Society. Thanks to John Gergley, Natalie Havlin, Elissa Sweet, and Adam Weimer for providing me with housing and hospitality during my research travels.

Throughout the development of this project I had so many valuable conversations with people whom I met as visiting scholars or during conferences. For this, I would like to thank Ira Berlin, Robin Blackburn, Arika Easley-Houser, Bronwen Everill, Caitlin Fitz, François Furstenberg, Amy Greenberg, Nick Guyatt, David Kazanjian, Paul Kramer, Gerda Lerner, James Loewen, Elspeth Martini, Tiya Miles, Jennifer Morgan, Angie Parker, Ousmane Power-Greene, Kisha Simmons, Matt Spooner, Marie Stango, Amy Van Natter, Lorenzo Veracini, and Michael Verney. Some of these interactions were very brief and others sustained over many years, but I want to recognize all of these people because their advice, criticism, and encouragement have remained with me to this day. I would like to extend a special thanks to Emily Conroy-Krutz. Her keen insights have consistently guided my thinking and pushed me to make the book better.

During various stages in the book's development I've also benefited from careful readings of my work by editors, conference commentators, and other colleagues. This list includes Dirk Bönker, Doug Egerton, Rashauna Johnson, Andrew Kahrl, Jason Opal, Nicole Phelps, Julie Seville, Bryant Shaw, Rachel St. John, and Rosemarie Zagarri. I am indebted to Shelley Hasinoff for providing a close reading of the entire manuscript at a critical moment in its development. A partial distillation of this book's research was previously published as "Situating African Colonization within the History of U.S. Expansion" in *New Directions in the Study of African American Recolonization* (University Press of Florida). I would like to thank Bev Tomek and Matt Hetrick, who served as coeditors of the volume and both offered valuable comments on my work. David Waldstreicher provided incisive feedback on the book as both the Early American Studies series editor and as editor for the *Journal of the Early Republic*, where an early version of Chapter 5 was published as "'The United States of Africa': Liberian Independence and the Contested Meaning of a Black Republic." The anonymous reviewers who commented on the manuscript for the University of Pennsylvania Press were also extremely helpful. Their criticism and perceptive observations dramatically strengthened the final book. The greatest thanks must be reserved for my editor at Penn Press, Bob Lockhart. Bob immediately grasped the stakes of this project and helped support, guide, and shape it in so many ways. Without him, the book would truly not be what it is today.

Finally, I was able to write this book only because of my family's unwavering love and support. They have given me the foundation to achieve things I would never have thought possible. I could not ask for two more encouraging parents than Diane and Bernie. From an early age, they taught me to work hard, be persistent, and trust myself, qualities that have proven essential to completing this book. My sister Jenna's warmth and humor have often lifted my spirits during the seemingly endless process of producing this book. I also want to thank Brian, Shelley, Sam, and Apple for their generosity, love, and support over the years. Amy deserves the most thanks of all. She has been there from the very beginning and shaped every facet of my work in innumerable ways. As an intellectual peer, she has been both my biggest supporter and my toughest critic. Most of all, she has simply loved me. That has meant more to me than I can convey here.